UNDERSTANDING FRANCE

Helen Drake

BRISTOL
UNIVERSITY
PRESS

First published in Great Britain in 2025 by

Bristol University Press
University of Bristol
1–9 Old Park Hill
Bristol
BS2 8BB
UK
t: +44 (0)117 374 6645
e: bup-info@bristol.ac.uk

Details of international sales and distribution partners are available at
bristoluniversitypress.co.uk

British Library Cataloguing in Publication Data
A catalogue record for this book is available from the British Library

ISBN 978-1-5292-2994-3 hardcover
ISBN 978-1-5292-2995-0 paperback
ISBN 978-1-5292-2996-7 ePub
ISBN 978-1-5292-2997-4 ePdf

Cover design: Qube Design
Front cover image: Shutterstock/Flag Stock
Bristol University Press use environmentally responsible
print partners.
Printed and bound in Great Britain by CPI Group (UK) Ltd,
Croydon, CR0 4YY

FSC
www.fsc.org
MIX
Paper | Supporting
responsible forestry
FSC® C013604

In loving memory of my inspirational
mum, Marjorie Joan Drake
(1926–2022)

Contents

List of Figures and Tables

Figures

Tables

List of Abbreviations

BBC	British Broadcasting Corporation
BSE	Bovine spongiform encephalopathy
CAC-40	Cotisation assistée en continue
CAP	Common Agricultural Policy
CCTV	Closed circuit television
CDRS	Contribution pour le remboursement de la dette sociale
CEP	Certificat d'études primaires
CFSP	Common Foreign and Security Policy
CJEF	Combined Joint Expeditionary Force
CNC	Centre national du cinéma et de l'image animée
CNPT	Chasse, Nature, Pêche, Tradition
COP	Conference of Parties
CPGE	Classes préparatoires aux grandes écoles
CSG	Contribution sociale géneralisée
DNA	Deoxyribonucleic acid
EC	European Community
ECB	European Central Bank
ECSC	European Coal and Steel Community
EDF	Électricité de France
EE-LV	Europe Écologie – les Verts
EEC	European Economic Community
EHPAD	Établissement d'hébergement pour personnes âgées dépendantes
EMU	Economic and Monetary Union
ENA	École nationale d'administration
EP	European Parliament
EPC	European Political Community
EU	European Union

EURATOM	European Atomic Energy Community
FDI	Foreign direct investment
FLN	Front de Libération nationale
FN	Front national
FNSEA	Fédération Nationale des Syndicats d'Exploitants Agricoles
GDP	Gross domestic product
GMO	Genetically modified organism
GP	General practitioner
HIV	Human immunodeficiency virus
IMF	International Monetary Fund
INSEE	Institut national de la statistique et des études économiques
INSP	Institut national du service public
ISIS	Islamic State
LCR	Ligue communiste révolutionnaire
LFI	La France insoumise
LO	Lutte ouvrière
LREM	La République en Marche
MEP	Member of European Parliament
MNR	Mouvement national républicain
MoDem	Mouvement démocrate
MRP	Mouvement des républicains populaires
NATO	North Atlantic Treaty Organization
NFP	Nouveau Front populaire
NPA	Nouveau Parti anticapitaliste
NUPES	Nouvelle Union populaire, écologique et sociale
OECD	Organisation for Economic Co-operation and Development
OIF	Organisation internationale de la Francophonie
PACS	Pacte civil de solidarité
PACTE	Plan d'action pour la croissance et la transformation des entreprises
PCF	Parti communiste français
PMA	Procréation médicalement assistée
PS	Parti socialiste
RECAMP	Reinforcement of African Peacekeeping Capacities

RIC	Référendum d'initiative citoyenne
RIP	Référendum d'initiative partagée
RN	Rassemblement national
RPR	Rassemblement pour la République
RTT	Réduction du temps de travail
SEM	Single European Market
SNCF	Sociéte nationale des chemins de fer
TEPA	Loi en faveur du travail, de l'emploi et du pouvoir d'achat
TEU	Treaty on European Union
TGV	Train à grande vitesse
TSCG	Treaty on Stability, Coordination and Governance
UDF	Union pour la démocratie française
UK	United Kingdom
UMP	Union pour un mouvement populaire
UN	United Nations
UNESCO	United Nations Educational, Scientific and Cultural Organization
US	United States of America
USSR	Union of Soviet Socialist Republics
VAT	Value added tax
WTO	World Trade Organization

Acknowledgements

David John Allen (1949–2012) was Professor of International Relations at Loughborough University and my partner. He died before I got this book under way but had he lived he would have encouraged me to keep the faith – and urged me to just get on with it. His memory lives on amongst those of us still committed to understanding Europe, and we remain grateful for his insights. I owe heartfelt thanks to Stephen Wenham of Bristol University Press for his remarkable belief in me and my abilities to rewrite *Contemporary France*, not to mention his patience. I would like my colleagues at Loughborough University's London campus to know how much I have treasured their warmth and laughs since I landed on the Olympic Park in the summer of 2017. What do I owe Brexit? It reinvigorated European studies in the UK and my motivation to keep going with this book – good. But it turned me back into the foreigner in France that I had once been in my 1980s student days: *au revoir*, freedom of movement. Amongst all this turbulence, without my Allen, Bray and Drake families, and my wonderful friends, there would be little point in all this. You have my eternal love and gratitude.

Preface

This work builds on my previous book, *Contemporary France*, published in 2011 by Palgrave Macmillan. The intervening years have been such an interesting time in France that I have taken the opportunity to rewrite much of what I wrote back then. A lot of the new material has been sombre – the suffering inflicted by mass terror attacks and the tightening of the state security apparatus, in a rising tide of violence; the disarray of the world order in which France is adrift and exposed; the personal indignities of socio-economic inequality; the pointless stigmatizing of France's Muslim citizens; and the impossibility of the political status quo. But there is also vibrancy and life. France's cultural scene is ever more diverse. In 2021, a vegan restaurant near Bordeaux was awarded a Michelin star. Polluted, urban spaces are being transformed into greener versions of their previous selves, Paris included. Community and solidarity are just as characteristic of France's street protests as violence and disruption. The Yellow Vests (*gilets jaunes*) movement of 2018–19 brought succour and hope to previously isolated individuals. Stifling, discriminatory, age-old social norms concerning gender, sex and sexuality have been exposed, gradually dragging the law into the 21st century. Technological developments connect the French with worldwide movements for progressive change – against sexual harassment, for action to halt the climate emergency. France still has a voice in Europe and the world, whatever its message.

The picture of France that emerges is of a country that has much in common with its European neighbours, including the questioning of EU membership itself. This comparative angle has shaped my thinking more acutely than last time around and is implicit throughout. Elsewhere, I have left the original text untouched: regarding France's history; when discussing the constitutional and institutional framework of the Fifth French Republic; when identifying where France is, still, in a class of its own. Overall, I would say that the story is one of impending transformation or, failing that, very uneasy stasis: the next chapter is highly uncertain. In this respect, France in the 2020s stands at a crossroads in thick fog. It has been here before, in its recent history alone. In this book I have tried to highlight clues to its likely path out, but I leave it to readers to tell the future for themselves.

Figure 0.1: Map of the regions of mainland and overseas France

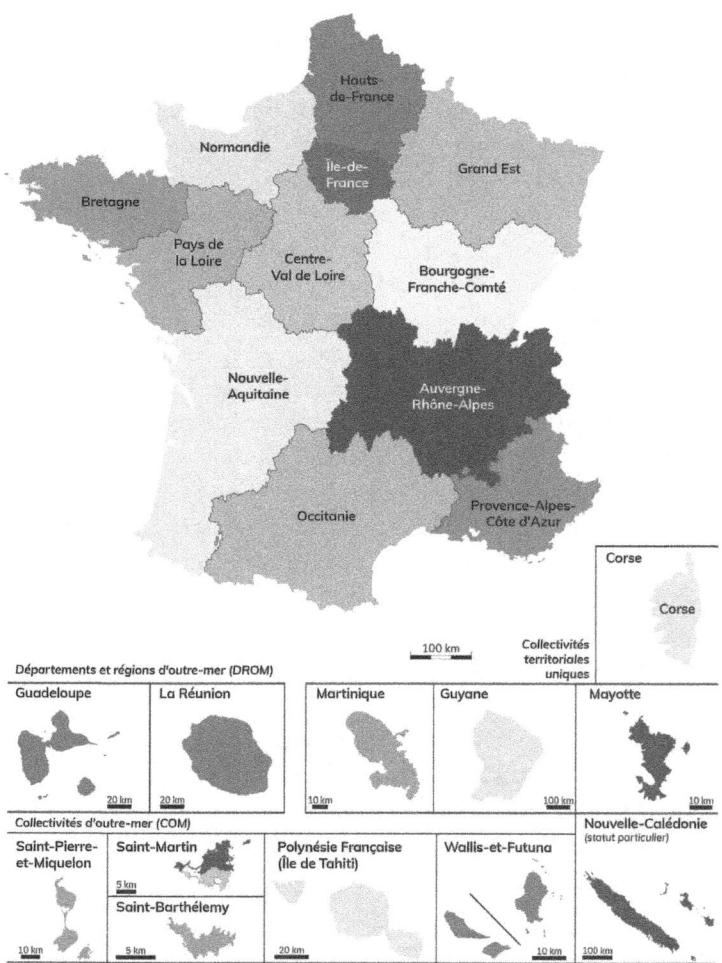

Source: DILA, vie-publique.fr © 2024. Cartography: Dario Ingiusto

Introduction

Contemporary France projects iconic images onto the world on an industrial scale. Anyone can conjure up a mind's-eye cliché of France; everyone has their favourite stereotype of French national character. All these pictures and all these emotions have played a vital part in the construction of French national identity. They point to a unified and proud French nation with a shared and lasting sense of history and its traditions. In reality, France is as disparate, disjointed and changeable as any other Western democratic country. Like many of its neighbours and allies, France faces serious challenges to its democratic way of life, if not its very existence: the climate emergency, geopolitical instability, repeated terror attacks on civilians, political turbulence and social alienation and inequality have all put 21st-century France's foundations under much strain.

In 19th-century France, local identities, customs, tastes and languages mattered far more to the French people than notions of nationhood, and important traces of those differences and traditions live on today. The wars, conscription, transportation and educational reforms of the turn of the 20th century went some way to 'turning peasants into Frenchmen', in Eugen Weber's famous terms (1976), but by the outbreak of World War II France remained a profoundly rural society with distinct regional loyalties. In today's France, some regional identities and cultures remain strong (especially for Basques, Bretons and Corsicans), but their political significance is patchy compared to contemporary differences of economic status and life chances between the French. These have given rise to dramatic uprisings such as the *gilets jaunes* – Yellow Vests – movement in 2018–19 that seriously damaged the authority of the newly elected President Emmanuel Macron.

In the second half of the 20th century, following a deeply traumatic war experience that is still not yet consigned to history, France transformed itself almost beyond recognition. The modernization agenda of the 30 years following the end of the war, based on economic growth, industrialization and internationalization, was so successful on its own terms – and internationally acknowledged in the case of flamboyant achievements such as France's high-speed train, the TGV, and the Franco-British supersonic aeroplane Concorde – that these years were dubbed the three 'glorious' decades (*les trente glorieuses*).

By contrast, the student riots and general strikes of May 1968 in France signalled that material comforts were insufficient to quell the quest for social and intellectual renewal that typified this icy period in the Cold War, and France was not alone in this respect. France subsequently embraced globalization – a choice not without its fierce detractors – and by the start of the 2020s, and even before the series of blows to the French economy struck by the COVID-19 pandemic and the 2022 Russian invasion of Ukraine, this development was entering a new, uncertain phase. The 'great metamorphosis' (Fourquet and Cassely, 2021: 13) of France's political and social economy that globalization had wrought, notably rapid deindustrialization over the space of less than 30 years and an accompanying decline in the fortunes of France's middle classes, posed seemingly intractable challenges for policy makers tasked with the long-term planning of post-metamorphosis France (dubbed *la France d'après* (after) by Fourquet, 2023), at a time when French society seemed typically pessimistic about its future.

France today is thus defined as much by its handling of current and future challenges as by its rich past, and in the following chapters we see how often France seeks to solve its contemporary problems in partnership with others, especially within the European Union (EU), and more broadly in multilateral organizations including the UN and NATO, and we assess the impact of this interdependence for the credibility of a political culture built on the credo of national sovereignty. Even where France's leaders, most notably President Emmanuel Macron, have explicitly redefined 'sovereignty' as the capacity to act (which can occur in cooperation with others), over and above its narrow legal definition (the inherent quality of a state), this still sits uneasily with more nationalistic minds in a France where Euroscepticism, for example, has steadily grown over many decades.

We probe the divide between France and the 'Anglo-Saxons' – the UK and the US – that still looms large in France, where President

Macron's fluent English evokes pride in some, while making others cringe; where McDonald's has its largest European market, and where Disneyland Paris shores up France's status as the world's number one tourist destination. We ask whether the philosophy of French republicanism, as summed up in the revolutionary slogan of *liberté, égalité, fraternité*, is an adequate guideline for public policy in the face not only of fast-moving social norms and costly expectations of the state, but of challenges – some ultra-violent – to the ideas and symbols at the very heart of republicanism itself. We see that in France an open, cosmopolitan and permeable society coexists with rigid and hierarchical codes of behaviour, the lingering social privileges of class and wealth, and increasing difficulties in bridging differences through peaceful, constructive channels. France is not alone in this uneasy coexistence of parallel lives.

In Chapter 1 (History and Legacies), we begin by acknowledging the significance of history to contemporary French life. It is physically prominent, educationally cherished but politically problematic, and France is definitely still coming to terms with the living past. Memories of the brutal injustices of France's colonial role and its subsequent battles of decolonization, especially in Algeria, are vividly recalled in the disquiet, today, among young French citizens of immigrant origin, many of whom experience discrimination on a daily basis. More sinister still is the perverse translation of such historical wounds by individuals radicalized by violent causes into heinous terror attacks on French soil, with all the backlash that entails in terms of ever-tighter state security measures, trigger-happy police law enforcement and a distrust of others that can be and has been weaponized for political ends. These are anxious times.

In Chapter 2 (France and the French) we see that, in any case, notions of *French* – meaning *national* – history were largely anachronistic before the late 19th century and the 'discovery of France' by the French themselves, to use Graham Robb's evocative term (2007). France was tribal and local for far longer than it has been a unified and 'indivisible' nation, as the 1958 Constitution has it. Diversity does still characterize France in the 21st century and in this chapter we review the variety of its physical geography and the cosmopolitanism of its population, and we assess the significance of these attributes for present-day policy. We probe the importance of notions such as *terroir* to the French way of life, as well as to the profitability of its tourist attractions and its products, and we navigate the complexities of French nationality and immigration legislation which imposes 'integration' both on newcomers to the French nation and on those who have resided long-term in the country, without perhaps ever feeling fully French. We consider the environmental challenges faced by France and the French, as well as the key policy responses to date, and the obstacles in the way of those answers. The *gilets jaunes* movement was itself sparked by government decisions, rational on their own terms, intended to accelerate France's transition away from fossil fuels (a carbon tax on motorists).

Yet diversity and interests (individual and especially collective) are supposed to be trumped by allegiance to a unitary nation, and the quest for this elusive state of affairs is an important aspect of French politics, as we see in Chapter 3 (Politics and the Republic). Republicanism (as opposed to, say, the monarchist or otherwise absolutist regimes that France has known in the past) forms the bedrock of French political culture and sustains a variant of democracy that both leans towards the abstract and looks back to the past. Over the course of its existence it has been periodically contested, and this is also true of the present day, although today's challenges are, as yet, more insidious and slow-burning than the bloody revolutions of history. Republicanism *à la française* has bred the notion that French politics is somehow exceptional, and thus incomparable to other liberal or social democracies, a claim that fades with every passing decade. The root of this claim to exceptionalism lies principally in the 1789 French Revolution, which spawned a style of politics in which claims to direct action, oratory and rhetoric are commonplace. Yet it is now more than a quarter of a century since France celebrated the bicentenary of its 1789 French Revolution, and representing the Republic has become an object of political competition: who owns it? Who belongs? Who does not? And who gets to say?

In this chapter, we see that the match between political supply and demand in France is far from perfect, and its opportunities still limited to a relatively small and exclusive elite. Even in France, democracy is imperfect and incomplete. These facts of French political life have created space for populist movements such as the far right National Rally (formerly the National Front), until recently kept out of power by electoral systems specifically designed to protect the French from themselves, but gradually 'normalizing' and finding space to represent its followers nationally as well as locally: the party's leader, Marine Le Pen, came second to Emmanuel Macron in both the 2017 and 2022 French presidential elections; the party won the most seats in the 2024 elections to the European Parliament; and it came first in the first round of the 2024 legislative elections. On the far left, Jean-Luc Mélenchon during the same period succeeded in aggregating many voices seeking a radical alternative path for French democracy but alienated supporters of a more moderate left-wing agenda. Support for France's traditional parties on both left and right crumbled dramatically in 2017, making way for Emmanuel Macron's version of a 'Revolution' (the title of his manifesto) that would modernize France once and for all, as he saw it, making it fit to face the planetary-scale challenges he correctly identified in the very near distance. Like most if not all hubristic French presidents before him, Macron failed to meet both his and others' expectations of him and, during his time in office, French politics became ever more turbulent, polarized and seemingly out of touch, with high rates of abstention and abysmally low public trust in politicians, and the sidestepping of France's political institutions by some of those seeking to be heard. Perhaps politics in its traditional sense was finally falling out of fashion, even in France, as in so many other countries.

In a similar manner, the structures and institutions of French government derive from a set of circumstances that, in 1958, at the beginning of today's Fifth French Republic, threatened the country's very existence. The system that emerged was designed for 'great men', specifically the Republic's founder, Charles de Gaulle, who trusted himself with control of the levers of political power. We see in Chapter 4 (Government, Governance and the State) that, over time and in the hands of mere mortals, this 'semi-presidential' system of power-sharing between a directly elected president and his (there has still, to date, been no female French president) handpicked prime minister (there have been only two women in this post since 1958), in a regime where powers are concentrated in the executive, has eroded political accountability at the very top of the state. Over time, this has diminished presidential authority itself, not to mention trust in the post and its incumbent. Quite aside from instances of political scandal (especially financial) at the top, French presidents and their governments can, if they wish, and they do, ride roughshod over parliament through constitutional measures designed – way back in 1958 – to stop parliament destabilizing the executive. But such measures are unpopular and expose the gaps of the semi-presidential regime where there could be dialogue, consensus and the accommodation of dissent within its framework. In September 2024, a motion to impeach President Macron was presented to the National Assembly by his opponents on the political left. However unlikely to succeed, it was yet another warning shot across the president's bows.

However, there is little political support for an outright transition to a Sixth French Republic and, instead, we see that France's constitution has been repeatedly amended in response to changing times; this may ensure the Fifth Republic's survival but not its health. We see too in this chapter that the French 'state' has a historical and symbolic importance that outstrips its actual functions but which ensures its survival in the face of challenges to its capacity to deliver services, justice and support to every French citizen, wherever they live or whichever life stage they find themselves in. Some see the French state as incapacitated by France's interdependence with the EU and we observe in this chapter how France has continuously sought to shape the EU and its decisions in the French image and interests (so-called Europeanization), but with limited results and at the cost of political destabilization. In parallel, successive French presidents, particularly on the left (François Mitterrand in 1983, François Hollande in 2014) have put their names to significant reforms of the structures of both the French state and French democracy through decentralization, 'deconcentration' and other alterations to the map of French territorial governance, with mitigated results.

Accordingly, in Chapter 5 (Society and Identity), we consider how well-equipped France really is, in terms of its politics, state and government, to deliver public policy that upholds the cohesion of the nation. When the French constitution states in Article 1 that France shall be a 'social' Republic, it is this national cohesion that it aims for. Achieving this ambition is arduous and contentious, and failings to achieve it are at the root of much of 'what ails France' (Granville, 2021), making headlines the world over, as in the case of protests against pensions and environmental reforms, to name but two examples. In theory, and according to the constitution, contemporary French society is organized along the strict lines of its republican ideals, namely the provision, protection and promotion of individual freedom (*liberté*), equality (*égalité*) and solidarity (*fraternité*). Achieving this balance is in reality, and inevitably, a tall order in France, whose population is large (68 million in 2023), ageing and diverse; where Catholic morality lives on as a cultural if not spiritual force, as seen in the backlash in the 2010s against 'marriage for all' legislation; where attitudes towards Islam and, to a lesser extent, Judaism, both significant minority religions in France, intersect with other social trends including women's rights, and with the very principle of *laïcité* – secularism *à la française* – that is enshrined in the constitution (France shall be a 'secular' republic); where scepticism and suspicion of the Anglo-American-style embrace of difference (at the level of both the individual and groups or communities) – not to mention 'political correctness' – troubles official discourse and policy; and where 'civil society' is traditionally an alien concept based on a 'repugnance' for British and American liberal, pluralistic societies, as Hayward (2007) has it. We investigate the welfare state in France, which incorporates safety nets for the elderly and the excluded, complete with gaps and deficiencies, as well as the world-renowned and staggeringly costly health system, and ask how the COVID-19 pandemic exposed its limits, and we enquire into the scope and limitations of an education system designed both to train an elite and to achieve more democratic goals, as befits a country that regards itself as one of the most civilized on earth.

Indeed, culturally speaking, France has an extensive past of elitist and grandiose activity, overshadowing the value of daily cultural practices. For at least 400 years, French leaders have spent heavily on cultural policies designed to project images of national splendour, in its chateaux, art, fashion, music and, latterly, technologies and sporting mega-events such as the 2024 Paris Summer Olympic and Paralympic Games. Culture in France is definitely political, and it is also commercially beneficial. Additionally, it is a matter of curated national identity: at the start of the 20th century, at precisely the time when nation-building and defence were seen as a matter of life and death, French regional languages suffered from repression, and the populations of France's colonial 'possessions' were bludgeoned with French culture in the form of the French language, not to mention the Catholic religion. In present-day France, questions of culture still have their dark side when they intersect with political pressures for a more exclusionary national identity. In Chapter 6 (Culture and

Leisure) we see, however, that culture and entertainment have now become accessible to virtually all in France, increasingly inside the home, and increasingly permeated by influences that lie well beyond the control of the state: culture as practised by people in their daily lives is an international, and often virtual, affair. Social media and the connectivity of the internet make a mockery of national boundaries, in democratic societies like France at least, and we do see the French state act (frequently in cooperation with others, within the EU for example) to set, or try to set, certain limits, for example on the use of the English language, or on the international trade in cultural goods, especially cinema. In these respects, France treads a fine balance between claiming that its culture is exceptional, worthy of defence, and acknowledging that culture is all the richer for its diversity.

In Chapter 7 (Economy and Business), we find much to bewilder the France-watcher. France is neither a classic liberal market economy nor a social market economy in the German style. It is traditionally highly critical of *laissez-faire*, 'Anglo-Saxon'-style political economy, but the French state is in retreat from market forces and has been for decades. Perhaps it is here that France was for some time genuinely in a class of its own, having crafted a unique model of socio-economic development and political economy that made way for a central role for the state (as financier and planner), despite the openness of its economy and its presence in all the important world economic forums. In today's France and particularly during President Macron's terms in office, the balance has shifted away from globalization as the favoured vehicle for economic competitiveness, and towards regional capacity-building to ensure the security of supply of food, energy and raw materials, and of national security itself. Also of note is the frequent pessimism the French express about the economy even when aggregate figures (inflation, employment) are relatively healthy. This tells us something about the bigger picture of the French political economy of growth at all costs, particularly at a time of acute environmental pressures, and of the disconnect between statistics and the lives and livelihoods they represent.

At the level of political language, we see that, in France, a struggle with the very morality of money for money's sake is often played out. This is probably a losing battle, given that France is no stranger to big business; on the contrary, many of its blue-chip companies are successful international leaders in their sector, and Paris is the world capital of luxury. Yet former President Sarkozy was mocked for openly embracing such values in his so-called 'bling-bling' behaviour; President Macron's fervour for France as a 'start up nation' was also viewed with widespread distaste if not derision; and former President Hollande's failure (2012–17) to make good on his manifesto promise to crush the world of finance contributed to the crumbling of the Socialist Party at the end of his mandate. In the economy, above all other areas of policy, France has tethered its fortunes to the EU and its single-currency Eurozone. Europe is France's biggest export market and, at present, its only hope for weathering the storm of competition from newly developing economies, not to mention China. President Macron made 'Europe' a cornerstone of his first presidential bid and set out, with some but limited success, to pursue France's 'Europeanization' process with calls for European-level economic 'sovereignty'. This meant generating, at EU level, the capacity to produce, finance, regulate, define and so on in response to the intense international disruptions to the economy suffered by France, along with its neighbours, from the very start of the 21st century, particularly the 2007–08 financial crisis, the COVID-19 pandemic and the 2022 Russian war on Ukraine.

Indeed, France is an international player, which, by virtue of it being a nuclear power, is one of only five permanent members of the United Nations Security Council, and this theme – France's international action, ambitions and limitations – characterizes our final substantive Chapter 8 (France in the World). France, as is the case for many other EU countries, finds that the state alone, in one country – even France – is powerless or, at best, insufficient to tackle, let alone resolve, the pressing and potentially most threatening of its problems: sustainably securing energy and food supplies; responding humanely to the mass migrations of people towards Europe despite political and popular pressures to close European doors; averting catastrophic failures to mitigate for climate change and biodiversity loss; and responding to similar-scale challenges from rapid developments in artificial intelligence and other advanced technologies. Nor are French foreign policy and diplomacy immune to budget cuts or changing geopolitical power shifts. Here, the security of the nation and the integrity of the French territory are potentially at threat, and it is the president's job to counter this. In the case of President Macron, the international stage was where he preferred to be, often drawing criticism for off-the-cuff, personalized diplomacy that shocked at home as much as abroad; this was his presidential prerogative, raising questions about the nature of French presidential power. As a former imperial and colonial player, France has experienced some angst in adjusting to its modest size and limited influence in the present day in a world seemingly populated by hyperpowers, rogue states, autocratic leaders and terrorists with nuclear weapons almost in their grasp. Paris accordingly works hard to influence peoples across the world using so-called soft power (the 'diplomacy of influence') as well as its military capacity, both of which are increasingly placed at the disposal of multinational and joint efforts to secure global peace and prosperity. Here, as in other themes explored in the book, we see how France cannot escape its history, particularly its past as Africa's so-called 'gendarme', a term that connotes both a peacekeeping, security role and the protection of certain French interests, from the use of its language to its access to raw materials and arms contracts. By 2023, a number of previously France-friendly nations in Africa had denounced French influence in the present day; France's failures (and their cover-ups) in the ghastly Rwandan genocide of 1994 had come to light; and France's costly military missions in the Sahel region of the continent, latterly designed and intended to ward off Islamist terrorism in those regions alongside international partners, had come to an inglorious and largely ineffective end. Here too, in this chapter, we see how France's membership of the EU is a core element of its foreign policy and diplomacy, but that the EU alone is insufficient to reach its goals and, we have said, is increasingly unpopular in France.

I wrote in the earlier version of this book (Drake, 2011) that France was no more or less likely to implode or fall victim to disaster, and no more or less equipped to face those prospects than its European neighbours or North American cousins. Perhaps this still holds although, since then, others with good reason to know have found France to be 'ailing' (Granville, 2021), 'deeply troubled' (Smith, 2021: x) and 'broken' (Ramdani, 2023). The same could arguably be said of the United States, certainly of Russia, even of China in certain respects and indeed, in the final chapter of this edition, I reflect on France in comparative perspective. Some of its problems are evidently home-grown, particularly the mismatch between the presidential powers as spelt out in the constitution and the realities of wielding power in a highly complex, open society. France's history and how it handles it are also unique to France. For these reasons, I consider that understanding France as a single country still matters. But many challenges are shared with other countries, regions and the world, and this perspective defined Emmanuel Macron's call for a 'revolution' at home (Macron, 2017). He fervently believed that France had the capacity and courage to face its future, and he set out to revitalize the country from root to branch. Like his predecessors, he underestimated the forces against him and overestimated his own abilities to govern, and during his two presidential terms, as we see in the following chapters, France edged ever closer to a reckoning of an as-yet-unknown nature.

1

History and Legacies

Introduction

History looms large in contemporary France. The teaching of history is central to French school curricula, and the writing of history by French scholars such as Fernand Braudel is renowned worldwide. Local councils and the central state alike invest in elaborate displays of the past to attract tourist revenues, and the passion for heritage (*le patrimoine*) is widespread in France. The popular theme park le Puy du Fou in the west of France, a rival to France's Disneyland Paris attraction outside Paris, successfully sells dramatic reconstructions of French history and heritage rather than rollercoaster rides. History and remembrance are physically everywhere in France, from the poignant war memorials in the smallest French village and the vast Allied cemeteries of northern France to the enigmatic brown signs beckoning motorists to exit France's motorways and explore local history and tradition. In imagining France's past, we conjure up regimes toppling in chaotic crisis; larger-than-life monarchs, emperors, dictators and presidents; and centuries-long, bloody wars, preferably waged against the 'English' or between religions. We are also invited to shudder at the sights and smells of the 1789 French Revolution and 'the figure of the sharp female called La Guillotine' (Dickens, 2000: 283).

French history is, indeed, characterized by much conflict and violence, and disagreements over the record find their way into contemporary French politics: legislation is passed and repealed as leaders attempt to forge and commemorate collective memories of painful past episodes, some still in living history, such as the German occupation of 1940–44 or the Algerian war of independence (1954–62). Historians still tussle over the causes of the French Revolution of 1789, and some protest at what they believe is the instrumentalization of history by contemporary politicians; others take issue with the glorification of French history: even le Puy du Fou is not immune to criticism of its framing of French history and its nationalist vibe. Many historical divisions have nevertheless been overcome, and the recurrent civil wars of the 18th, 19th and even 20th centuries do now seem to be a thing of the past, although there are still fault lines as well as new lines of battle, and we explore them in this and subsequent chapters.

Contemporary France is firmly wedded to a republican political regime – despite arguments about what that republicanism means in practice – with royalism limited to a passion for the UK royal family (the deaths of Princess Diana and Queen Elizabeth II in 1997 and 2022, respectively, were big news in France, and King Charles III was given a lavish state welcome in September 2023); to prurient curiosity, *Paris Match*-style, for the playboys and girls of the Monaco dynasty; and to support for a strong, personalized presidency (although we will see in Chapter 3 that no recent presidents have satisfactorily lived up to the idea of a 'republican monarch' imprinted on the regime by the example of its first president, Charles de Gaulle). The Catholic Church, historically a pillar of French society, coexists with republicanism – and with other faiths – but has no role in political life in a formally secular state. Support for communism, so marked in post-war France, has declined to, almost certainly, the point of no return; a legislative edifice, however imperfect, is in place to pacify intra-French tensions between the sexes, genders, generations and races; and relations are peaceful with those neighbours with whom relations have been most troubled in the past – namely, the 'English' (the UK is referred to as *l'Angleterre* – England – in France) and Germany.

But this does not mean that 21st-century France can finally take its history for granted; far from it. France today is effectively one state, one territory (albeit spread across different continents), one people and one nation: a single, 'indivisible' entity, as the 1958 constitution proclaims. But it also struggles to digest the consequences of certain episodes of its history and, in particular, its past as a colonial power, specifically its 19th-century conquest of parts of North Africa, above all Algeria. Andrew Hussey's provocative notion of the 'long war between France and its Arabs' (Hussey, 2015) is as haunting in 2024 as a decade ago, if not more so. The horrific instances of mass terrorism perpetrated in France in 2015 and 2016; the sporadic but no less shocking killings of individuals who in certain cases symbolized for their attackers the French state and its history, such as the slaughter of French history teacher Samuel Paty in 2020; the episodic reemergence of antisemitic acts across France: all of these grisly developments point to a country where historical scores are still being settled. They are, moreover, distorted and refracted not only through the prisms of France's domestic situation today (including ongoing problems of discrimination and police violence against minority ethnic individuals) but by wider geopolitical forces (including the US 'war on terror'; the UK and US's abject failures in Afghanistan, Iraq and Libya; the raging Arab–Israeli conflict) that have created opportunities for allegiances other than to the French nation and its bloody history.

In this chapter, we review the emergence of the modern French nation-state from the Roman Empire. We track its evolution into the *ancien régime* – the old order – of the medieval and Renaissance monarchy, which laid the foundations for the strong, centralized state for which France is still known today, and on which aspects of its identity are shaped. We consider the eruption of patriotic nationalism associated with the 1789 French Revolution, and the sense of exceptionalism that it has bequeathed to contemporary France: an idealized belief in the universal and exportable values of democracy, human rights and egalitarianism. The chapter then focuses on the exceptional transformations undergone by French society, economy, markets and politics from the mid- to late 20th century to today's post-Cold War era. We emphasize the reconstruction of French identity undertaken by Charles de Gaulle in the 1960s, and the 21st-century challenges to the French sense of national self. The 20th century in so many ways challenged the very identity and existence of France, and existential angst is a problem that current politicians have not fully banished from their mindsets. We balance images of political chaos with a sense of the conservative and continuous forces that are just as much part of the legacy of France's past. We spend time with the violent repercussions and distortions – the legacies – of France's history that continue

15

to reverberate through the country today and prevent any sense of complacency about the past.

The making of the French nation-state

When discussing prehistoric, ancient and medieval France, contemporary notions of *national* identity – let alone national *consciousness* – are anachronistic, since these periods all established the diversity – regional, cultural, tribal – that, to this day, challenges aspirations to French national unity. The Romans conquered the native Celts in 1 BC, assimilated them, then left them to successive waves of invading barbarian (foreign) tribes. Prehistoric man and woman had already left traces of social organization, the evidence of which is best known in the shape of the cave paintings at Lascaux in the Dordogne region of south-west France (on public show in replica form) and the eerie standing stones of Brittany.

From Roman Gaul to Renaissance France

Under Roman rule, France was known as Gaul and, of the tribal invaders, the fifth-century Germanic Franks lent their name to what is now France. The Romans left their physical marks on Gaul, many of which still stand today (including the Pont du Gard and the Maison Carrée, both in Provence). Significantly, Julius Caesar's *pax romana* brought stability and shape to Gaul, by means of what we would today call centralized language and communications policies, and a unitary legal system. These were all enforceable by legions of Roman soldiers, immortalized in Goscinny's popular cartoon illustrations of the plucky and comic Astérix facing down the intruder.

The Catholic Church slowly took over from the Roman Empire as a source of minimal cohesion between disparate peoples. Clovis, king of the Salian (northern) Franks, converted to the Christian faith in the late fifth century, and many followed his example, giving them something in common, although hardly a nationality as we now understand it. The combination of Clovis and church was significant in shaping medieval France, where Paris and its region, the Île de France, were already emerging as the epicentre of power; today, the area is France's biggest and richest region. Clovis's descendants were the Merovingians, by all accounts long-haired and loutish, and with the time and energy to extend the kingdom to Burgundy and Provence. But their lax rule allowed aristocratic rivals to emerge, and from these emerged the Carolingian line, via the well-known historical figures of Martel and Pepin. The best-known son of the Carolingians was Charlemagne. Crowned Holy Roman Emperor in AD 800, his legendary influence was a civilizing force in the 'Dark Ages' (the ninth and tenth centuries), even naturalizing Viking invaders. His immediate legacy was the territory of West Francia, the physical template for contemporary France, but after his death his empire disintegrated, shrinking by the tenth century to an area little bigger than today's Île de France region.

Anglo-French rivalry marked this period in France, and cross-Channel competition still exists today, albeit within a stable and friendly partnership: war is unthinkable between the two formerly and frequently warring neighbours. William the Conqueror's victory in England in 1066 rebounded against the stability and territorial ambitions of French royal authority insofar as his successors mounted repeated challenges to French monarchs over a lengthy period, which included the Hundred Years' War (1337–1453) and the burning of Joan of Arc by the English. But by the end of the war the French had made considerable territorial gains from the English contenders, including the large and rich province of Aquitaine in the south-west, thus consolidating the royal domains. The quest by the English to colonize this region nevertheless continued well into the 21st century in the far more peaceful shape of British exiles seeking the 'good life' in rural France. Until Brexit, that is, when the UK's decision by referendum in 2016 to leave the EU slowly punctured this phenomenon. This time, the English had defeated themselves.

In other respects, too, these were centuries of consolidation, the impact of which is still felt today. King Philippe Augustus (1180–1223) paved Paris, and the foundations of the spectacular gothic cathedral of Notre Dame de Paris were laid in these years. When on 15 April 2019 Notre Dame almost burned to extinction, the shock was immense: another blow dealt to a potent symbol of France, not long after the 2015 and 2016 lethal mass terror attacks on the republican values of free speech (*Charlie Hebdo*) and free society (Paris, Nice). The Sorbonne University was established in 1257 and, with it, the roots of Paris's contemporary reputation as a seat of learning and knowledge, as well as the growing role of the

French language, alongside Latin, in these fields. By the 14th century, French royal prestige was high and, by the early 15th century, the territory of France had expanded to resemble its contemporary shape. Papal authority had, for a while (1309–77), been established in France, in Avignon, and a sense of national identity was emerging around these developments. The Renaissance of the 16th century strengthened this feeling, and many of today's extrovert symbols of utter Frenchness – the chateaux of the Loire, the Louvre museum, French literature, the French language (the King's *langue d'oil*, or language of the north) – date from these days.

The ancien régime*: the emergence of the modern French state*

The France of the *ancien régime* – the old, or 'former', pre-revolutionary order of the 17th and 18th centuries – was ravaged by religious strife and wars. The Wars of Religion (1562–98) brought bloodshed and a waste of human talent: the Saint Bartholemew's massacre of six thousand French protestants on 24 August 1572 stands out as a particularly bloody historical date. Under the reign of Louis XIV (1643–1715), the French Huguenot Protestants were eventually exiled, taking much creative and intellectual know-how with them, including to London, which became a regular haven for French exiles seeking safety or freedom in the centuries to come; the 'French London' of the 21st century is very much the heir of these early pioneers (Huc-Hepher, 2021). But these earlier years and these battles also gave France its first Bourbon king, Henry IV. Having converted to Catholicism and offered limited tolerance to the Huguenots in the form of the 1598 Edict of Nantes, he ushered in the 1600s. That epoch was known as *le grand siècle* ('splendid century') and it marked a revival in the standards of the French monarchy measured in terms of ruthlessness, authoritarianism, images of greatness and expense, all in the name of French nation- and state-building.

Henry IV's immediate successors, Louis XIII and Louis XIV, established the most sumptuous period of French royal history ever, and their names and those of their ministers (Richelieu, Mazarin, Colbert) are engraved on the French psyche as symbols of when France was great, however troubled. Their 'absolutist' systems of authority in which kings were deemed to answer to no one but God, ensured new levels of administrative efficiency, as did Richelieu's *intendants*, precursors of today's departmental *préfets* (see Chapter 4). This was also a time of ostentatious greatness and wealth, ranging from works of architecture (the palace of Versailles, near Paris), art and culture; the creation of the Académie française by Richelieu in 1635; the royal patronage of manufacture and science; and imperialism (1648 saw the Treaty of Westphalia sealing victory over the Hapsburgs). Despite serious popular uprisings against royal authority – which, in retrospect, were a dress rehearsal for the French Revolution – France was strong and the monarch powerful. But aggressive foreign policies were ruinously expensive, and taxation systems required the cooperation of potential challengers to royal authority in the shape of the regional *parlements* (courts) and the aristocratic lawyers that peopled them.

By the time of the outbreak of the French Revolution in 1789, 'France' and the 'French' had, thus, neither been created by any continuous, strategic action on the part of a single dynastic leadership, nor by a spontaneous, popular process of unification at a given point in time. Instead, the French state and nation had emerged from centuries of war (foreign, civil, religious), waged by leaders of varying abilities and desires but sharing a quest for power, and whose authority was always and inevitably vulnerable to challenge, and luck. 'Society' was highly disparate, composed of groups – the noble aristocrats, the bourgeoisie, the clergy, the peasants, the workers – enjoying or suffering vastly different sets of privileges and opportunities, which created permanently combustible mixtures of resentments. A form of centralizing authority did appear over time, albeit in a punctuated, often chaotic manner, in the shape of authoritarian – royal and clerical – structures intended to save costs and consolidate power by the imposition of norms of language, religion, justice and taxation. These met with varying success.

1789–1799: a decade of revolution

The French Revolution of 1789 was a decisive episode in French history. Its impact is still felt in contemporary French political culture, even though the process by which democratic, republican politics subsequently took root in France was long, tortuous and frequently deadly. The French Revolution was, in all respects, dramatic. It produced a set of apocryphal characters, amply represented ever since in literature, film and art, and it engaged a series of battles at home and abroad that still resonate in France today, however faintly. It lent a patriotic dimension to the formation of French identity and gave root to the modern-day concepts of nation and nationalism. The French Revolution was not a sudden event, nor did it change France overnight, but its best-known effects were momentous, particularly for its losers and their interests (and heads). The *ancien régime* was definitively repudiated by the physical elimination, by guillotine, of its leading figures, including the king and queen, and by the abolition of noble and feudal privilege through destroying the 'orders' of the old system – the clergy, nobility, lawyers and crafts- and guildsmen.

The Revolution had no initial blueprint, and the line between the Revolution and the republicanism of present-day France is over 200 years long, broken and rejoined in several places. The ideals of the revolutionaries, as expressed in the 1789 Declaration of the Rights of Man and the Citizen, spawned the vocabulary of contemporary democratic French politics: popular sovereignty, the rule of law, equality before the law, free speech and political representation. Today's constitution, moreover, begins with explicit reference to the 1789 text. But two centuries were needed for these notions to become embedded as standard political practice, and they are still being revised in line with contemporary social norms, as we see in later chapters.

The Napoleonic Empire, 1799–1815

By 1799, army officer Napoleon Bonaparte was sufficiently admired for his victories in the revolutionary wars waged by France across Europe that he was able to exploit the confusion of the revolutionary decade and take power by a *coup d'état* on 18–19 Brumaire (9 November) 1799 – and subsequently prosecute his own, Napoleonic wars in Europe. He was appointed First Consul for ten years but, after only five, on 18 May 1804, he had himself crowned the first emperor of his new hereditary empire. Napoleon's regime maintained the revolutionary ideal of popular sovereignty but perverted it into the shape of a presumed bond between the people and the great leader himself. Within this bond, and under his charismatic, authoritarian, guidance, the people could express their will in carefully manufactured plebiscites but not in free elections, nor did they enjoy free speech or a free press, which were curtailed and censured in these years. Echoes of this style of personalized leadership have persisted into contemporary France and especially its provisions for a powerful president, as we elaborate in Chapters 3 and 4. When President Nicolas Sarkozy was elected in May 2007, bringing another short-ish Frenchman to power, comparisons, comic and serious, with Napoleon Bonaparte were common media currency.

The backbone of the French state in the Napoleonic era, also still recognizable today, was a professional, elitist bureaucracy, trained up in the new *lycées* – senior schools – established during this time, and on which state senior schools are modelled in France today, although the model is showing its age, as we see in Chapter 5. Napoleon also controlled the church in the form of a Concordat signed with Rome in 1802. Finally, and significantly for contemporary France, he governed the whole of the French territory by means of a uniform legal system – the Napoleonic codes – and an administrative machine answerable to the emperor, and which rewarded its faithful servants with the newly created *Légion d'honneur*. But Napoleon's domestic reforms could not guarantee the success of his wars and he abdicated in April 1814, after his military retreat from Russia, and before making his 100 days comeback that ended in 1815 in further military defeat at the famous Battle of Waterloo at the hands of Britain's Duke of Wellington, a confrontation lavishly depicted in Ridley Scott's 2023 film *Napoleon*.

Nineteenth-century restorations: monarchy, empire and republic

Which, if any, regime would secure both national reconciliation (internal stability) and military success (external prestige), and in what circumstances? The default setting of the 19th century was a restored, constitutional monarchy, trapped between the historical pulls of authoritarianism and, on occasions, the revival of revolutionary republicanism. The context was burgeoning industrialization, mass literacy, the rise and rise of the property-owning bourgeoisie; the Romanticism of 19th-century art, literature and philosophy; and new signs of the French propensity for glamour and glory. These were the years when Baron Haussmann drove the tank-friendly wide *grands boulevards* into Paris, bearing their characteristically well-proportioned buildings that are so distinctive of today's French capital city; the

Arc de Triomphe was completed; colonies and territory were won (including Algeria, the so-called 'jewel' in France's empire, which would give rise to so much pain and bloodshed into the 20th and 21st centuries, as noted elsewhere in this chapter). Universal male suffrage and the eventual abolition of slavery in the colonies were also legacies of the 19th century.

But the popular uprisings of 1830 and the workers' revolution of 1848 drove the monarchy (the Bourbon King Louis XVIII and the Orleanist 'citizen-king' Louis-Philippe, respectively) out for good, with the latter living out his final years in exile in England and replaced by the Second Empire under Emperor Louis-Napoleon Bonaparte (1851–70) and the Empress Princess Eugénie. These rulers indulged in a socially liberal lifestyle that was itself swept away by the Paris Commune of 1870 after France's military defeat by Prussia which had brought about the painful loss of Alsace and Lorraine. These beginnings, endings and convulsions were all versions of a civil war that the 1789 Revolution had not definitively resolved.

1870–1940: the Third Republic

Politically speaking, France in the 19th century oscillated between popular claims for more freedom, equality and fraternity (electoral reform, better working conditions) and brutally repressive responses by a variety of authoritarian regimes. The Third French Republic (1870–1940) lasted nearly ten times longer than its predecessors combined. French republicanism had by now matured, spurred on by the raised consciousness acquired through free and lay education, free expression, free association, and gains in workers' rights, most visibly the 40-hour week and the holiday entitlement of 12 working days, which brought leisure into working people's lives, and into the economy. By 1905, church and state had been legally separated, as they are to this day in secular France (see Chapter 5), ending both the overt power struggles between the Catholic Church and the state and, more broadly, signalling the removal of the religious factor in public and political life. However, the realities of this separation – known as *la laïcité* – still give rise to much debate in 21st-century France, as we develop in subsequent chapters. It was no coincidence that, in this climate, it was deemed safe to reinstate the symbols of

1789: the *Marseillaise* as the national anthem, 14 July as a public holiday, and the revolutionary rally-cry *liberté, égalité, fraternité* etched onto public buildings. The blooming of French arts in this *belle époque* was matched by advances in science and engineering, regularly showcased to the world in exhibition form. The Eiffel Tower stands today to remind us of this period.

Free and compulsory education was also a conduit in this period for the imposition of the French language, and for prescribed children's stories of how France became France. These were all vehicles for raising the consciousness of the existence of a *nation*, France. Patriotism was, indeed, tangible – its dark side a spirit of revenge (*la revanche*) towards Germany following the 1870 defeat, and the ugly xenophobic nationalism encapsulated in the writing of racialist Maurice Barrès. The fear of the outsider was especially targeted against the notional Jew and at Bolshevik Russia. The Dreyfus affair of these years – the cooked-up, covered-up condemnation to a penal colony for treason of an innocent Jewish French army officer, Alfred Dreyfus – divided the nation, right down to the family unit, and rocked the Third Republic to its very roots. Intellectual and writer Emile Zola's *J'accuse*, his yowl of protest at the conniving of the institutions of the state, reverberates, still, more than a century later.

Ominously, these narrow definitions of French identity based on concepts of race, territory and roots, as exposed by the Dreyfus scandal, offered fertile ground for what was to follow a generation later, namely the Holocaust and France's part in it (see below). Despite this, the horrors and vast human losses of the World War I battlefields (most notoriously, the Somme and Verdun) united the French more than they divided them, and the republicans maintained France's status as a world presence and cultural pole of attraction. But population growth was low, swathes of the economy were weak and inefficient, and centuries of French hegemony on the European continent were evidently at an end.

The Third Republic did not withstand the German invasion of France in June 1940. Germany's intentions were overwhelmingly aggressive, fuelled by the ruinous reparations imposed on it by the Versailles settlement. The reasons for France's capitulation, appeasement and collaboration with the occupier include the attraction, for some, of a French place in a Germanic, Aryan Europe.

The collapse of the Third Republic in 1940 into the authoritarian Vichy regime resonated with the introverted, virulent nationalism that had shadowed the successes of the Third Republic and to which Bolshevik Russia was more alien and hateful than Nazi Germany.

The post-war transformations of France

It is no exaggeration to describe the decades in France that followed the shocks and aftershocks of World War II as transformative. Domestic politics, France's place in the international system, its relations with the US, its economy, its society, its self-image: all these found themselves challenged. If a nation-state can experience existential angst, then this was the condition of post-war France. Beyond physical reconstruction and the settling of scores, the priority for France's post-war leaders was to rebuild the identity of France to, somehow, deal with the trauma of the war years and its repercussions, including the rapid loss of the French Empire and the latent civil war between supporters of Vichy and de Gaulle's Free French. This was done through appeals to myth, nostalgia and selective memory, and by a series of history-making decisions around goals that would characterize France for at least the next 50 years, namely modernization, Europeanization, decolonization and the quest for international greatness – *la grandeur*.

France's World War II: tales of occupation, resistance and liberation

In the confusion of the rout of the French military by the invading German army in June 1940, the government of the Third Republic fled, abdicating responsibility to the hero of the World War I battle of Verdun, Marshal Pétain, by now well into his 80s, for extracting the best treatment possible from Germany, via an armistice. Marshal Pétain, who, after the war, was sentenced to death but permitted by de Gaulle to serve life imprisonment instead (Jackson, 2023: 275), along with Prime Minister Pierre Laval (put on trial and executed in 1945), seized the opportunity of this dramatic change in France's fortunes to instigate a domestic revolution of his own. This was a *révolution nationale*, based on a crude design to turn back the clock to an imagined pre-republican, halcyon era of national purity. Executive authority in the new regime, based at Vichy in the – initially – unoccupied zone, was concentrated in Pétain's role; the mantra *travail, famille, patrie* (work, family, country) replaced the revolutionary *liberté, égalité, fraternité*, and the French Catholic Church was co-opted into the venture. Traditional values, as the Vichyites saw them, had returned, and would restore the French nation to its former greatness – despite the awkward fact that by 1943, the entire country was effectively under German occupation.

Vichy had its winners and enthusiasts beyond the regime's leaders. Collaboration with the German occupier was a spectrum of behaviours and activities, with active resistance at one end of the scale and enthusiastic cooperation at the other, and many French people fell somewhere in between. There was one obvious exception: Charles de Gaulle. General de Gaulle, military officer under Pétain's command in World War I, was drafted into the first of the Vichy governments as junior defence minister, but fled to London following the June 1940 armistice to raise British support for the French resistance; the rest is history.

The story of de Gaulle's war continues to fascinate because it reveals the fragility of his enterprise, namely to organize the 'Free French' – those military and civilians from mainland France and France's African colonies who, like him, rejected the Vichy settlement – into a fighting force and a homeland, guerilla-type resistance movement. De Gaulle was repudiated on many occasions by the wartime leaders of the US and the UK, President F.D. Roosevelt and Prime Minister Winston Churchill, who made repeated efforts to persuade Vichy France – legitimate France, as the Allies saw it – to join the war. The resistance movement itself was internally split, yet it was from within the resistance movement that the skeletal structures and policies – and, importantly, the legitimacy of the first post-war government – took shape, and loyalties and reputations formed. The French Communist Party gained public acceptance, for example, for its role in the resistance; and it was also from within the resistance that the most mythical and symbolic aspects of de Gaulle's leadership qualities derived.

This mythologizing of de Gaulle's actions in the Vichy period was fundamental, from de Gaulle's perspective, in enabling France and the French to emerge from the war with some sense of national unity around the idea that the French Republic had been maintained

Figure 1.1: Omaha Beach, Normandy. Memorial to the Allied Forces of Operation Overlord (Author)

despite Vichy and thanks to the resistance movement. This narrative extended to the glorification of the role of French forces in the Liberation of 1944–45, although today's memorials to the critical role played by the Allies in this drama tell another story (see Figure 1.1).

The *épuration* (purges) – the summary punishment or execution meted out in 1944–45 to tens of thousands of French people for their alleged wartime collaboration – was the most visible evidence of this black and white view of events. The ambiguities and grey areas of Vichy should have humbled the French but, for as long as de Gaulle was in charge, humility was not in the French national interest.

Modernization, Europeanization and decolonization

The confusion and ambiguities of the war years constituted a context ripe for yet another French civil war. Instead, somehow, in the dangerous international climate of the Cold War, the turbulence was channelled into the creative chaos of the Fourth Republic (1946–58). This regime instigated a programme of domestic reconstruction on the one hand and, on the other, international rehabilitation through decolonization and the anchoring of France, however ambiguously, to the Western camp in the Cold War. But it was still riven with divisions, which, in 1958, exploded into near-civil war surrounding the loss of France's most prized colony: Algeria.

By 1946, de Gaulle himself had already withdrawn from the provisional government that took power following the liberation of France in 1944, inter-party unity having proved elusive in the context of the emerging Cold War. In particular, the French Communist Party, buoyed in popularity and membership by its association with active resistance, could not reconcile itself to the dose of capitalist conservatism that would have made it a parliamentary ally of the socialists and centrists. The Catholic, centrist MRP (le Mouvement des républicains populaires) had limited appeal thanks to its confessional character; the Socialists were split on many issues; Pierre Poujade's nationalist movement challenged stability; and de Gaulle's supporters continually undermined the regime and its leaders during the 12-year period that became known as de Gaulle's 'crossing of the desert' – his self-imposed exile at home in Colombey-les-Deux-Eglises (now a tourist attraction).

This was not a good basis on which to rebuild the shattered French nation, reconstruct the economy, or assist the country to adjust to its post-war role in the world. Of these three objectives, most successful was socio-economic revival: international influence and a new external identity for France would come later, with de Gaulle's return as president of the Fifth Republic in 1958. Ambitions of social progress were enshrined in the 1946 constitution: women now had the vote, and new systems were instituted for state-led, 'technocratic' economic planning. This indicative, five-year rolling 'plan' produced a startling reversal of fortunes, typified by economic growth and real changes to daily lives. The French population began to grow, in part through rising immigration, in part because of a post-war baby boom (the population grew by over 12 million over the 30 years from 1946). Thus were born French consumers, henceforth protected from the worst misfortunes by a burgeoning welfare state (*l'état-providence*). New towns and homes were built and equipped to far higher standards than many were accustomed to: new generations of French people became fans of the cars, refrigerators, washing machines, televisions and telephones and other home comforts that they saw their American counterparts enjoying in films, and even in their own neighbourhoods (in the case of the US forces stationed at NATO's then HQ outside Paris). Urbanization, industrialization and tertiarization altered the image of a profoundly rural country, itself previously transformed by the tractor. New jobs – on production lines, in supermarkets – were created, altering socio-professional hierarchies, and France laid the foundations for its successes as an exporting nation. These were modern times: the beginning of the 'trente glorieuses' – the 30 'glorious' years of economic expansion from 1946 to 1975.

The international context to such expansion was the emergence of a bipolar world order in which the Cold War between the USSR and the US held their allies and satellites to ransom by various means. Thus, under pressure from the US in the form of the European Recovery Program (the Marshall Plan), innovative thinkers in post-war France got to work. Under the specific guidance of French international businessman Jean Monnet, they proposed a groundbreaking scheme for Franco-German reconciliation in the form of a potentially Europe-wide protected market for coal and steel: the 1951 European Coal and Steel Community (ECSC). This was a market opportunity for France that has significantly shaped French economics to the present day (see Chapters 7 and 8) and by 2000 had led to the adoption in France of the single European currency, the euro. But this form of European unification was also a face-saving solution to forging a new friendship with Germany and, by 1958, French leaders had agreed to expand the experiment to the civilian use of nuclear technology and the entire market economy. These developments created EURATOM (the European Atomic Energy Community) and the EEC (the European Economic Community), respectively.

Despite further encouragement from the US, the leaders of the Fourth Republic could not agree to extend these new forms of European cooperation to military and defence; thus the ECSC and EEC emerged as precious successes during a period marked by foreign policy humiliations. These included the loss of French Indochina in 1954 (searingly rendered in Eric Vuillard's ironically entitled novel *An Honourable Exit* (2023)); the climb-down to the US in the Suez crisis of 1956; and the growing unrest in Algeria, which was, administratively speaking, French territory but whose indigenous citizens were lesser in the eyes of the law. All of these developments drained the Fourth Republic of resources and legitimacy but, by 1958, it was Algeria's guerilla freedom-fighters, the FLN (Front de libération nationale – National Liberation Front) that brought the French army, losing lives and face, to the point of rebellion against the Paris politicians. Once again, *in extremis,* the French Republic seemed to need an injection of strong political leadership to contain revolution and maintain national unity. Who better than another saviour figure? Charles de Gaulle's personal aura, military credentials and political backing combined to make him irresistible to the army and government alike. In June 1958, the Fourth French Republic parliamentarians voted de Gaulle in as prime minister and in September 1958 the French people, voting by referendum, agreed to his conditions for a new, Fifth French Republic. In 2023, this regime celebrated 65 years of existence with remarkably little fanfare.

Gaullist France in the Cold War years

As first president of the Fifth Republic between 1959 and 1969, de Gaulle set ambitious goals that guaranteed further transformations of the identity of France and, in particular, the face that it projected to the outside world. This world, as de Gaulle saw it, was characterized by an unstable and unfair distribution of power between the USSR and the US, which he set out to challenge; this was his 'Yalta complex', in reference to the February 1945 summit at which the borders of Europe and respective spheres of influence had been determined by the Allied powers but to which France had not been invited. Thus, de Gaulle oversaw the development of a French nuclear deterrent, independent of American technology or strategy, and designed ostensibly to reach any target, not just the Soviet threat (the so-called *tous azimuts* doctrine). He also established a truly history-making friendship with the West German chancellor Konrad Adenauer that laid the foundations of the 'Franco-Saxon' (Hayward, 2007) European Communities of the 1970s and 1980s.

France, Europe and the US

De Gaulle's intentions for the Franco-German relationship (in the absence of cooperation from the UK) were that it should constitute the bedrock of a third, European, military power in the world, a vision known in French as *l'Europe puissance*. This ambition and this terminology still have currency in contemporary French political discourse, but they were ambiguous from day one. How would this bloc relate to NATO, for example, whose aims are also the military protection of (then) Western Europe? De Gaulle's response in 1966 was shocking: he expelled NATO's HQ from France and withdrew France from the organization, a posture not reversed until 30 years later under Presidents Chirac and then Sarkozy (see also Chapter 8). Simultaneously, de Gaulle proposed to turn the EEC into a 'Union of States' with common policies in matters of defence, culture, education and the economy. But these efforts were unsuccessful since the EEC's other members, notably Germany, were reluctant to take such steps towards destabilizing the European order in the dangerous Cold War years. De Gaulle's legacy in terms of European integration have, instead, been a strong French commitment to Europe's Common Agricultural Policy, a highly structured form of Franco-German cooperation (see Chapters 7 and 8), and testy relations with the UK.

Domestically, de Gaulle's stand-off with the US was reflected in his strident derision of American cultures and taste. This was a stance with firm roots in the Fourth Republic, when high-level protests against the import of Coca-Cola to France coexisted with generous but reluctant market access accorded to US-produced feature films. At stake in these battles was national identity, and the tussle between France and the US for global influence through culture, market economics and military reach continues to this day (see Chapters 6 and 8).

Founding the Fifth French Republic

De Gaulle's identity wars extended to the nature of the regime itself in France. The Fifth French Republic was in itself a transformation, albeit with echoes of previous – non-republican – regimes. From 1958 to 1962, de Gaulle, as president, overrode party and parliamentary politics to rule by a series of public referenda as he moved towards the shocking decision to accord Algeria its independence in 1962. This was a policy that almost cost him his life, courtesy of factions of the military and European settlers (known as *les pieds noirs*) for whom the expulsion from Algeria was a traumatic, impossible experience.

Table 1.1: Presidents of the Fifth French Republic

Charles de Gaulle	1959–69	Re-elected 1965 by first direct election of the Fifth Republic
Georges Pompidou	1969–74	Died in office
Valéry Giscard d'Estaing	1974–81	One seven-year term
François Mitterrand	1981–95	Two seven-year terms
Jacques Chirac	1995–2007	One seven-year term and one five-year term
Nicolas Sarkozy	2007–12	One five-year term
François Hollande	2012–17	One five-year term
Emmanuel Macron	2017–	One five-year term; re-elected 2022

De Gaulle was, despite appearances, a realist, and shedding Algeria was for him a price to be paid for France's international credibility and strength.

In 1962, such was his legitimacy at the time, de Gaulle unconstitutionally amended the constitution itself in favour of a henceforth directly elected president. Thus, even after his death, the Fifth Republic would have a strong executive president. This dramatic proposal succeeded, again by referendum, and we see in Chapter 4 that this provision for a popular, directly elected president makes the French head of state one of the most powerful leaders in the Western world, within a unique regime. We will also see in that chapter that presidential authority entrusted to mere French mortals has inexorably waned, not in letter but in spirit; by 2024 there had been eight presidents (see Table 1.1). But in the 1960s the instability of governments and the stranglehold of factional interests that had thwarted France's previous republics were now replaced by a more stable political life, institutionally at least.

Revolution? May 1968

The essence of Gaullism in de Gaulle's own day was his ability to reinvent French national identity as required by dramatic events,

31

while simultaneously striving to shape the course of these events. De Gaulle probably did possess an extraordinary talent of insight into domestic and international realities, yet he was no magician, and the forces of change eventually escaped his control and cost him his grip over the country. His version of the French Republic had created a patrician framework of power, heavily reliant on his own personal legitimacy. But he was an ageing and increasingly eccentric figure in the France of the late 1960s, in a context – Vietnam, the Beatles – typified by cultural and political consciousness-raising at home and abroad. His political style became an anachronism, and was challenged – in full, televised view of the world – by what became known as the 'events' (les événements) of May 1968. In Paris, a student-led youth revolt spread to workers, who organized a general strike throughout the country. The police were a key figure in this situation, notorious for the brutality with which they suppressed the riots in Paris. That force was reminiscent of the repression of the 19th-century French revolutions, not to mention the shocking quelling in 1961 of a peaceful pro-Algerian liberation march in Paris, which saw innocent victims thrown into the Seine river by the forces de l'ordre (the head of which was none other than Vichy collaborator Maurice Papon; see below). Repeated cases of police violence continue, moreover, to plague relations between the security forces and citizens in France today, reaching a particular nadir during the gilets jaunes movement of 2018–19. The 1968 events, indeed, took on a revolutionary aura, driven by angry, well-educated young people new to political activism, in debates open to all, and subject to no apparent rules. They deployed a new vocabulary of political slogans ('it is forbidden to forbid'; 'under the pavement, the beach') and extolled personal freedom from social or cultural taboo.

But de Gaulle lost neither his head nor, initially, his presidential position and, in the immediate aftermath of May–June 1968, even saw his parliamentary majority reinforced, as conservative forces in French society once again rejected a revolutionary future. But by then de Gaulle perhaps saw himself as the new ancien régime, a barrier to the next necessary phase in France's modernization. Within a year, he had resigned as president after losing the fifth and final referendum of his presidency, and less than six months later he was dead. The immediate legacy of 1968 was a raft of reforming legislation (in the education sector, for example, to respond to the students whose protests had ignited the events; and further moves towards workers' rights), albeit of limited impact. The more lasting legacy was political: the parties of the left had, in May 1968, failed to unite sufficiently to channel the events towards a peaceful overthrow of the Fifth Republic that they claimed to detest, yet the events of 1968, in removing de Gaulle from the scene, opened a decade in which the right became weakened by its own divisions, thus easing the left's passage to power in 1981, after 23 years of opposition.

The 'glorious' years of fast economic growth and social transformation that had characterized the previous post-war decades were severely curtailed by the economic turbulence of the 1970s. The breakdown of the global Bretton Woods financial system at the start of the decade, and the intense pressure on the price of crude oil at the end, exposed underlying weaknesses in the French economy (see Chapters 7 and 8), such as the heavy hand of the state in micro-economic decision-making, significant trade deficits, and a weak currency. French leaders turned the screws: President Valéry Giscard d'Estaing, a political figure independent and distanced by a generation from de Gaulle's close circle, tried to call a halt to unskilled immigration in the mid-1970s and persuade migrant workers to return home, and to seek currency protection within a European monetary system, with very limited results. His final prime minister, Raymond Barre, turned to austerity measures to stem rising inflation and unemployment, again with little success.

The power of the French presidency as interpreted by de Gaulle was still evident in the form of world-renowned feats and achievements in many fields: the civil nuclear energy programme, the laying down of the high-speed train (the TGV – *train à grande vitesse*) network, the Pompidou Centre and Montparnasse Tower constructions in Paris, and the Anglo-French Concorde supersonic aeroplane were all intended as symbols of French *grandeur* for international, as much as domestic, consumption. France was more socially liberal under Giscard, with new rights for women, for example. Modernization also took the shape of technological developments including France's quirky Minitel, an innovative precursor to the era of personal computers and the internet. French households were given free hardware with connectivity via the telephone that became much loved for its messaging (*messagerie*) functions, especially the telephone directory and dating services. It was cheap, practical and accessible to all, but was soon overtaken by more advanced digital technologies. Giscard notably worked for détente in the Franco-American relationship but he was undermined by would-be heirs to Gaullism from within his majority, rallied by future president Jacques Chirac, and the communist left allowed itself to be lured into electoral alliances with the reinvigorated Socialist Party under the leadership of François Mitterrand.

Change and continuity: François Mitterrand's France

Mitterrand had once memorably described de Gaulle's leadership as a permanent *coup d'état*, yet, once he himself was elected to the powerful presidency in 1981, he reported back from the sumptuous Elysée Palace that the function, in fact, suited him rather well, and he went on to consolidate, not overturn, the Fifth French Republic. Mitterrand's 14-year presidency (1981–95) was the longest there will ever be under the current constitution and, in many respects, he and his socialist governments set France on the tracks to the 21st century: overturning 'traditions' such as the death penalty; encouraging the tolerance of difference, between genders, races and ethnicities; modernizing industrial structures; embracing new technologies and, more reluctantly, the market; and making France a powerful leading member of the European Union. But when the 21st century came a decade early in 1989, in the form of the collapse of the Soviet Empire, Mitterrand suddenly aged, both literally and in contrast with the challenges of the new times. His own past began to catch up with him, too, and France's 'work of memory' in relation to painful 20th-century events was under way.

The socialist experiment?

Was François Mitterrand a socialist? He brought the left to power in the Fifth Republic by presenting himself, successfully, as the leader of the *whole* of the French left. In reality, the French left was deeply divided. In keeping with an electoral platform written by the Socialist Party for candidate Mitterrand, and including a handful of Communist Party ministers, the Fifth Republic's first socialist governments, from 1981 to 1983, embarked on a large-scale programme of nationalization (of banks and industry), along with a raft of social reforms designed to improve the conditions of France's working classes. These included longer statutory holidays, a rise in the minimum wage, a wealth tax, a ceiling of 60 years on the retirement age, and other redistributory measures. This programme set France apart from its EEC neighbours in its pursuit of socialism in one country – with drastic results. Capital fled from the country, France lost international credibility, Communist Party ministers were fired, and three currency devaluations followed in quick succession in 1982 and 1983 under the guidance of France's finance minister, Jacques Delors.

Delors went on to become a central figure in the aftermath of this failure. Appointed president of the European Commission by Mitterrand in 1984, Delors piloted, from Brussels, what became known as the Single European Market programme (the SEM – see Chapter 7). This comprised a swathe of European-level legislative measures designed to complete the provisions of the original 1957 Treaty of Rome in favour of the free movement, within the EC, of goods, capital, services and people, by means of the removal of existing barriers of all kinds. Delors would have been unsuccessful without the support of French president Mitterrand and his German and British counterparts, Chancellor Helmut Kohl and Prime Minister Margaret Thatcher. The programme that they all sanctioned was predominantly one of economic liberalization and deregulation, and its implementation in France set new targets for the economy designed to bring economic gains in the form of industrial competitiveness (see Chapter 7). As a French socialist who had campaigned in 1981 to 'break with capitalism', however, Mitterrand's policy U-turn, as it came to be known, cast the Socialist Party into a confused state regarding the market economy, with no clear sign, still today, of a satisfactory resolution. The Mitterrand–Delors duo, argues Morelle (2021), set France on a track of 'unmaking' France, a claim with some credibility that we revisit in subsequent chapters below.

Taking European cover in order to implement domestic economic reforms – in other words, instrumentalizing Europe – set 1980s France on a course that thus far has proved irreversible, although Euroscepticism, as we see in Chapter 3 below, has installed itself as a permanent challenge at the heart of French politics. François Mitterrand went on to only very narrowly (50.8 per cent) persuade his population in a referendum in 1992 that the Maastricht Treaty – designed to create a single European currency alongside new European-level powers in matters of security and defence – was the correct answer to the new circumstances of a reunified Germany and a spent Soviet Union, whatever the cost to independent policy-making (see Figure 1.2). There was continuity and logic to this European commitment and close partnership with Germany; in the early 1980s, Mitterrand had already supported Chancellor Kohl in his decision to allow the installation of US short-range missiles targeted at the Soviet Union. In the final decade of the Cold War, Mitterrand had turned out to be a far more enthusiastic Atlanticist than most had predicted.

Mitterrand's domestic legacy is complex: he sponsored socially liberal measures, and he set in train a significant programme of decentralization that is still ongoing (see Chapter 4). In addition, he sanctioned spending on popular cultural events (see Chapter 6) and tended to the national pride and the international face of France by means of an architectural legacy (the pyramid in the Louvre courtyard being the most striking, shocking at the time) that has helped to maintain the status of the French capital as one of the ten most visited cities in the world. He survived an unprecedented episode of power-sharing – known as *la cohabitation* – when he was forced to appoint his long-time opponent Jacques Chirac as prime minister following the defeat of the left in the 1986 legislative elections (see Chapters 3 and 4), and he emerged from the experience as a sort of father figure whom the nation was content to re-elect in 1988 for an equally unprecedented second seven-year term.

Age, illness and the past eventually caught up with François Mitterrand, who died in January 1996. He had remained enigmatic to the end: the first the general public knew of his second family – Anne Pingeot and their daughter, Mazarine – was when *Paris Match* published their photos, shortly before they gathered at his graveside next to his wife, Danielle. As for the secret of his long-standing prostate cancer, that emerged only after his death when his doctor, Claude Gubler, committed his account to publication in a book (*The Big Secret*) that sold tens of thousands of copies before being withdrawn from the shelves and pulped. Mitterrand

Figure 1.2: 'Yes or no?' The referendum on the Maastricht Treaty, 20 September 1992. The draft treaty text ran to about 70 pages and was sent to each French voter. Here we see the cover page and the 'yes' and 'no' voting slips (*bulletins de vote*) (Author)

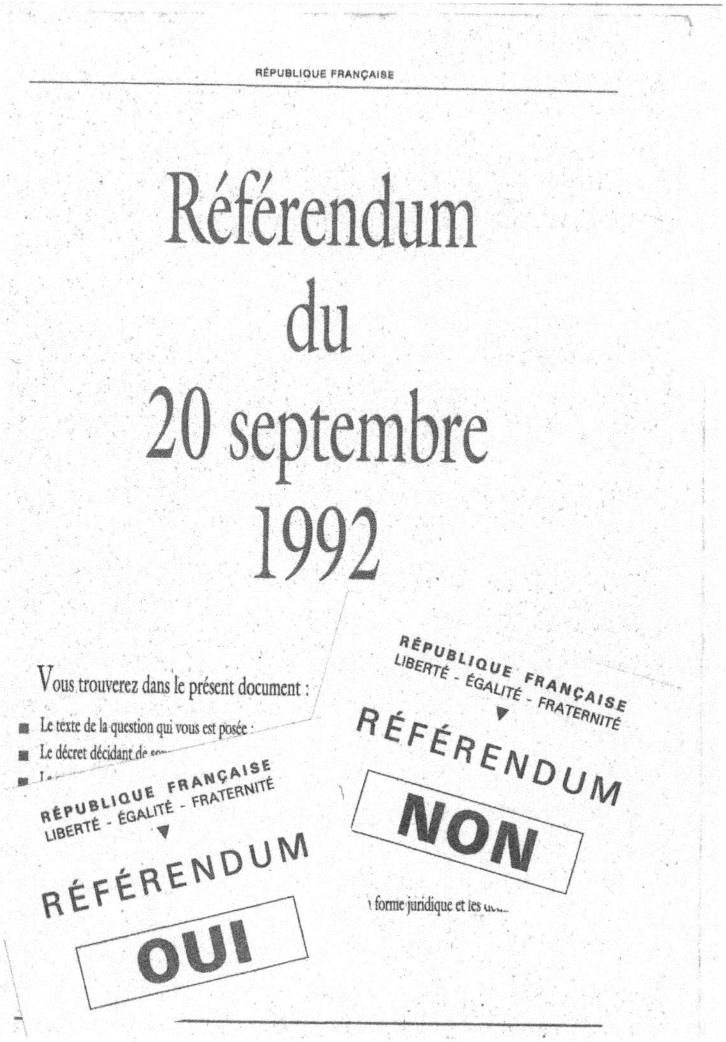

had already subjected himself to questions about the exact nature of his involvement with the Vichy regime in World War II, and details of his interest in the 1930s in far-right activities were by then already known. Fourteen years in power was, also, excessive by contemporary democratic standards, and during Mitterrand's presidency the far-right National Front began its as-yet-inexorable rise. Its then leader, Jean-Marie Le Pen, scored 15 per cent (nearly 4 million votes) in the first round of the 1995 presidential election and subsequently increased his share to nearly 20 per cent in 2002, and his votes to over 5 million. Twenty years later, in the second and final round of the 2022 presidential elections and as we see in Chapter 3, his daughter had taken this vote share to over 13 million votes and broken through with almost 100 seats in the National Assembly (the lower house of parliament) for her party, now named the National Rally. Domestically and internationally, French identity was challenged by the developments of the late 20th century and, in 1995, France elected Jacques Chirac (on his third attempt) to assist France in the transition from one century to the next. This would involve a reckoning with the recent, 20th-century past.

From Jacques Chirac to Emmanuel Macron: France enters the 21st century

In 1989, France had celebrated the bicentenary of the storming of the Bastille prison in 1789, prompting some historians to conclude that, 200 years later, France had finally embraced the present and relegated its revolutionary past to distant memory. This was controversial but less troubling for contemporary politics than the events of the mid- to late twentieth century, still within living memory, that cast a shadow over the present. The extent of the complicity of Vichy officials with the German occupiers in the deportation to concentration camps of French and foreign Jews, and the truths of French repression in its colonial territories, especially Algeria, were the objects of legal, media and political attention in the very first years of the 21st century. Those reckonings were soon joined by the indescribably painful work of digesting the meaning of the repeated terror attacks that rocked France from 2012 for an entire decade.

War trials

Jean-Marie Le Pen's attitudes during the 1980s had encouraged a small minority of intellectuals and academics to trivialize – to revise or even 'negate' – France's responsibility in the World War II deportation of French and foreign Jews from France to Nazi concentration camps; this, predictably, had led to outrage, as well as the outlawing of such speech. At the same time, the painstaking pursuit of war criminals had caught up with a number of French high-ranking collaborators, and the 1990s saw the high-profile trials of two of these. Paul Touvier, in 1994, was found guilty of crimes against humanity and sentenced to life imprisonment for his role as leader of Vichy's Militia police. In 1998, Maurice Papon, a regional official (general-secretary of the *préfecture* of Bordeaux) at the time of his orders for the deportation of French Jews, was found guilty of complicity in such crimes and sentenced to ten years in prison (he was released after three years on the grounds of ill health, and died in 2007).

Most notoriously, both men had gone on to exercise political influence in the decades after Vichy. Papon, as head of Paris Police in 1961, had failed to prevent or stop the bloody repression and murder of Algerians demonstrating in Paris to support the cause of Algerian independence (see above). This continuity was an important aspect of the trials because it demonstrated the complicity not just of individuals such as Touvier and Papon but of the machinery of the French state itself, in some of the darkest moments of French history. Similarly, the revelations in the 1990s, by victims and perpetrators alike, of the French army torture of Algerian nationalists (FLN) during the Algerian war reminded the French that such atrocities had occurred within the framework of the Republic, and effectively with its blessing. It took until 2018 for a French president, Emmanuel Macron, to explicitly acknowledge this fact of France's past. Not all were shamed by these revelations in comparison with their shame in losing Algeria itself. President Chirac's response to these developments was to decree symbols of truth and reconciliation, including a day of national homage to the victims of the Algerian conflict, the first of which took place in September 2001. In 1995, he also instigated the official recognition of the role of the French state in the crimes of the Vichy regime, and promised to pay in full, in accordance with a law of 1994, the retirement pensions of veteran colonial soldiers. However, it was not until a Council of State ruling in 2002 that action was taken in this respect. The Catholic Church, for its part, had issued an apology in 1997 for its complicity with the crimes of Vichy.

President Chirac's gestures to curtail the nostalgic perspective on 20th-century French history were not without their opponents, or twists and turns. In 2005, he was forced to repeal legislation requiring teachers to ensure that the 'positive role' of France in its former colonies was part of the school curriculum, and his successor, Nicolas Sarkozy, on the very night of his election to the presidency on 6 May 2007, declared that France had no call to demean itself by 'repenting' for the past. President Macron, for his part, refused to apologize on behalf of France for its colonial rule of Algeria, believing such apologies to have less substance than the actual hard graft of reconciliation, although he did apologize to France's *harkis*, the many thousands of Algerians who had fought for France in the Algerian war of independence but were subsequently mistreated by the French state. Contemporary France has, thus, taken responsibility for the complicity of the French state in crimes against humanity by treading a cautious, tricky path to a point somewhere between denial and repentance, and between the twin pulls of domestic voices considering that France's leaders have either gone too far or not far enough in their acknowledgements that French history can and should be exposed to the norms of the present day.

Ending the past?

President Sarkozy's promises to break with the past were comprehensive; they were to apply to virtually all areas of French public policy-making and national life, starting with getting the French 'back to work' after a decade of the 35-hour working week. Yet, during Chirac's presidency, many steps had already been taken towards embracing the 21st century. Domestically, the 1958 constitution had been amended to include the commitment to 'parity' in national elections in an attempt to increase the number of women in leading roles in French politics and parliament, but implementation of this provision would be slow. From 2002 onwards, the constitution also included the mention of the Republic as being henceforth organized on a 'decentralized' basis, in recognition of the ongoing project to devolve power, resources and responsibility – and some, very limited autonomy – to France's regions and towns, as we see in further detail in Chapter 4. The length of the presidential mandate was also reduced, during Chirac's presidency, from seven to five years, making cohabitation less likely, although not impossible, and bringing France closer into line with comparable democratic systems. This would have a significant impact on presidential power, reducing its capacity for long-term, visionary action, as we develop in Chapter 4. Reforms to the market economy, instigated during the late 1980s, continued as public utilities were partially privatized and deregulated, and France upheld its performance as an exporting nation.

There were also domestic defeats and controversies for President Chirac. In 2004, he brought into law a toughening of the rules regarding *la laïcité* (secularism). The law banned the wearing by pupils in state schools of the 'conspicuous' signs of religion, especially the Muslim headscarf (*le voile*) and, although it won strong support in parliament and in public opinion, it projected a repressive image of France to the outside world, and was seen by its opponents as playing into the hands of the National Front in the fear it suggested of the power of Muslim culture in contemporary France. These dynamics only strengthened in subsequent years, as the French tussled with the implementation of the principle of *laïcité* in a population that was becoming ever more diverse, culturally and in terms of religious affiliation (see Chapter 5).

Conclusions

By the close of the first decade of the 21st century, France had elected a president intent upon extricating France, as Nicolas Sarkozy saw it, from the straitjacket of history, and making France a country like any other. For President Sarkozy, nothing was off limits – not the 1789 Revolution; not the 1968 cultural near-miss revolution so fondly remembered by France's baby-boom generation, in power during the 2000s; not the 'French social model', where workers' rights are carefully balanced against market imperatives; nor even the solemnity of presidential office. One decade later, by 2020, France had dispensed with a one-term socialist president, François Hollande, along with its mainstream political parties of left and right, bringing to power the curious iconoclast Emmanuel Macron.

Given the strength of history in France as a social science discipline and the passions of living and selective memories, any presidential ambitions to rewrite France's past would inevitably be very limited in practice. Nevertheless, the hold of history – ancient, medieval, revolutionary, recent – over contemporary France is undoubtedly loosening and in many ways France in the mid-2020s does look a lot more like other countries than it did even only 20 years ago. It is definitely of its times; the most recent, big structural changes and upheavals were nearly half a century ago, and Franco-French civil wars are a thing of the past: today's divisions and challenges are matters of and for policy, not grand historical principles. However, they are still significant and France's political class struggles to contain them. Domestically and internationally, France faces problems that are common across Europe – the contested place of Islam in society, the economic challenges of global markets, national security – and it is increasingly turning to its neighbours and partners for ideas and assistance in resolving the most pressing of these.

2

France and the French

Introduction

Contemporary France has a strong sense of national self, largely flowing from the history explored in the previous chapter. But that history, we have seen, is complex and contested; so too, unsurprisingly, is this selfhood. Indeed, and as with other Western countries, French national identity finds itself undergoing permanent renegotiation to keep up with the times. Physically speaking, the six-sided outline of mainland France – 'the Hexagon' – is synonymous with France itself. The country has not always been this shape, however, having traumatically lost its eastern provinces of Alsace and Lorraine to Germany between 1870 and 1919 and, again, for the duration of World War II. Moreover, until the 20th century, when transportation and education became widespread, the geometric shape of the country was not even familiar to many of its own citizens.

Furthermore, the notion of the Hexagon limits that imagined space to what the French call the *métropole* or mainland France, when in fact France physically spills out into seas and continents around the globe as far as the Pacific, comprising territories where calls for independence from France challenge the rhetoric of national unity. Similarly, French citizens communicating and (mis)informing themselves in cyberspace pit the French state's capacity to craft national identity against the power of US corporations such as Facebook and Google to generate new allegiances – and new (un)truths. Also challenging France's monopoly over its own identity is France's membership of the European Union (EU) and, beyond that, of many international organizations and binding international agreements. The Hexagon, Hayward (2007: 47) says, is a shrinking piece of an ever-expanding puzzle and, indeed, French governments have, over the past 70 years, voluntarily and constitutionally transferred powers (euphemistically termed 'competences') to the institutions of the EU. The very physical borders between France and many of its neighbouring EU countries have been rendered largely irrelevant by French membership of the EU's passport-free Schengen zone, by way of example, other than in times deemed to warrant temporary restoration of these barriers, and these facts of EU membership have come under increasing pressure.

Demography itself is a serious subject in France given the country's history since the 19th century of low birth rates and generations decimated by war. Throughout much of the 20th century, France turned to its colonies for supplies of workers and fighters, intending to limit them to just those roles, rather than subsequently absorb them into the nation with full rights; this was a blind spot that by the 1980s had caught up with France and has challenged it ever since. Accordingly, France's population in the present day is cosmopolitan and multiethnic, shaped by successive waves of immigration throughout much of the 20th century, as well as by the diversity of those who can trace their ancestors back to times before the territory was as unified as it is today. It is also growing, although that growth rate is slowing, for now.

But French policy today on immigration, race, ethnicity and belonging is strikingly fraught with contradictions and strife as the quest for a unified national community saps the energy of policy makers navigating all sorts of realities including mass migration to Europe, and concerns about France's capacity to secure the nation. The 2024 Immigration, Integration and Asylum law amply illustrates this bind, in which France is far from alone in Europe. Just as significant, these challenges blight the daily lives of those who struggle to live a life free from discrimination on the grounds of their origins. In 2009, President Sarkozy declared that being French means belonging to a particular 'civilization' and respecting certain 'values' and 'customs' (2009): not all values and behaviours are equal in France, he proclaimed. By way of example, said Sarkozy, France is a country where there is no place for the *burqa* and in 2011 the wearing of this garment was duly banned from the public place.

Ten years later, French police were to be found ordering women to undress themselves in public where they had had the audacity to wear a *burkini* – modest swimwear – on French beaches. This troubling clash of women's rights over *their* bodies with the protection of the *national* body from certain claims to self-expression or, above all, to group belonging, is an ongoing dilemma for contemporary France.

In this chapter we address these key aspects of French national identity associated with its territory and population and explore the challenges and opportunities facing both. First, we begin with the matter of territory – the physical manifestation of France – and challenges to its integrity from open borders, transport, digital technologies and human mobility, among other factors. We look at *la terre* – the land, its resources, its management and its mythical qualities – and at *le terroir* – the combination, in a specific area, of soil, climate and location that fuels the claims to distinction and authenticity made for French food and wines, and for its tourist charms. Today, less than 20 per cent of the French population lives in the countryside, only a tiny minority of them are farmers, and traditional-style small-scale farmers are literally dying out. Yet the rurality that typified French life well into the 20th century has put French agriculture and its produce on a political and cultural pedestal. At the same time, many living in rural areas, and with some justification, feel like second-class citizens, neglected by the state and its services, and their grievances fuelled the *gilets jaunes* movement of 2018–19. Under these headings, we include an evaluation of how France is placed to withstand the challenges of climate change and energy insecurity, and explore the responses crafted by French leaders at national and international levels.

Second, we then focus on the French themselves – who are they, where are they from, who belongs and who does not? In the words of the so-called 'great debate' on French national identity launched by President Sarkozy in 2009, 'what does it mean to be French' in 21st-century France? This includes an overview of questions of race, ethnicity, culture and religion; of policy on immigration, nationality and citizenship; and of trends and developments in beliefs and attitudes in these regards. In conclusion, we reflect on the balance of these forces currently shaping France and the French within the bounds of their own country and nation. The French Constitution

(Article 1) declares the French Republic to be 'indivisible', and that is hard to achieve.

La terre, territory and *le terroir*

Most of the boundaries of France are natural (principally, mountains, rivers and coasts), and France contains a great variety of physical features, as well as a range of climatic zones. These are factors that help explain why in 2022 France welcomed almost 80 million international visitors, making it the world's favourite tourist destination (Statista, 2024), and why France's agricultural products range from beets in the north to olives and lemons in the south. Wine is produced in all four points of the French mainland, as well as in between, and accounted, also in 2022, for around 16 per cent of all French agricultural production (Ministère de l'agriculture et de la souveraineté alimentaire, 2024).

France faces the English Channel (or la Manche, as it is called in French), and this coast offers high cliffs, fishing villages and the World War II landing beaches. On the northern reaches of this coast, near the Channel port of Calais in particular, the beaches and their environs are also nowadays the site of makeshift camps struck by irregular migrants seeking to make the perilous journey across the Channel to reach the south coast of England. French police patrol these beaches and routinely dismantle these temporary dwellings, some of the efforts funded by the UK seeking to deter migrants from making the journey. Such expenditure has, however, proven insufficient to prevent the tragic deaths of many would-be refugees before they reached the UK, and inefficient in destroying the business model of the criminal people-smugglers.

The Atlantic coast for its part is famed for its sands, its surf and, towards the far south-west, its huge sand dunes and views of the Pyrénées mountains and, beyond them, Spain. This is also the terrain of the Basque country, straddling the Franco-Spanish border, home to a distinctive language and culture. On the Mediterranean, the Côte d'Azur has been a favourite with tourists, artists, retirees and second-home dwellers for several centuries. In the early 1960s, many of the European settlers fleeing Algeria on independence – called *pieds noirs* by native Algerians – also made their homes here as best they could after the trauma and material losses of their flight. It is a culturally and economically rich region of the country and votes largely for politicians promising to conserve and protect its privileges. Inland, France is separated by the Alps from Italy, by the Pyrénées from Spain, by the Vosges from Germany, by the Jura from Switzerland, and by nearly 200 kilometres of the Rhine from Germany. The Alps and the Pyrénées are over 50 million years old, and Mont Blanc in the French Alps, at 4,897 metres, is West Europe's highest peak. The Alps are also where the impact of climate change on France is at its most stark: the visible retreat of the glaciers and the unpredictability of snowfall testify to this phenomenon.

The four major rivers of France (the Loire, the Garonne, the Seine and the Rhône) and their tributaries and parallel canals offer spectacular limestone gorges, canyons, flat plains and beautiful navigable waterways, as well as their famous settlements: Paris on the Seine (the birthplace of modern France); Lyon on the Rhône, where it meets the Saône river; and the chateaux that line the Loire, including former royal abodes. The Massif Central alone includes extinct volcanoes, giving peaks of distinctive shape. East of Paris, by contrast, the land is flat but fertile, and in the north-east was traditionally home to important industrial centres (for coal and steel, for example) and where France's rapid deindustrialization from the 1980s onwards has left its distinct mark on lives, livelihoods, politics and physical geography alike.

These physical features are all accompanied by distinctive (but all temperate) climates, including an oceanic zone on France's western coast; continental weather patterns to the north-east; and the Mediterranean and mountain climates, historically and still much sought-after but now also subjected to extreme weather phenomena with severe consequences, such as the wildfires of summer 2022 in the south, and the repeated flooding in certain parts of the north over the winter of 2023–24. Together with the exotic locations of its overseas *départements*, the attractions of Paris and its many vibrant regional cities, France for now remains a country of much appeal.

France and its overseas territories

Mainland France, which in fact includes the island of Corsica, accounts for over 95 per cent of the country's population and over 80 per cent of its territory, with the rest accounted for by 12 overseas territories and communities, home to around 2.8 million people (see Figure 0.1, the map of mainland and overseas France, p xvi). These are spread right around the globe and were acquired when France was a colonial power. Most are islands. This legacy of colonialism is increasingly a factor as all parties struggle to rebalance their relationships in keeping with today's problems and expectations. The result is a patchwork of different models of administrative governance, differing degrees of autonomy from Paris, and an array of explosive, political tensions.

In the Pacific Ocean are the 150 islands of French Polynesia, Wallis and Fortuna and New Caledonia. In 2024, this latter territory erupted in violent riots as a long process designed to reconcile the island's indigenous – Kanak – and settler populations came to a head. Under the terms of the 1998 Nouméa Agreement, the island had undergone a process of public consultation by referenda as a route to potential independence. The first two votes only narrowly confirmed the status quo but the last referendum, held in 2021 during the COVID-19 pandemic, suggested a population now categorically opposed to independence (96 per cent). However, it had been boycotted by independentists and in 2024, when the French government legislated to remove a block on recent settlers having a vote (part of the Nouméa agreement), the situation degenerated, placing the native islanders' quest for self-determination, in a context of socio-economic hardship, back on France's troubled political agenda.

Five of the overseas territories are in the tropics, four of which – Martinique and Guadeloupe in the Caribbean, and Mayotte and Reunion in the Indian Ocean – are mountainous islands and a fifth, French Guyana in South America, is largely covered by rainforest. Both Guyana and Martinique voted to become a single overseas authority (*collectivité d'outre-mer*, as is the case for Saint Pierre and Micquelon in the Atlantic Ocean). Under Article 74 of the French Constitution, this status provides greater autonomy from Paris than the status of department-region currently held by the territories of Guadeloupe, Reunion Island and, since 2011, Mayotte (although Guyana and Martinique are also still categorized as overseas department-regions). Under Article 73 of the French Constitution, national rules apply in key policy domains, with some exceptions for adaptation to local circumstances.

France's overseas territories (which include, in the Antarctic, its unpopulated southern territories) have been of strategic importance to France, affording it an extensive maritime presence, support for its space industry and, until the end of the 20th century, a testing ground for France's nuclear weapons. They are also part of France's tourist business, and tourism is a vital source of income for these distant regions of France. State agency Atout France estimates annual tourist revenue from France's overseas territories at around 2 billion euros, with the territories welcoming over 1.7 million tourists in 2022 (Atout France, 2024). Politically, though, they are minefields, lagging significantly behind mainland France on many criteria. Gross domestic product (GDP) per capita is below the French national average. The cost of daily living is higher, especially for food. Unemployment is higher, as is the rate of school dropouts, and more people depend on state welfare. Indeed, they are costly to the French state and they are, moreover, sore reminders of France's colonial past, as well as its involvement in the slave trade. They continue to be sites of serious unrest and challenge within and to the French Republic – as Leigh Turner wrote of the UK and its overseas territories, conflict between mainland and overseas France is 'pre-programmed' (Turner, 2024) – but they generate very little debate in French politics or society (again, not dissimilar to the UK).

Habitats, mobility and transport

Visitors to mainland France itself, coming from more crowded European countries such as the UK or the Netherlands, are invariably struck by how spacious the country is. France may be smaller than the US state of Texas, with a population nearly three times as big, but, to a European visitor at least, France feels big in a North American way, with proper distances between urban sprawls despite the spread of out-of-town shopping centres and housing across the country. France is less than half as densely populated as the UK and Germany. Of its surface area, 80 per cent is rural but only 20 per cent of the population live there, and the vast majority of those are not farmers. Agricultural land has been lost over the decades to other uses, not only urbanization but also forestry: well over one quarter of France's land is covered by forest.

Despite these statistics, France still constitutes a large share of the EU's agricultural land (approximately one fifth), and this is used for meat and dairy herds, cheese and wine production, and the cultivation of sugars and cereals. This production makes France the world's sixth largest exporter of agricultural goods, and the main agricultural producer in the EU. Barely 3 per cent of the working population actually works on the land, however, and agriculture accounts for little more than 2 per cent of GDP, even though agricultural production itself has grown (as has the average farm size), and agribusiness itself generates trade surpluses, France's main agricultural and food exports being wine, spirits, dairy and cereals. But these surpluses have been declining, and farmers in the dairy and beef industries struggle to maintain their incomes and competitiveness, particularly given the gradually decreasing support for agricultural production from the EU's Common Agricultural Policy (CAP) as the EU expands its membership and resets its spending priorities (see Chapters 7 and 8), and in the face of ruthless retail pricing.

Around two thirds of the population are estimated to live in urban areas and one third in rural surroundings, when measured by population density (as opposed to the built environment). Around 7 per cent of the total population live in *communes* (see Chapter 4) of 500 people or fewer. Traditionally, a 'rural' lifestyle implied working the land for agricultural output or subsistence. In contrast, today's so-called 'neo-rurals' (*néo-ruraux* or '*rurbains*' – urban, city people aspiring to a rural lifestyle) practise a wide variety of activities in the countryside, linked principally to tourism or the service industries, or they exercise professions where advanced communications technologies make location irrelevant. Clashes of interest between farmers and their neo-rural neighbours – over the environment and the use of precious resources such as water – are not uncommon. The number of second homes in France today, principally in the countryside, is estimated to be around 4 million and, in some parts of France, particularly in the centre and south-west, British and other European migrants have, in some cases, populated and revived otherwise dying rural communities over several decades.

However, following the UK's decision in 2016 to leave the EU – Brexit – there is some evidence of a reversal of this trend, since 'Brits' (Drake and Collard, 2008) no longer enjoy uncomplicated rights of freedom of movement, including residency, within the EU. Furthermore, second-home ownership per se is increasingly coming at a cost, as growing numbers of local authorities find themselves permitted to charge high local taxes on these residences

Figure 2.1: France for sale? Ring England. The Dordogne, south-west France, 2000 (Author)

(*la taxe d'habitation*) to address housing shortages that may be particularly acute in their locality, in some cases exacerbated by the enthusiasm in France as elsewhere for Airbnb short-term rentals (France being one of Airbnb's biggest markets). These movements towards the countryside, confirmed in the 2021 census, go some way towards correcting the significant rural exodus that marked the *trente glorieuses* – the modernization years – between the 1950s and the 1980s in France, when people moved to the cities en masse in search of work. That flight from the countryside had itself echoed earlier movements away from the rural France that is still, today, mythologized as the 'real France'; Graham Robb (2007: 330) expertly describes how, in the late 19th century, '[t]he rural population was flowing away to the cities, leaving the countryside exposed to the forces of Nature and foreign invasion. It was the patriotic duty of every French citizen to go on holiday to unpopular places.'

However, some people – of course – continue to move to Paris and its rich region – the Île de France – and other urban areas in search of work and a different life. The picture is now more balanced, but contemporary France is still unmistakably urban, and has been since the 1960s; the most notable aspect of this development has been the growth and popularity of France's medium-sized and large towns – its regional cities – such as Bordeaux, Grenoble, Lyon, Montpellier, Nantes, Nice, Rennes, Strasbourg and Toulouse. These come complete with modern transport systems, including trams, and a distinct and vibrant cultural life of their own.

The number and variety of such cities is, indeed, one of France's many attractions: France has over 40 cities of 100,000 inhabitants or more (excluding Paris). Compared with the post-war decades in France, the lifestyles of urban and country dwellers are more alike, and today's principal distinctions are between those living comfortably, whether urban or rural, and those living in less favourable surroundings, especially in France's outer-city suburbs

Figure 2.2: Green Paris? Electric trams (Author)

and estates – *la banlieue* and *les cités*. However, it was predominantly the grievances of rural inhabitants, feeling unfairly targeted by a new diesel ('carbon') tax, being more reliant than town- and city-dwellers on their private vehicles, that sparked and sustained the *gilets jaunes* movement in 2018–19 (see also Chapters 3 and 5) and subsequently prompted public policy attention towards these problems.

Indeed, these patterns of human migration and habitation cannot be divorced from the development in contemporary France of efficient and fast long-distance travel networks, especially by rail and road, juxtaposed with large swathes of the country where public transport for short, daily journeys including the commute to work is a less viable or tempting option than the car. It is possible to drive in a single day from France's Channel ports to its Mediterranean coast, thanks to France's network of toll motorways: the distance between the Channel port of Boulogne to the Mediterranean resort of Nice is just under 1,200 kilometres, which, according to ViaMichelin (2024) could be driven in around 12 hours at a cost of approximately 200 euros. Low-cost airlines still offer a wide choice of options for travelling between regional airports in France (and its European neighbours), although regional airport construction projects have met with stiff local resistance on environmental grounds; and in 2023 the government decreed, also for environmental reasons (the actual impact is contested), that short-haul flights were now forbidden for journeys that could be completed by train in less than 2.5 hours. High-speed motorway and rail networks bring all major points of the country within reach of each other, as well as offering links between France and other European countries, both on the continent itself and to its nearby neighbour, the UK. The world-famous TGV (*train à grande vitesse*) high-speed trains run on a network that has both seen a dramatic expansion since the early days in the 1980s and an equally dramatic opening to market competition. Travel times have been significantly cut, to the point where the Paris–Strasbourg journey (nearly 500 kilometres) takes a little over two hours, compared with the four hours of the past.

France used to be notorious for a transport network where all lines radiated from Paris; times have changed. The Channel Tunnel, opened in 1996, now provides a fixed rail and road link between Britain and France. The rail journey by Eurostar takes a mere 20 minutes to get under the Channel and has brought regional cities of France – as well as the cities beyond its borders, in Belgium, the Netherlands, Germany, Spain, Italy and Switzerland, for example – within easy and comfortable reach of the UK (London, at least). Rail and road passengers do not always have to change in Paris. Car ferries still link several French Channel ports (Calais and Boulogne in the east; Dieppe, le Havre, Caen, St Malo and Roscoff towards the west) to the UK and to Ireland, giving drivers a choice between these more sedate methods of breaching the Channel and the high-speed 'Shuttle' link offered by the Channel Tunnel (car drivers and passengers, and also freight, are transported, in their vehicle, in metal coaches, through the Tunnel).

Thus, transport technology has added a further layer to the centuries-old relationship between France and its neighbours. This very openness has compounded the sense of a loss of France's traditional, agrarian identity allowing certain politicians to tap into veins of nostalgia for the 'real' or 'deep' France – the so-called *France profonde*. This is an expression that defies sensible translation, although Celia Brayfield's *Deep France* (2004) does justice to the ideas that it conveys, namely positive connotations of tradition, authenticity and what is 'real' and 'true' – and their many ambiguities. For the French and their politicians, 'deep France' signifies the road travelled in half a century of modernization, for better or for worse. At the end of World War II, one third of the French population was living off, or otherwise connected to, the land. This was a population described as 'peasant' (*une population paysanne*), and the French term for peasant – *le paysan* – can still trigger nostalgic sentiments in contemporary France. The symbolic status of farmers, today, is encapsulated in the term *le paysan*, which does translate directly as 'peasant' but also conveys the positive meaning of guardian of the land as a way of life. Moreover, it relates to a significant (but not cohesive or unified) social class in France that survived well into the mid-20th century. The modern-day *agriculteur* is the business-like, entrepreneurial, usually educated, usually industrialized descendant of this traditional figure, with a consumer lifestyle very similar to that of city-dwellers. They are, moreover, emblematic of the productivist turn taken by French agriculture in the 1950s and 1960s (as seen in Chapter 1). Designed to generate growth and, ideally, even it out across the territory, this was a characteristic of the socio-economic boom of the *trente glorieuses*. These were the early days of the EU's

CAP and its support for the overproduction of foodstuffs. It was also the heyday of the centralized planning of France's territory known as *l'aménagement du territoire*.

In today's France, far more actors and interests are involved, alongside or instead of the central state, in planning out the use of the land, with small *communes* having considerable responsibility for planning permission, and regions closely associated with the handling of EU financial aid (see Chapter 4 for a further discussion of the many and complex layers of local government in France). In rural France, today, agricultural production must be balanced with economic development (especially job creation), the preservation and stewardship of the environment and, crucially, the promotion of the tourism that is so significant to France's economy (representing around 3 per cent of France's GDP) and which sustains, in turn, rural life itself.

Tourism and diversity

Indeed, the tourist to rural France will find themselves regaled with opportunities to sample a wide diversity of produce, of *paysages*, and of physical beauty. Regions, *départements* and *pays* (groupings of areas with common 'projects') all advertise their *terroir*, its distinctiveness, and its specialities. *Terroir*, we have said, is at the root of some of France's most famed and iconic produce, including its wine and cheeses (see Figure 2.3).

Steinberger (2009: 19) summarizes the idea of *terroir* as 'location, location, location' and as 'a central organizing principle of French viticulture'. Stephen Bayley, writing nearly two decades ago, hears the French explain *terroir* as 'the mystical union of landscape and weather and personality which gives specificity to a great wine' (Bayley, 2002). Clearly, the precise meaning of the notion of *terroir* varies according to the palate of the gastronome and the balance sheet of the producer. Thus, by way of example, when driving across small roads in central France, we may come across *la route des produits d'origine contrôlée transcorréziens* ('the road of produce of certified origin from the Corrèze') in what is a deeply rural department of France.

Furthermore, rural France works hard to attract and to entertain its tourists, both national and international. Events and attractions are clearly signposted, and the smallest of villages stage art exhibitions

Figure 2.3: Cheese, cheese and more cheese (Author)

open to all, usually free, often run by volunteers organized into special interest *associations*, and made possible courtesy of good amenities including the *salle des expositions* (exhibition space) or the tiny local tourist office. These frequently display an impressive array of brochures and flyers for local accommodation, organized events, and advice on the many ways that the area can be enjoyed by the visitor. Furthermore, most small villages have clean public toilets and *aires* – public spaces – for picnicking in the shade, and at a proper table with proper seating. Certain villages qualify as *villages étape* by virtue of the quality of their services (and if they have fewer than 5,000 inhabitants and can be found less than five minutes or kilometres from a free – not toll – stretch of motorway, or dual carriageway), and these villages are clearly indicated on the highways and motorways that run past; in the words of the scheme's website, it's a brand of quality. Beyond the village, France has 58 'natural regional parks', defined by their mission of sustainable development, 11 'national parks' (including in overseas France), 359 nature reserves, over 1,000 historical monuments (*monuments historiques*), numerous classified sites of interest (*sites classés*) and 53 UNESCO World Heritage sites (UNESCO, 2024). The whole of France is, thus, way-marked for the tourist: at the entrance to small villages on both national and departmental roads, large signs display the amenities and attractions on offer; even huge hypermarkets advertise distinct regional produce. Rural and regional France, we observe, is both intrinsically appealing and big business.

Energy and the environment

In France, the matter of environmental protection and climate change mitigation is complicated by the fact that, for all its natural attributes, France is relatively poor in natural resources, especially fossil fuels. Three quarters of France's energy production comes from nuclear power (with less than 6 per cent from renewables) but in 2022 France was still relying on oil and gas to meet around 45 per cent of its energy consumption; it is also home to one of the world's largest oil companies, TotalEnergies. French production of nuclear power gradually declined after 2000, then steeply so in 2022. Russia's invasion of Ukraine in the same year exposed the risk of this trajectory and by 2024, the building of new reactors had been announced, setting the scene for conflict with those opposed to nuclear energy and its risks. The beginnings of the French nuclear programme in the 1970s, at the time of a serious world oil price and supply crisis, gave rise to green movements, but these were largely unsuccessful in withstanding the force of the French state in their day, and green politics in France today still lacks the force and support one might imagine (see Chapter 3). Today, France's moves to reduce its greenhouse gas emissions by 40 per cent by 2030 and achieve carbon neutrality by 2050 (while maintaining dynamic alignment with EU-wide targets) are opening up both new fault lines in society (we saw that the *gilets jaunes* revolt was sparked by a new carbon tax deemed unfair on motorists with no viable alternative modes of transport) and new front lines in political competition (see Chapter 3). Other climate mitigation measures including onshore wind turbines and the construction of huge water reservoirs for agricultural use have come up against strong environmental opposition. Competition for the use of scarce resources is setting in and new environmental battle lines are being drawn.

France, like other countries, has suffered the negative effects on animal and human health of harmful pathogens such as the BSE (bovine spongiform encephalopathy) – 'mad cow' – epidemic in the mid-1980s; and of course the SARS-CoV-2 or COVID-19 pandemic in 2020–22. It has had to weigh up the risks and benefits of genetically modified organism (GMO) crops: since 2008, the commercial cultivation of GMOs has been banned in France, which must again also align with EU legislation in the matter. France must also navigate what some in France see as the globalization of junk food – *la malbouffe*; and must face up to trends that, while relatively weak in France, are not absent, including support for better animal welfare and rights, and even veganism (the Parti animaliste contested the 2024 European elections in France). In 2023, France sided with other EU member states in permitting the continued use of pesticides such as glyphosates, despite previously voting against the renewal of their use, known to cause human and environmental damage but deemed vital to support agriculture in its slow transition to more environmentally friendly practices in a highly competitive market.

In 2002 a 'Charter for the Environment' was appended to the 1958 French Constitution, indicating the state's commitment, symbolic and legal, to the weight of the environmental factor when planning for economic growth. A rolling programme of environmental debate and policy-planning (known as the Grenelle initiative) was put in place but key measures (such as a carbon tax on individuals and companies) subsequently withered, for lack of judicial and political support. In 2015, France took credit for its climate diplomacy when at COP21 in Paris the world's leading polluters reached a landmark agreement to limit global temperature increases to 'well below 2 degrees', and ideally 1.5 degrees, in this 21st century. The environmental agenda in France is, thus, driven by political considerations and the clash of interests, set against a broader concern with the impact of climate change. In this domain, many actors and interests galvanize for and against change, making reform as difficult in France as elsewhere.

Just as France is increasingly turning to its neighbours and seeking to maximize its influence in international forums to resolve its environmental dilemmas, so its identity as a nation cannot be divorced from France's international context. France, we have said, is a country open in 3D to forces and flows of all kinds. These include the movement of people, and the French population is, indeed, cosmopolitan and ethnically mixed, the result of a long history of immigration. These characteristics have given rise to all sorts of public policy dilemmas in a nation where abstract ideals of national unity, and equality between its nationals whatever their ethnic origins, are increasingly hard to fulfil. Deciding who has the right to be on French soil and what they can do when they are there – work, marry, vote, receive welfare assistance, acquire nationality – are all matters of public policy that cannot be made either in isolation from France's neighbouring countries or from the EU or other international bodies – or, indeed, from the rest of the world, many of whose inhabitants would and sometimes, tragically, do die for the freedoms of France.

Who are the 21st-century French?

France has a population of 67.9 million, almost 8 million larger than at the start of the 21st century and still growing, but more slowly than in previous years These figures still make France the second most highly (but not densely) populated country in the EU27 after Germany (84.3 million inhabitants). In the first decade of the 21st century and for the first time in 30 years, the birth rate in France rose to an average of two children per woman, the highest in the EU along with Ireland, and far above the EU average of 1.48. However, by the 2010s the birth rate in France had begun to fall and in 2022 INSEE reported that the lowest number ever of babies since 1946 had been born in France (723,000), representing a birth rate of 1.8 (INSEE, 2024). At the same time, the French population is ageing, as in other European countries. In 2022, French women, along with their Spanish counterparts, had the longest life expectancy, at 85.3 years for women; the equivalent for men was 79.3 years. This figure was lower than in 2019, following excess deaths due to COVID-19 and extreme weather events, particularly heatwaves. In 2022, one fifth of the French population was aged 65 or over, a figure that has been steadily rising for decades and that is typical of EU countries. In today's France, the political problems of demography are no longer those of the past, when declining birth rates and total population size spelt an existentially dangerous growth in the differential in population size between France and its enemy, Germany. Today's most challenging demographic issues concern the need to bolster the labour force and to sustain the costs of providing welfare to an ageing society (see also Chapter 5) and the issues that arise from links drawn between racial, ethnic, cultural and religious identities on the one hand and, on the other, definitions of what it means to be French.

Immigration and emigration

In France, nationality is, historically speaking, not seen as a fixed characteristic of an individual. Laws have evolved in line with political thinking linked to demographic and other social challenges as perceived by the government of the day. Nationality and citizenship have not always even been synonymous. At the time of the *ancien régime*, it was sufficient to pledge loyalty to the King to be deemed a 'citizen'. The vocabulary of citizenship itself emerged from the French revolution at a time when citizens were defined by their ancestry – their blood – and not by their country of residence – their 'soil'. Being a 'foreigner' did not preclude an individual from fighting France's wars (hence, la Légion étrangère or the French Foreign Legion, which still recruits to this day). This regime was known as *jus sanguinis* and lasted into the middle of the 19th century. Since then, the principle has been that children born in France (on French soil) to foreign parents can be French (*jus soli*), but under increasingly tightening conditions. France allows dual nationality and proposals made in 2015 by then President Hollande to potentially strip dual nationals of their French nationality, in the context of anti-terror legislation, were controversial and failed to make it through the French parliament; Hollande subsequently said that he regretted proposing the idea. In 2022, 114,483 individuals acquired French nationality, of whom 59,904 did so through automatic naturalization. In 1999, the former figure had been closer to 150,000. As of 2023, when a new immigration bill was being debated, as we see later in this chapter, the rules for acquiring nationality were as follows:

• A child is automatically born French if at least one parent is French, or if the child and at least one of its parents were born in France.
• A child born in France of two immigrants who have not acquired French nationality is not born French. The acquisition of French

nationality is automatic at the age of 18, if the child has been resident in France for at least five years since the age of 11; can be requested by a child at age 16; and children in this category over the age of 13 can also acquire French nationality through their legal guardians if they have been resident for five years.

In terms of their origins, moreover, the French have always been a mix of peoples: *at least* one in five French people is deemed to have *at least* one foreign ancestor in their family tree (Brame, 2006: 40). In 2022 it was estimated that around 10 per cent of the French population, or approximately 7 million people, were immigrants, roughly the average for the EU27. This is a figure that has risen since the middle of the 20th century, when 5 per cent of France's population was of immigrant origin. In France, an immigrant is someone born abroad and of foreign nationality who stays for at least a year; someone can be foreign (*étranger*, not French) but also not an immigrant if they are born in France but to foreign parents. In 2022, over a third (2.5 million) of these immigrants had acquired French nationality, 4.5 million had not, and 0.8 million were foreigners born in France. Almost half of France's immigrant population had been born in Africa and almost a third in other European countries. In 2022, one quarter of births were to one or two parents of foreign nationality.

France has no significant tradition of emigration, unlike the UK or Ireland. However, emigration is not negligible and at the turn of the 21st century London was said to be France's sixth or seventh biggest city, reflecting the numbers of young French people who had made their way across the Channel, attracted by job opportunities, varied lifestyles and less discrimination (Huc-Hepher, 2021; Lequesne, 2020). Brexit subsequently put an end to cross-Channel mobility on this scale. The French diaspora is also to be found in North Africa (Morocco) and North America and is seen as part of the French body politic, enjoying full voting rights for life and supportive of Emmanuel Macron in both his presidential victories.

Migration vs mobility: (some) Europeans and the rest

One specific aspect of French citizenship is the case of the European (EU) citizen on French soil under the terms of the EU's freedom of movement provisions. Since the 1992 Maastricht Treaty's provision for the creation of the European citizen, EU nationals, with very few restrictions, can move, settle and reside as they wish in the 26 other member states. Once there, they are free to exercise the provisions of their EU citizenship should they so wish, including the right to vote (at local and European elections) and to stand in these elections; and also to work, seek health care and other welfare benefits, and so on. These were all rights notably lost by France's substantial British population when the UK voted for Brexit in 2016.

Key dimensions of citizenship are, thus, divorced from nationality and, for some opponents of the nearly defeated 1992 Maastricht Treaty in France, this was deemed a serious threat to national sovereignty. Prominent 'sovereignist' critics at the time even talked of the 'treason' of allowing non-French nationals any right to vote on national soil. This argument resonated as it did in part because of the ongoing refusal in France to grant voting rights to long-term residents who do not have French nationality. This group includes, primarily, France's postcolonial populations from North Africa. Successive presidents and their political parties have suggested that these populations should have the right to vote in local elections but, so far, they have lacked the courage to instigate the change and in the current climate of tightening rules, as seen later in this chapter, that looks unlikely to change.

Unlike the governance of intra-EU mobility, where France is bound by collective rules that it has signed up to as part of its EU membership, France has sovereignty over its immigration policy regarding non-EU nationals, free to determine who it admits. Implementing this in practice is vexed. Historically, France has engineered and welcomed immigration, including of colonial cohorts, predominantly for economic reasons, especially to fill jobs in the industrializing economy of the 20th century, or to fight wars. In today's France, this economic imperative has returned to drive demand for immigrant labour as the country seeks to reindustrialize and secure its economy in a more perilous geopolitical climate (see Chapter 7), particularly following a fall in unemployment figures during Macron's presidency. But the issue is politically contentious. From the 1950s onwards, the expectation was that these workers would return to their home countries in due course (when no longer needed). There was no specific attempt to build a nation around and including its immigrants and, in this respect, France is distinct from the US. More recently, however – and, in particular, since the decolonization of France's North African and sub-Saharan African 'possessions' in the 1950s and 1960s – immigrants increasingly have come to stay and brought their families with them (and still do, naturally); family reunification, alongside immigration for work and asylum-seeking, is the largest driver of immigration to France. Family reunification makes immigrants visible because they need mainstream, family housing (they are not just single males in basic hostels) and their children need school places. Accordingly, 'immigration' and, crucially, the 'integration' of immigrants has increasingly, and especially since the 1980s, been treated by French governments as a 'problem' of public policy.

Indeed, by the 2020s, such issues had become highly politicized, instrumentalized by populist politicians (see Chapter 3), conflated with issues of race, culture and security, and seemingly intractable as a public policy challenge, as in so many other Western nations. It is complicated – again, as in many of France's neighbours – by the migratory movements of people in the 21st century fleeing war, persecution, discrimination or otherwise miserable lives in their home countries and seeking refuge somewhere they think will be safer and more welcoming; many are at the mercy of unscrupulous criminal gangs. The scale of such irregular movements towards Europe intensified in the 2010s as the consequences of the US and its allies' 'war on terror' played themselves out in Iraq and Afghanistan, as Syria's civil war churned on, and as societies unravelled in conflict in so many countries in Africa and the Middle East. International conventions on asylum-seeker and refugee status have been confounded by what by 2015 was largely dubbed in the EU a migration *crisis*, referring to the increased scale of these movements and the inability of European countries including France to devise a strategic, unified, rational response. In France, in the context of the appalling terror attacks of this period, it was easy for certain politicians to turn up the dial on their anti-immigrant, scare-mongering rhetoric, exploiting public ambivalence towards immigration, ignoring the case for immigrant labour, acute in certain sectors including medical practitioners (see Chapter 5), and this has become a staple of contemporary French politics (see Chapter 3). Accordingly, policy in France on who belongs and who does not, who can visit, stay, work, retire or not, is complex, and frequently changes in line with the politics of the day; the trend is for ever-tightening rules as France, along with many other European countries, struggles to balance these migratory and political pressures against a geopolitical and environmental context making the mass displacement of peoples around the world more, not less, likely.

Le Monde (2024) reported that the 2023 government bill 'To Control Immigration and Improve Integration' was the 30th reform of immigration and integration law in France in 40 years. As the bill made its passage through France's two houses of Parliament, the spectrum and relative strength of political views were evident. The government's original text demonstrated its wish to balance labour market needs in priority sectors including construction and social and medical care, by easing the conditions for regularization of irregular workers and issuing longer-term residency cards to attract skilled labour, with an emphasis, as in many if not all previous reforms, on tightening the requirements for non-French inhabitants eligible for residency to demonstrate their allegiance to the Republic (by swearing to uphold the republican principles of the freedom of speech and conscience, of gender equality, of respect for the symbols of the Republic).

Such conditions were unsurprising at a time of headline news of cases of violence, physical and symbolic, against those very principles and symbols, these headlines themselves to be understood in the febrile context of France's experience of terrorist acts from 2012 onwards. During the *gilets jaunes* movement, some of France's most revered historical monuments including the Arc de Triomphe in Paris were daubed with graffiti. Far, far more tragic and sinister were the fatal attacks on persons who in France are at seen as being the heart of the country's republican identity. These included history teacher Samuel Paty, brutally assassinated outside his school in October 2020 by a refugee of Chechen origin following a class in which M. Paty sought to engage his students in debate on the freedom of expression, with reference to the cartoons of Mohammed that had triggered the killing of the cartoonists of the satirical paper *Charlie Hebdo* in 2015. Certain pupils and their parents had taken to social media to complain against the teacher, effectively putting a target on his back – and were subsequently tried for complicity in his murder. Three years later in Arras, in the north of France, French teacher

Dominique Bernard was stabbed to death in his school by another radicalized individual, known to the police and who, gruesomely, was a former pupil of the school.

Such trauma has played into the hands of those seeking to restrict immigration and the government's 2023 bill was notably hardened by senators from the political right seeking more restrictive measures for France's undocumented inhabitants, concerning for example their access to health care. Such arguments, in France as routinely in other countries, are couched in terms of controlling immigration by minimizing the 'pull' factors that could encourage them, despite evidence that migratory 'push' factors are typically more compelling (the reasons for migrating) For those seeking more generous provisions, such arguments are proof that fears (real or manufactured) about immigration have in France, as in many other European countries, spread from the extreme politics of the far right into the political mainstream, which in its bid to compete for votes for the extremes finds itself adopting the latter's language and policies alike.

Immigration and integration: changing the rules

Immigrants in France have been expected, and explicitly so, to assume a common identity – that of the French citizen. In colonial times, the goal was no less than the 'assimilation' of any foreign bodies into the nation through the coercive power of the (Catholic) church and state. In the present day, the seemingly more neutral concept of 'integration' drives French policy concerning the melding of ethnic and racial differences into the Republic. The principle of secularity, known as *la laïcité* (see Chapter 5), plays the role previously held by the Catholic religious establishment, and political competition dictates the legislation framing the rules for belonging to the nation. In these expressions of state power in this matter, France is aligning itself with most other EU member states, and also with common EU policy in this domain.

Here, legislation is frequently used as a blunt tool to manage these relationships. In today's France, national identity has come to be determined through an increasingly narrow lens that links 'Frenchness' to ever more stringent criteria. At the same time, measures to identify and combat discrimination have found their way into the public policy domain, despite the fact that concepts such as the 'right to difference', 'minorities' and even 'communities' are alien to French political culture (as we see in Chapter 3). Namely, in France, all (legal) residents are guaranteed equality before the law by the constitution itself, irrespective of race, religion or ethnic origin. Difference in these respects is deemed irrelevant from a political or policy perspective, and the state legislates to remove difference from the public policy equation: not only is there no special treatment, for example, for adolescent schoolgirls wishing to wear the Islamic headscarf; in public (state) schools, they are banned from doing so (see also Chapters 3 and 5). Such markers of personal identity have come to be deemed as signs of non-allegiance to the French nation and the more visible the gap from the norm, the more potentially consequential for life chances; in practice, the Muslim veil or other head-coverings have been stigmatized. Hence, skin colour and surname have demonstrably gone hand in hand in France in recent years with discrimination in the job and housing markets, in police treatment, in opportunities for jobs in politics, and in the state more broadly.

But is France a racist society? Academic research points to a French society that is growing more, not less, tolerant of difference and that is less, not more, racist than previously (Mayer and Tiberj, 2021), while voting in ever larger numbers and across a growing age range for political figures such as Marine Le Pen or Eric Zemmour (see Chapter 3), who encourage the fear of others; simultaneously, French governments issue ever tighter rules on what it means to be French. The question remains open and loaded: daily discrimination on ethnic grounds is a fact, and racist acts are well-documented. President Macron in November 2023, in the context of the Israeli–Palestinian war of that period, singled out antisemitism as a particularly virulent strand of such prejudice that remains as 'odious', he said, as at the time of the Dreyfus affair and as described then by Emile Zola (see Chapter 1; Macron, 2023a), and the following day several political parties and their followers took part in peaceful marches against antisemitism across the country. In Paris, the march was attended by France's far right party the Rassemblement national, which, as developed in Chapter 3, argues that it has moved far beyond its virulently antisemitic history. This conflation of immigration and national identity typically overestimates the extent to which immigration concerns people compared with other dimensions of 'Frenchness' (beyond nationality and origins) that, in recent years, have come to be posed as problems of public policy. These revolve around the treatment, in French politics and society, of individual and group identities, and questions of discrimination on these grounds.

Beyond the debate: legislating for identity?

The very language of what we might broadly call 'identity politics' – which is embedded in policy-making norms in certain other European countries, including the UK, and certainly in the US – sits very uneasily with the French republican traditions that we explore at greater length in the following chapters. In many respects, even the notion of 'identity' itself, when applied not to the nation but, rather, to groups or individuals within it, is treated by much of the mainstream of French politics and society as unwelcome political correctness imported from the 'Anglo-Saxons'. Such perspectives have been heightened by the emergence of so-called 'woke' culture and its emphasis on individual identities defined by gender and sexuality; these are all developments whose opponents could and do point to their conflict with the 'indivisibility' of the nation.

The practice of ethnic monitoring, for example, used as a customary tool elsewhere for if not combating then at least recording and monitoring unfair discrimination (in the job market, in particular) on the grounds of subjective prejudices of race and ethnicity, is treated in France with suspicion, and even collecting statistics to compile records on an individual's ethnicity is highly problematic. Indeed, the very terms 'ethnicity' – let alone 'race' – are, by and large, deemed illegitimate categories of social difference by a wide spectrum of opinion in France. It follows that the idea of quotas or other forms of positive discrimination (or affirmative action) to achieve a more ethnically diverse and representative body politic or labour force is anathema to most French – in theory. In practice, certain organizations (in the education system, as we see in Chapter 5) do find ways to level the playing field, taking an individual's neighbourhood as a proxy criterion for ethnic origin per se.

Yet France does have a race problem, particularly in association with its population of North African – ex-colonial – origin. In the 1980s, at the time of President François Mitterrand's Socialist

Party governments, a head of steam built up in the form of social movements to combat racism directed at these populations in particular. Children of France's postcolonial immigrants, known as *les beurs* (slang for 'Arab'), involved themselves in the struggle. Such activity made the problem of prejudice in this context visible but fell short of significant or systemic measures designed to combat its consequences. Neither did the *mouvement beur* prevent the rise of the far right as a political force (as developed in Chapter 3). In the following decades, and under pressure to implement a growing body of EU law, France began to tackle discrimination per se, more broadly defined. This remains a contentious public policy field, but a vital one, as evidence of discrimination comes to light. In this context, anti-discrimination legislation has been proposed, hotly debated and sometimes passed, and new public bodies have been established to feed and shape the debate, and to implement the law; pressure groups and watchdogs also exist outside the framework of the state.

Conclusions

In 2008, then President Nicolas Sarkozy commissioned a report headed by one of France's most eminent female politicians and public figures, Simone Veil. The task was to investigate whether the diversity that characterizes the French should be written into the constitution itself as an organizing principle of the French Republic. 'Respect' for the diversity that constitutes French identity would have taken its place beside the existing statements in the constitution that France itself 'shall be organized on a decentralized basis' (Article 1), that its regional languages are part and parcel of the 'heritage' of France (Article 75-1), that it 'ensures' the equality of French citizens before the law, whatever their cultural, religious or racial origins (Article 1), that it formally 'respects' all religions (with the exception of some banned sects (Article 1)) and that and 'favours' one specific type of positive discrimination, namely the 'equal access' of men and women to elected political office, and to social and professional responsibilities (Article 1).

The Veil Committee found that such a constitutional amendment, and the scope for positive discrimination that it would offer, were not necessary to fulfil the constitution's existing commitments to freedom, equality and fraternity. By the time of President Macron's second presidential mandate, the acknowledgement of 'diversity' itself as a founding principle of the Fifth French Republic was still apparently a step too far that did not feature in his various proposals to update the French Constitution. Yet we see in the following chapters how French politics has come to be characterized by the prominence of figures worrying the open wound of differences between the French, regarding not only the distinctions raised in this chapter (of location, origin, race and religion) but also socio-economic inequalities and their consequences (see also Chapter 5). Debates around the recognition or not of this diversity in practice is a feature of politics in France today.

3

Politics and the Republic

Introduction

Politics in contemporary France draws on a strong sense of history, and French political identity is anchored in the past. In a society where the status quo is deemed to represent over 200 years of democratic achievement and social progress, promoting change is a politically risky business. Not embracing change or keeping up with evolving demands and developments is equally perilous. Today's Fifth French Republic was itself designed to tame French political life via the shock of new and revitalized institutions, and to marry France's tumultuous past to the demands of the present. 2023 marked the 65th anniversary of the regime, making it the second-longest-lasting of France's republican experiments (as seen in Chapter 1), but the occasion passed with very little fanfare or ceremony.

French politics in the 2020s indeed looks very different to only a decade previously and those voices calling for yet more change – including of the very system itself – are electorally popular. France's youngest ever president, Emmanuel Macron, was elected in 2017 on nothing less than a manifesto of 'Revolution' (Macron, 2017), brought to power by the momentum of a new political movement named for the idea of movement itself: En Marche! (and for the president himself: EM). France's traditional political parties emerged from that election in tatters, while movements further to the left and right did well. The very notions of 'left' and 'right', moreover, are themselves becoming stretched in a political landscape characterized by a multiplicity of causes, movements and groupings, some more ephemeral than others. Five years later, in 2022, Macron was re-elected after a first term in which he had faced ferocious resistance, symbolized the world over by the *gilets jaunes* (Yellow Vests) movement, to changes amounting to far less than a revolution, and he had shelved or failed to reach certain of his more far-reaching goals, including electoral reform.

In 2022, the mainstream opposition parties performed even more poorly than in 2017 and those on the extremes and margins even better. Calls for a new – Sixth – Republic were by now nothing new. Abstentionism was at an all-time high in both the presidential and the parliamentary elections in 2022 and populism – political figures claiming not to belong to the established elite and promising the illusion of a quick and easy break from the past, and simple solutions to complex problems – was as vigorous in France as in many of its neighbours and allies (See Tables 3.1 and 3.3). As elsewhere in the democratic world, moreover, trust in French institutions was low (after an ephemeral bump during the COVID-19 pandemic), as was interest in politics itself (trends tracked over many years by Sciences Po, 2024). Evidence suggested that, while a large majority of the French still believed democracy to be the ideal political system, they disagreed on what form this should take (Léon and Gallard, 2023).

By the time of the 2024 legislative elections, calls to defy the European Union were winning serious votes in a country known for its historically outsized influence on EU affairs and for having rebuilt its identity in the second half of the 20th century around its EU membership (as seen in Chapter 1). Most strikingly, the party that was for so long a pariah of French politics – the Front national (FN – National Front) – was by now a purportedly detoxified movement, renamed the Rassemblement national (RN – National Rally), present across the country's media and finally established in French parliament. Having won almost one fifth of the National Assembly's seats in the parliamentary elections of June 2022 to form the largest single opposition party in the chamber, it then came first in the first round of the 2024 legislative elections. Pushed back in the second round a week later, it nevertheless maintained its position as the single largest parliamentary party, with now 126 seats (plus 17 allies who had gone rogue from the centrist Republican party; see Table 3.3).

A young person voting for the first time in the presidential election of 2022 (when a quarter of young voters aged between 25 and 34 voted for Le Pen in the first round) could very well have been unaware that 'Marine' and the RN were contemporary, sanitized versions of a party previously notorious for the brutality and racism of its founder, Marine's father, Jean-Marie Le Pen, and his supporting cast, some with connections to the German Third Reich (Ramdani, 2023: 74). Where in 1987 Jean-Marie Le Pen dismissed the death camps (gas chambers) of the Holocaust as a 'point of detail in the history of world war two', Marine Le Pen today marches alongside France's traditional parties in protest against antisemitism, and the party couches its distaste for Islam, now France's largest minority religion (see Chapter 5), in the languages of rights, particularly of women, of national security in the face of terrorism perpetrated on occasion by radicalized Islamist extremists, and of patriotism.

The chapter addresses all of the above by, first, surveying the core characteristics of French political culture, which revolves around the meaning of republicanism. This is a culture that has bred a sense of what is called 'exceptionalism' in French politics that, for its critics, can be seen as a brake on reform. The chapter then, second, reviews how political parties and voters alike have evolved to arrive at the circumstances of 2024 as previously described. We see how a trend – again, not unique to France – for formerly mainstream parties to hold leadership primary elections (as in the US) has produced candidates from the extremes of these parties, thus widening the gap between left and right and hollowing out the centre ground. We explore the very meanings of 'left' and 'right' in a political system dominated until as late as the 1990s by the influence of Gaullism and communism, where the left did not come to power until 1981, nearly 25 years after the founding of the Fifth Republic and where, as we saw above, France's traditional political parties are now all but extinct. We assess the parties and movements on what are no longer the margins of French politics (the National Rally on the right and France Unbowed or la France insoumise (LFI) on the left under the leadership of Jean-Luc Mélenchon), driven by charismatic figures who fit squarely into pre-republican traditions of political leadership, as seen in Chapter 1.

We consider, third, the most compelling of the issues currently finding political expression in France, including the Yellow Vests movement: new fault lines emerging out of the climate emergency and measures to address it; the insecurities arising from antisocial behaviour and terrorism itself and the responses to these; differences around France's place in the world – how interdependent, how sovereign should it be? – and the scandals and ethics of public life. We review the forms that political action in these matters is taking, both at grassroots and official levels: alongside attempts at direct democracy ('great debates', citizens' conventions and greater scope for referenda), these include violence perpetrated by protesters and the state alike, yet more relics from France's historical repertoires of political action.

The picture of French politics to emerge from this overview is troubled and troubling: a society that is in so many respects on the move, open and exposed to trends that transcend the nation, but combined with a political class seemingly hamstrung by its traditional culture and historical inheritance, and relatively lacking in diversity (of age, gender or class). These legacies and their drag on society are the message at the heart of France's populists who seek new political alliances across Europe and who in 2024 targeted elections to the European Parliament (EP) as a stage for their brand of politics. Perhaps social change is happening at such a speed and on such a scale that, in the context of such forceful global trends as climate change and technology, it has swept away the 'French exception' of the past two centuries and made the preservation of representative, republican democracy itself as challenging in France, birthplace of modern democratic politics, as elsewhere in Europe and North America.

French political culture

French political culture is often described as 'exceptional'. This characteristic revolves around the French Revolution, and 1789 is, indeed, the key to understanding the emphasis in contemporary French politics on events that happened well over two centuries ago. We saw in Chapter 1 that the violent transition from the *ancien régime* of absolute monarchy to the Republic remained a work in progress for much of the 19th century, and contemporary French politics has

Table 3.1: The 2024 European Parliament (EP) and French legislative elections

Election	Principal parties/groups	Vote share %/seats won
		Seats won (out of 81)
European Parliament	La France Revient! Jordan Bardella and Marine Le Pen	30
	Besoin d'Europe (presidential group)	13
	Réveiller l'Europe (PS and allies)	13
	La France insoumise (LFI)	9
		Vote share (%)
Legislative, round 1	Le Rassemblement national	29.26
	le Nouveau Front populaire (NFP)	28.06
	Ensemble (presidential group)	20.04
		Seats won (out of 577; 289 needed for an absolute majority)
Legislative, round 2	Le Nouveau Front Populaire	193
	Ensemble (presidential group)	165
	le Rassemblement national (FN) (and allies)	126 (+16)
	la Droite républicaine (formerly LR)	47

The table shows the startling performance of the RN in the 2024 EP election and in the first round of the French legislative elections of 2024, coming first in both. It also shows how, in the second round of the legislative elections, it was then pushed back by tactical voting into third place, behind the Nouveau Front Populaire (NFP) and the presidential group. This left the National Assembly (and president) paralysed by three roughly equal-sized political blocs, none of which enjoyed an absolute majority and two of which (the NFP and Ensemble) were composed of different parties, movements and factions. The table confirms the RN's national breakthrough in terms of National Assembly seats: from zero in 2012 to eight in 2017, 88 in 2022 and 126 in 2024. Finally, the table reminds us that the prime minister, Michel Barnier, appointed by President Macron after these elections and after much hesitation, came from the party that ended only in fourth place (la Droite républicaine, formerly LR).

its roots in both pre- and post-revolutionary times, revolving around a so-called republican monarch – its president – and giving rise to stereotypical styles and forms of political action (more strikes! more demonstrations!).

Republican democracy

Republicanism is at the heart of French political identity and, in the contemporary French context, denotes a nation of sovereign citizens whose general will is served by the French state under the leadership of the French president. The original republican ideal of direct democracy, symbolized in 1793 by the execution of the monarch Louis XVI, is encapsulated in the slogan enshrined in Article 2 of the current French Constitution of 'government of the people, by the people and for the people'. During the Revolution itself, the leaders of the 'Terror' under the First Republic were the first to pervert these new democratic ideals into a zealous and totalitarian form of rule. Over time and in response, French republicanism in practice has come to mean parliamentary, representative democracy, upon which in the Fifth Republic, emerging as it did from a time of extreme threats to the country's stability, is grafted a dose of direct democracy in the form of recourse to referenda, tolerance for the voices of the 'street', and a directly elected president (see also Chapter 4). Populist politicians, as we see below, activate this legacy of direct democracy to encourage people to contest the representative institutions of which they are themselves part and/or to which they aspire. French republicanism is still a consensual political doctrine but there is disagreement over which form that republic should take.

Political style

Styles of political action that typify France find their roots in this revolutionary legacy. Direct action by the French against their rulers was already a means of protest under the *ancien régime* but the French Revolution legitimized such methods and institutionalized them by means of the republican credo of *popular* sovereignty. The anarchist movements of 19th-century France compounded these radical tendencies and key social advances of the 20th century, for example in labour law, can be linked to organized, popular protest in the context of industrialization. In contemporary France, direct action in the form of strikes, protests and mass demonstrations are still as much part of the political process as parliamentary debate; sometimes they are successful in reversing government action (as in the case of the 'carbon tax' that sparked the *gilets jaunes* movement in 2018–29), but both parliament and street can equally be overturned by executive political will. In 2022 this fact of French political life dramatically played itself out over President Macron's reform of pensions and specifically the retirement age (see also below and Chapter 5), when neither rancorous, largely inconclusive parliamentary debates nor mass popular protest deterred or prevented the government from passing its desired legislation. Also inherent in French political style is the recourse to impassioned political rhetoric and oratory, reminiscent of the revolutionary patriots.

Myths, symbols and stories

Thus, the 1789 French Revolution lives on in contemporary France in a method and vocabulary of politics that prioritizes equality and fraternity between French citizens and the primacy of the secular, rational French state. This is an approach to the past that relies heavily on the use of symbols and myths to suggest an uninterrupted and undisputed political history, largely in order to bolster contemporary French political identity. These include quintessentially French icons such as the French tricolour flag; the mystical Marianne – the allegorical female face and bust of France found on certain French stamps and euro coins, for example; and the Republican motto itself, enshrined in the 1958 constitution and engraved since the late 19th century on many public buildings, of *Liberté, Égalité, Fraternité* (Liberty, Equality, Fraternity). Such symbols and myths from the past are an important dimension of present-day French politics because they give the sense of an undisputed, continuous, national political history designed to unify a nation proud of its achievements and pedigree. Hence, when demonstrators deface symbolic edifices such as the Arc de Triomphe in Paris or public schools and libraries, they are contesting this republican story, consciously or otherwise. When terrorists target the Eiffel Tower, tourists and national sporting events, they seek to undermine foundations of national pride. Indeed, the 200-plus-year-old history of French republicanism has been

Table 3.2: 200-plus years of regime change

Absolute monarchy	Louis XVI	1774–92
First Republic		1792–1804
First Empire	Napoleon I	1804–14
Monarchy	The Restoration	1815–30
Monarchy	The July Monarchy	1830–48
Second Republic		1848–52
Second Empire	Napoleon III	1852–70
Third Republic		1870–1940
The French State	The Vichy regime	1940–44
The Provisional Government	Headed by Charles de Gaulle	1944–46
Fourth Republic		1946–58
Fifth Republic		1958–present day

punctured on many occasions by other non-republican regimes, including empire in the 19th century, and dictatorship in the 20th, as seen in Chapter 1 (and in Table 3.2), and these reactions against republicanism have left traces in the present-day regime.

The political party system: from bipolarity to breakdown

French party politics in the Fifth French Republic has been shaped by the electoral rules of the regime created back in 1958 specifically to encourage parties to form electoral alliances or 'poles' that would support stable government. This was a reaction to the breakdown of the multiparty parliamentary regime of its predecessor, the Fourth Republic, which had proven unable to govern in the crisis of Algerian independence (see Chapter 1). It took over two decades after 1958 for France's political parties to coalesce into a bipolar system formed of two blocs (poles) of left and right that subsequently governed for another two decades, alternating and sometimes sharing power between themselves, with little room for extremes. By the start of the 21st century, this system was straining to contain its own contradictions and by 2024 had collapsed under its own weight in the face of growing trends in political behaviour not unique to France: voter abstentionism (a disinclination to engage with or trust the politics on offer) and distrust; polarization (the widening of the gap between political opponents and the inability to bridge it); and populism (promises to bypass the messy compromises of democratic politics and solve complex problems with simple solutions and no pain).

A turning point in the party system had come in 2002. In the first round of presidential elections in that year, the candidates of the main parties on the left and right – the incumbent prime minister (Lionel Jospin) and president (Jacques Chirac), respectively – had fared extremely badly (winning vote shares of only 16 per cent and 19 per cent, respectively), drained of popular support by contestants from smaller movements to their left and right (one quarter of votes in the first round in 2002 were cast for candidates who won less than 5 per cent of the vote; this figure has since doubled). The incumbent prime minister, Lionel Jospin of the Socialist Party, did not even win his way through to the second round of voting, the first time in 33 years that a candidate from the mainstream left was absent from the final round of voting. Jean-Marie Le Pen, leader of the French far right, did make it to that stage but was subsequently beaten in the second round by President Chirac by 82 per cent of the votes as France formed a so-called 'republican front' against Le Pen. Abstentionism, at 30 per cent, was also unprecedently high, as was the proportion of spoilt ballot papers, at nearly 4 per cent. By way of comparison, in the first presidential election in 1965, the first-round winners, President de Gaulle and François Mitterrand, polled 76 per cent of the votes between them.

Five years later, in 2007, despite the ongoing backdrop of abstentionism and support for parties, movements and causes such as the National Front, the Trotskyite left, Euroscepticism, street protest and violence (such as the urban riots of October–November 2005 and youth protests against reform of employment law), for the first time in nearly 30 years, the French electorate (see Table 3.3) returned a sitting majority party, the centre-right UMP (Union for a Popular Movement – Union pour un mouvement populaire). People voted in very high numbers (a turnout of 84 per cent in both rounds of the presidential contest); they concentrated their votes in the first

Table 3.3: Changing voting patterns, presidential elections
rounds 1 and 2, 2007–22

Year	Candidates/parties	Vote share (%)
2007		
Round 1 (top 4)	Nicolas Sarkozy (UMP)	31.18
	Ségolène Royal (PS)	25.87
	François Bayrou (UDF)	18.57
	Jean-Marie Le Pen (FN)	10.44
Round 2	Nicolas Sarkozy (UMP)	53.06
	Ségolène Royal (PS)	46.94
	Abstentions	*16.03*
2012		
Round 1(top 4)	François Hollande (PS)	28.63
	Nicolas Sarkozy (UMP)	27.18
	Marine Le Pen (FN)	17.90
	Jean-Luc Mélenchon (Left Front)	11.10
Round 2	François Hollande (PS)	51.64
	Nicolas Sarkozy (UMP)	48.36
	Abstentions	*19.65*
2017		
Round 1(top 4)	Emmanuel Macron	24.01
	Marine Le Pen (FN)	21.30
	François Fillon (UMP)	20.01
	Jean-Luc Mélenchon (LFI)	19.58
Round 2	Emmanuel Macron (LREM,)	66.10
	Marine Le Pen (FN)	33.90
	Abstentions	*25.44*
2022		
Round 1 (top 4)	Emmanuel Macron (Renaissance)	27.85
	Marine Le Pen (RN)	23.15
	Jean-Luc Mélenchon (LFI)	21.95
	Éric Zemmour (Reconquête)	7.07
Round 2	Emmanuel Macron (Renaissance)	55.88
	Marine Le Pen (RN)	41.45
	Abstentions	*28.01*

Source: Ministère de l'Intérieur et des Outre-Mer, 2024

The table shows rising abstentionism, the growing vote for the National Front/
National Rally and the far right in general, the disappearance of the traditional
parties of government, and the persistence of the vote for the far-left candidate
Jean-Luc Mélenchon but his failure to break through to the presidency.

round of the presidential contest on the contenders from the two main French parties, ensuring a return to a left–right contest in the second and final round; and in that vote they returned a decisive victory for Nicolas Sarkozy of the UMP, who made strong scores in both rounds of voting. In the ensuing legislative elections, the French electorate voted in an absolute majority of UMP deputies, sealing the new French president's institutional power. Those 2007 elections, therefore, suggested that France had reverted to the bipolar logic of party and electoral politics in the Fifth French Republic and that the mainstream French political parties *were* fulfilling their representative role. A decade later, in 2017, nothing could have been further from the truth (also see Table 3.3). A closer look at French political parties, voters and key political issues reveals the forces at play that have kept French politics on a rollercoaster ride, and points towards likely future developments.

Winners and losers on the French right

The 2007 elections therefore marked a significant achievement for the main party on the French right, the UMP. Formed in haste after the presidential elections of April–May 2002 by former prime minister Alain Juppé to carry Jacques Chirac to victory against Jean-Marie Le Pen in the second round of the presidential election, as seen above, and to contest the June legislative elections of that year, this successor to the RPR (Rally for the Republic – Rassemblement pour la République), in the very unusual circumstances of the 2002 election aftermath, found itself able to unify much of what previously had been a rather fragmented centre-right ground. This was an important but ultimately short-lived development for a party that had grown out of the Gaullist movement and had uneasily grafted onto the numerous traditional forms of the French right, ranging from counter-revolutionaries and liberals to authoritarian and nationalist movements towards the far right of the spectrum.

The Gaullists: from the RPR to the Republicans

During his time in office between 1958 and 1969, President Charles de Gaulle relied primarily on the support of the French nation, which he tested in a succession of referenda, rather than on a single party, and he resigned when he lost his fifth plebiscite in 1969 (as seen in Chapter 1). His supporters, during and following his presidency, organized themselves into movements they called *rallies* and *unions* dedicated to defending the new Republic and de Gaulle's vision of a restored French identity. Party organization was secondary to these aims; indeed, de Gaulle blamed the party politics of the Fourth Republic for rendering the National Assembly incapable of producing durable government majorities (and the constitution in Article 4 reminds parties to 'respect the principles of national sovereignty and democracy'). Consequently, the Gaullists defied classification. Their politics at the outset were the restoration of France as an independent global player via a strong currency, economy and image, all headed by a strong leader.

The 1965 presidential election in which de Gaulle had to fight a second-round contest against François Mitterrand (subsequently leader of the left and French president, as seen in Chapter 1), demonstrated that even a leader with such unique credentials as de Gaulle required some sort of party machinery (known as an *appareil*) in order to mobilize the electorate. For de Gaulle's successors, the need for a supportive party was even more pressing since they could not, by definition, rely on de Gaulle's aura and authority to attract the votes of the French. On the death in 1974 of Georges Pompidou, de Gaulle's immediate successor, the French elected as president a centrist, liberal, Atlanticist politician, Giscard d'Estaing. His prime minister, future president Jacques Chirac, reformed the Gaullist movement into its most organized structure yet under the name of the RPR: the Rally for the Republic. Its members sought to differentiate themselves from Giscard's supporters – the Independent Republicans – by a shift to a more independent – Gaullist – foreign policy line, and an emphasis on the traditional economic statism of Gaullist politics (see Chapter 7). The uneasy relationship between the RPR and Giscard's subsequent new federation, the UDF (Union for French Democracy – Union pour la démocratie française) was a contributory factor in the defeat of the right in the 1981 elections in favour of the French left.

Under Chirac's party leadership during the 1980s, the RPR nevertheless began to look more like other West European conservative parties, with an emphasis on free-market economics and attempts to oppose and curb the social liberalism of the ruling French left; this was, in a specific economic context, characterized by

France's commitment by the mid-1980s to the EC's goal of completing the single European market by 1993 (see Chapter 7). Nevertheless, 'Europe', the market economy and matters of society continued to hamper unity within the RPR and complicate alliances with those also claiming to be from the right and centre-right of French politics.

Sovereignists, centrists and liberals

The 1992 Maastricht referendum in France, in which the electorate was asked to accept or reject the terms of the EU's Maastricht Treaty (as seen in Chapter 1; see also Chapters 7 and 8), constituted an opportunity for a certain strand of thinking on the right in France to express itself forcefully. The so-called 'sovereignists', led by RPR heavyweight Philippe Séguin, argued that the treaty eroded the French republican notion of national sovereignty on at least two accounts: the treaty created 'European citizens' with voting rights in other EU member states, so detaching citizenship from nationality (as seen in Chapter 2), and it involved a transfer of powers from Paris to Brussels in monetary policy, in preparation for the introduction of the single European currency in 2002. Their arguments were eloquent and, although the RPR's leader, Jacques Chirac, voted in favour of the treaty (his ambition to be president trumping his 1970s' Gaullist opposition to European integration), he did not exhort his party to do the same. The centre–right split on the issue and the referendum was barely won (by 51 per cent of the votes), 'sovereignism' having its supporters on the left as well.

Subsequently, the sovereignist rump broke away from the RPR to contest the 1999 EP elections, and the climate encouraged similar-minded individuals such as Philippe de Villiers to break away from the pro-European UDF and campaign, henceforth, on a very narrow anti-European, anti-immigration and anti-Islam platform. In this way, the 1990s were problematic for the RPR, which could not speak for all of its leading figures, let alone electorate, on a matter as important as France's future role and influence in the European Union.

Simultaneously, the RPR, seeking dominance within its camp, or 'pole', had to find a way to coexist with so-called market liberals such as Alain Madelin's Démocratie libérale members. These people thought and behaved more like other European conservatives in their desire to cut back the French state in favour of a more open and free-market economy. In the context of France's state-centric political culture, as seen above, openly espousing economic liberalism remains politically risky, and this fact of French political life goes some way to explaining the fate met by Macron's 'revolution'. Less risky is the label of 'centrist', a space occupied by François Bayrou. Bayrou, heir to France's Fourth Republican Christian Democratic tradition and head of his group MoDem (Democratic Movement), represents a conviction that the centre ground of French politics can lead an autonomous existence. His alliance with the RPR, in and out of government, was conditional at best, fractious at worst and when, in December 2024, he was appointed prime minister in a turbulent political context characterised by extremes, his centrist credentials arguably hindered the work of creating political consensus.

By 2007, neither the liberals nor the centrists had succeeded in establishing a strong electoral presence outside an alliance with the once-again-renamed party – now the UMP – leaving the UMP dominant in a – by definition – unbalanced 'pole' on the right, making French politics at this end of the spectrum at this point looking more 'bipartisan' than 'bipolar'. Less than a decade later, by 2015, the UMP had once more renamed itself, this time as the Republicans (les Républicains). This was symbolic of its image as defenders of the regime at a time when the space in the centre had provided opportunities for newcomers to break through and establish themselves on a ticket of change. First came the National Front, moving in from the fringes of the French far right (and in 2024 its successor, the National Rally, taking some of the Republicans with it), then Emmanuel Macron, to widespread surprise.

From the National Front to the National Rally: still a Le Pen family affair?

The National Front was largely dormant in the Fifth Republic until the 1980s, when, under its leader Jean-Marie Le Pen, it made its first electoral breakthroughs in elections to local French authorities and the EP (and fleetingly to the French National Assembly during France's short-lived experiment in 1986 with proportional representation). The party's roots can be traced back to the antisemitic, authoritarian and militaristic ideas and groups of the early 20th century, and to Petain's Vichy regime of the '*État français*' (French state), intended to turn the clock back on republicanism to a mythical time of the traditional values of '*travail, famille, patrie*' – work, family and country (see Chapter 1). Le Pen himself developed into a startlingly effective, indefatigable, rally-style political leader capable of rousing, manipulative political rhetoric. Despite the National Front's internal rivalries (which in 1998 led to a break-away in the form of the MNR (National Republican Movement – Mouvement national républicain), led by Le Pen's former lieutenant Bruno Mégret), the French National Front rose in political prominence to the point where, by the 1997 legislative elections, it could legitimately be described as France's third biggest political force (Shields, 2007) after the RPR and the Socialist Party, and the second biggest component on the political right, ahead of the UDF. By 2011 it had a new leader, Le Pen's daughter Marine, who four years later, in 2015, excluded her father from the party – perhaps a sham rift – as part of her so-called detoxification or 'de-demonization' (*dédiabolisation*) process.

The political context that established itself from the 1980s onwards was an important contributory factor to the rise of Le Pen. This included the weak opposition of the mainstream right to key policies of the left in power at the time such as François Mitterrand's commitment to European integration; and the social liberalism of the left (the end of the death penalty, a softer immigration policy environment, the tolerance of cultural differences, the promotion of cultural diversity, and the fight against racism). The repeated occurrence of *cohabitation* (power-sharing between a president and prime minister from rival political parties, with the president opposed by the parliamentary majority) between left and right (1986–88, 1993–95, 1997–2002) provided further scope for Jean-Marie Le Pen to depict the mainstream left and right as converging around a centre ground of politics designed, in his terms, to drag France into a multicultural, globalized mire. The decline of the French Communist Party (le Parti communiste français – PCF) at this time (see below), and the failure of other new entrants to the political game (such as ecologists and greens) to organize sustained opposition to the traditional left–right politics was grist to the mill of a talented leader and orator such as Le Pen, who, at a time of rising unemployment, played shamelessly on people's fears for their jobs, their neighbourhoods, their safety, their identity, even their lives.

During this period, the FN succeeded in influencing the political agenda in matters not only of immigration and cultural identity but also, albeit to a lesser extent, regarding France in Europe, and the economy. The rules of the political game kept Le Pen away from power at the national level, since neither the RPR nor UDF were, back then, prepared to treat the FN as an electoral ally (with some exceptions at local and regional levels), in 2002 forming a 'republican front', as we saw, to block Le Pen's journey to the Elysée. The party's electoral successes were limited to those contests (European and regional elections) fought under full or partial proportional representation and to a handful of municipal victories in its stronghold in the south-east of France (in the mid- to late 1990s, four towns in that region were controlled by the FN). In addition, Le Pen polled between 10 per cent and 20 per cent in the presidential elections of 1988, 1995, 2002 and 2007 – representing almost 4 million French voters in the last of these contests.

The nationwide implantation of the FN and the strength of its electoral support, however dispersed, ensured that in the 1997 legislative elections it was able to maintain candidates in many second-round contests alongside the mainstream left–right opponents (so-called *triangulaire* contests), a fact that split the right-wing vote and contributed to the unexpected success of the left in those elections. These achievements brought Le Pen and the party visibility and, just as important, resources in the form of broadcast airtime, and media attention in general, public funding (at national and EP level), and the opportunity at local level to try out its policy of *la préférence nationale* – the preferential treatment of 'native' French people regarding welfare and other benefits.

Today's National Rally under its figurehead, Marine Le Pen, claims to have separated the party from this past via the process of '*dédiabolisation*' – that for its critics, with some justification, is little more than a smokescreen for nationalist, exclusionary politics. Under her leadership, the party's achievements have been remarkable. It has pitched itself as a party than can govern, tracking voter concerns to do so. In the name of security it encourages voters to make connections between France's Muslim population, terrorism by Islamist extremists, and immigration. To tackle cost of living challenges it highlights for voters the costs of climate change mitigation measures, and it defends ecological nationalism. To voters' sense of powerlessness and lack of trust in politicians it paints a rosy picture of a future France freed from its many international constraints, 'taking back control' of its borders from the EU, and all delivered by a party that promises to only ever directly heed the people's voice. Le Pen herself restyled her political image – becoming 'Marine' for the purposes of the election – including refreshed communication skills, leaning into the trivia and titillation of the social media age, posting herself striking tender poses with cats.

Has it all worked? Yes. In 2017 and 2022 Le Pen faced off Emmanuel Macron in the second round of the presidential election, breaking through the 10 million vote barrier in the second round of the 2017 election, and exceeding 13 million five years later. In 2022, the RN was notably no longer the pariah of French politics and there was no large-scale republican front to block her, unlike its predecessor, the FN, in the 2002 contest (see Table 3.3). In 2022, moreover, the Le Pen dynasty now had a contender as the representative of the ultranationalist fringes of French politics: former mainstream journalist Eric Zemmour, convicted in 2022 of racist hate speech and who attracted over 7 per cent of the votes (almost two and a half million people) in the first round of the presidential election, exceeding the total score of the candidates of the formerly mainstream left and right parties combined.

The RN's own electoral base had widened and in 2022 its voters returned deputies to the National Assembly in 89 constituencies across the country, where previously it had had only eight representatives, making it the largest of the opposition parties in the National Assembly, and thereby embedding the party further still in France's republican institutions. 'Marine', parliamentary deputy and leader of the RN's parliamentary party, had by then entrusted the presidency of the RN to a well-spoken, young, energetic man from outside the Le Pen family who made much of his humble upbringing in social housing, Jordan Bardella, who was already representing the party in the EP (see Figure 3.1). (This appointment would perhaps prove particularly prescient should the prosecution of Marine le Pen (and 24 co-defendants) for illegal party funding connected to her time as European Parliament deputy be successful and ban her from political office for five years.) The duo brought the party into first place in both the 2024 June elections to the EP and the first round of the 2024 French legislative elections, ending up with 143 seats in the National Assembly and, thereby, wielding unprecedented political leverage over a weakened President Macron.

Figure 3.1: The end of the Le Pen family affair? Electoral posters spanning 30 years, showing Jean-Marie Le Pen, Marine Le Pen and Jordan Bardella, party leader and would-be prime minister, 2024 (Author)

Emmanuel Macron: from movement to renaissance

France had by 2022 twice elected its youngest president ever, Emmanuel Macron, only 39 when first elected in 2017. Previously presidential adviser and then minister during François Hollande's presidential term, and having never previously stood for election, Macron's run for the presidency was a surprise, as was his victory. His win and his electorate in 2017 were populated by France's remaining fervent pro-Europeans (Europe being a key priority of Macron's campaign; see Chapter 8) and by the urban, affluent, well-educated and somewhat aged French who saw him, correctly, not as a revolutionary at all but as a defender of their interests; the circumstances of 2017 gifted him a lucky break. By his youth, his lack of electoral baggage, his political toolbox (he ran an Obama-type campaign, mobilizing grassroots-level voters via the 'march' of his supporters across the country), and his plans for a 'revolution', he was a disruptive element (Drake, 2018).

President Hollande had not sought a second term; the old parties on the left and right had run leadership primaries that returned candidates with strong but small followings in their respective parties, one of whom, François Fillon, former prime minister under Nicolas Sarkozy, was undermined by investigations into financial wrongdoing for which he was subsequently charged and convicted. Le Pen herself faltered in the live televised debate with Macron between the two presidential rounds and Macron went on to victory. But five years later, after a first term in office scarred by the *gilets jaunes*, growing personal unpopularity and the immense challenges of combatting

Figure 3.2: A fresh-faced Emmanuel Macron campaigns for his first presidential mandate in May 2017. The strains of office are visible in his campaign for re-election five years later, in May 2022 (Author)

the COVID-19 pandemic, Macron's victory was narrower. His movement had lost its momentum, and in the June 2022 legislative elections also lost its parliamentary majority (subsequently further reduced in the 2024 parliamentary elections), despite optimistically renaming itself Renaissance. Abstention had risen again. The far right had exceeded its 2017 performance and on the left of the spectrum politics now revolved around the divisive figure of Jean-Luc Mélenchon, supporter of a Sixth French Republic based on direct democracy and a break with capitalist excesses.

The French left in a globalized France

Where Gaullism has shaped the contemporary French right, communism is key to understanding the French left. When the French Socialist Party (PS) finally came to power in the Fifth Republic in 1981, it was the beginning of the end for the French Communist Party (PCF). By 2022, both parties had collapsed to almost certainly the point of no return as their electorates turned to other figures across the political landscape, and to other forms of political action beyond the vote.

Socialism and communism à la française

French socialism and communism took shape in the early 20th century in response to domestic industrialization and the communist revolutions in the first decades of that century in Russia. The two movements split in 1920 over their differences regarding the Bolshevik revolution and their own willingness or not to work within the electoral politics of the Third Republic. The experience of World War II was crucial in lending the PCF a form of credibility in response to the active part played (or claimed to have been played) by Communist Party members in the resistance of the Free French to the German occupier (see Chapter 1). Relations between de Gaulle and the PCF, however, then, as later, during the Cold War, were undermined by de Gaulle's suspicion of the PCF as a Soviet satellite (and the party never explicitly converted to Eurocommunism unlike, for example, its Italian counterparts), by the PCF's hatred of a regime and president (de Gaulle) whom they branded as dictatorial, and by the Communists' rejection of the emerging mass consumer, capitalist society. Yet the PCF was a stronger party than the Socialists for much of the Fourth and Fifth Republics, in part due to stringent internal party discipline and the loyalty of its followers and in part for its promise of a more authentic (i.e. less Gaullist) French Republic based on a break (*rupture*) with capitalism.

The Socialists' fortunes were revived at the start of the 1970s by the arrival of François Mitterrand as leader. In 1981 (as seen in Chapter 1), the PS was able to win the presidency from the political right, and to win parliamentary majorities for all but four of Mitterrand's 14 years as president, which lent him and the PS considerable authority and power. The PS also constructed a power base throughout France in its regional and local authorities, and a sizeable presence in the EP. Mitterrand's success in gaining power was due in no small part to the tactical deals he made with the PCF; these ranged from an uneasy 'common programme of government' in the 1970s to including Communist ministers in his government from 1981 to 1988. Socialist Party prime minister Lionel Jospin, from 1997–2002, similarly brought Communist leaders into his *gauche plurielle* – a 'pluralist' left alliance. But Mitterrand's biggest triumph was to persuade Communist and Socialist voters that he, Mitterrand, was the sole leader of the left; and that Communist followers' only chance of representation in the Republic was to vote for him as president.

Mitterrand's victory came at a high cost for the PCF, compounding the impact of factors external to France, especially the ending of the Cold War in the late 1980s, of internal problems such as the party's reluctance or inability to update its ideology, and of growing political competition. The PS itself, however, once in power, never fully cohered around Mitterrand's compromises on the socialist manifesto that brought him to power. After an abruptly terminated 'socialist experiment' from 1981 to 1983 (see Chapter 1), Mitterrand pinned his political survival and career on adapting French socialism and France itself to new rules, especially those of the expanding and deepening European Economic Community, as it then was. This created a fault line within the party that never repaired. In 2005, now having been in opposition for a decade, the PS officially supported the EU's Draft Constitutional Treaty along with the RPR government and President Chirac. However, former PS prime minister Laurent Fabius campaigned against the text, taking much of the PS vote with him in a result that by 55 per cent killed the treaty.

The PS failed to win back the presidency from the right in 2007 when its candidate was not the party's leader, François Hollande, but his then partner-in-life Ségolène Royal. She had won the party's primary for the nomination, and embodied change by virtue of her age, gender (she would have been France's first female president), interest in participative democracy and, paradoxically, her lack of party roots and experience, which was less divisive of party unity than that of the party heavyweights. But she failed to defeat presidential opponent Nicolas Sarkozy and it was ultimately François Hollande who won the presidency back for the PS in 2012 for one term after a dramatic twist in the party's fortunes: expectations were high that Dominique Strauss-Kahn, former International Monetary Fund IMF director and from the wing of the PS that *did* support further European integration, would win the nomination. Following his highly publicized arrest for sexual assault in New York in May 2011 (charges were eventually dropped, although much additional sleaze subsequently came to light), Strauss-Kahn exited the picture and the party picked Hollande to contest the election. In his campaign, candidate Hollande declared big finance his enemy, talked tough on the EU's austerity measures following the 2008–09 global financial crash and looked set to swing the country back to a more radical form of French socialism. But his party haemorrhaged support over his five-year term as radical change failed to materialize. By 2012 the political space had already become more crowded, with over 30 per cent of votes cast for presidential candidates outside the mainstream left and right in the first round of the presidential election; by 2017 this was nearer 50 per cent, with alternative offers on the left a significant part of the picture.

From the Left Front to France Unbowed: the journey of Jean-Luc Mélenchon

The level of support for political formations to the far left of the PS was already high by previous standards in the 2002 presidential elections, when far-left candidates attracted between them over 10 per cent of the votes that might otherwise have gone to the PS candidate, incumbent prime minister Lionel Jospin, and which thus cost him a place in the second round of those elections. Some of those candidates represented movements and personalities with a long life in the Fifth Republic. Arlette Laguiller, for example, leader of the Lutte ouvrière (LO – Workers' Struggle), stood in every presidential election from 1981 until her retirement from politics after the 2007 presidential vote. Olivier Besancenot emerged in the 2000s, leading the Ligue revolutionnaire communiste (LCR – Communist Revolutionary League). In 2009, Besancenot renamed the LCR as the Nouveau Parti anticapitaliste (NPA – New Anti-capitalist Party), thus removing all mention of 'communism' from its title in the hope of broadening its appeal. The NPA's message revolved around the sort of challenge to France's Europeanized, globalized economy that, formerly, the PCF would have articulated on behalf of, principally, those implacably opposed to the opening of national trade borders and deeply committed to challenging the domination of capital over labour. The electorate for these movements was very small and, like the then FN, they were kept away from political power by the system's play of majoritarian elections and electoral alliances; they were also fragmented, rejecting any systematic alliance on this end of the political spectrum.

What this constellation arguably lacked was a leader around whom it could revolve and cohere. Enter Jean-Luc Mélenchon, previously minister, local politician, and senator for the PS, who over the course of the 2010s gathered pace as the figure to lead this charge on the status quo, with startling results. He founded the Left Party (Parti de gauche) in 2008, which in 2009, along with the PCF, fought the EP elections as the Left Front (Front de gauche), returning Mélenchon as MEP and building his electoral credibility to the point where in the 2012 presidential elections he (for the Left Front) came fourth with 11 per cent and nearly 4 million votes. By 2017, Mélenchon had once again reformed his supporters into the grouping that has now become synonymous with his achievements and to its critics, notorious for its raucous conduct in parliament, its uncompromising policy stance and its defiance of pragmatic, coalition politics: France Unbowed or la France insoumise (LFI). Under this banner, Mélenchon rallied almost 22 per cent (7.7 million) of the votes in the first round of the 2022 presidential elections, this time coming third, after Marine Le Pen, and much more narrowly missing qualification for the second round. Had Mélenchon faced Macron in that round, rather than Marine

Le Pen, the result could have been the first big political shock of 21st-century French politics, akin to Mitterrand's election in 1981. Mélenchon's brand of radicalism offered a link back to the history of the French left, when it had offered an alternative to the status quo, not an *n*th version of the same. Where much of the traditional, working-class, less-educated electorate of the French left had by now been tempted by Le Pen, who stressed the conservation and restoration of any number of interests and values, Mélenchon rallied those, especially the young and of immigrant origin, and including those with high levels of education, tantalized by the prospect of a fresh start that would finally dismantle vested interests and tackle existential emergencies as the party defined them. Mélenchon showed himself to be a talented political performer, engaging with methods familiar to younger generations versed in digital technologies, and drawing on oratorical skills that echoed France's early revolutions, as seen above. Following his close result in the 2022 presidential election, he persuaded the remnants of the traditional French left – the PS, the PCF and France's ecologist representatives (Europe Ecology–The Greens or EE-LV, subsequently renamed Les Écologistes), whose candidates had fought the 2022 election separately, with disastrous results, to form a new parliamentary grouping, NUPES (the New Ecological and Social People's Union). The June legislative elections of that year successfully returned 131 NUPES deputies, who formed a parliamentary group under Mélenchon's leadership, the unity of which was soon tested by the pressures of opposing Macron's flagship policy on the reform of France's pensions, by rivalries between the leaders of its various constituent parties and, by December 2023, by differences over the Israeli–Palestinian war that pointed to the end of the road not only for NUPES but probably for Mélenchon's leadership of an alternative left politics. The French left headed divided once more into the 2024 EP elections but in a dramatic twist came together only weeks later (this time under the historically resonant label New Popular Front – NPF) to push back the RN in the second round of the 2024 legislative elections. This deprived the RN of the absolute majority they had anticipated and which would have given them the right to expect to form a government and pick a prime minister. But a wary, defiant president overlooked the NPF too for government, and plunged French politics into a period of great uncertainty.

Figure 3.3: Machos, racists, golfers and the rich all vote. Do you? Exhortations by Jean-Luc Mélenchon's France Unbowed (la France insoumise) to register and vote in the 2024 European Parliament elections (Author)

French politics and 21st-century problems

The struggles of France's political parties are not only a function of the electoral rules of the Fifth Republic regime that superimpose artificial alliances between them if they are to win power, at the risk of denaturing them, as seen above. Nor can they be explained away merely as a reflection of the radicalism of France's revolutionary, fractious past permanently seeking expression. These factors are relevant, but the reality is more complicated, namely that France's politicians are as challenged as their counterparts in other countries by sociological, demographic and cultural changes inside and outside of France. Class, religion, education and geography still matter, but these pillars of electoral behaviour have been confounded by the individualistic premises of late capitalism, from remote working

95

patterns and 'bullshit' jobs to the entertainment and, especially, news that is delivered and tailored to personal devices via social media and its algorithms. Deep inequalities of wealth, income, opportunity and living standards, particularly in a country professing equality (*égalité*) as one of its founding principles, have significant consequences for people's expectations of politics. In this context, at the intersection of such trends and faced with existential fears and daily worries, voters are increasingly turning away from the new *old régimes* and seeking solutions elsewhere.

Les gilets jaunes: *the Yellow Vests*

Sparked by a proposed rise in fuel tax and lowering of speed limits in 2018, what became the *gilets jaunes* movement took root in one individual, Priscillia Ludosky, appalled at the rise in the cost of filling her fuel tank, and her social media network. It spread across the country as people donned the eponymous high-vis yellow vests all motorists in France are required to carry in their vehicles. They staked out roundabouts and motorway toll booths on France's roads, discussing their grievances between themselves and with passing motorists. French journalist Florence Aubenas (2023) writes movingly of her encounters with individuals not accustomed to participating in collective action but finding comfort and camaraderie in these new communal spaces. The movement rolled out in 18 'Acts' over the course of 18 months in 2018–19 and in the cities, especially Paris, the demonstrations attracted participants drawn to violence, threats were made on the president's life and police brutality cost lives and inflicted life-changing injuries. In response, President Macron launched a 'Great National Debate', travelling through France to speak at town hall meetings where people had been encouraged to register their grievances and suggestions in *cahiers* or ledgers. This was a process with strong resonance of the historically significant consultation carried out in the months leading up to the French Revolution in 1789. Unlike Louis XIV, Macron survived and kept his head. His government did withdraw the most unpopular proposals, particularly the 'carbon tax' on fuel, and there was no cohering of the *gilets jaunes* into a new political force with electoral traction. But the eruption of this moment in French political life pointed to underlying, ongoing fault

Figure 3.4: The end of the road for Jean-Luc Mélenchon's bid for power? (Author)

lines in French society that were finding their expression outside the ballot box as well as driving the transformations of French electoral politics as seen above.

The environment, ecology and climate change

The environment and climate change was one of these cleavages, pitting defenders of the natural world against established interests and traditions and creating opportunities for politicians, in crude terms, to side with saving the planet or saving voters from the costs of making the definitive transition away from fossil fuels. Ecological activism in France dates back to the 1970s' protests against France's nuclear energy programme and its land-based nuclear missiles. Action to defend rural traditions and livelihoods has also been part of France's party political landscape, notably in the form of the Hunting, Fishing, Nature and Tradition movement (CNPT, subsequently renamed the Rurality Movement), which contested elections during the 1990s with modest results. It includes the 'French wine terrorism' of the 1960s (Smith, 2016). In today's France, these conflicts of interests play out most visibly (and, frequently, violently) in protests over large infrastructure projects such as regional airports, railway tunnels, the installation of onshore wind turbines, the planting of genetically modified crops (still banned in France, as seen in Chapter 2) and the construction of large reservoirs to irrigate agricultural land. The state response to what it sees as eco-terrorism has been harsh, including violent repression and the outlawing of certain activists and their groups.

Radical activism to highlight the climate emergency in France, as in other countries, deems traditional party politics incapable of addressing the urgency of action to prevent climate collapse, and conventional politics has indeed proven limited to effect change. Green parties in France have won some parliamentary representation in France and the EP, and some seats in government when the PS were in power, most recently during the presidency of François Hollande (2012–17), when France also hosted the international diplomatic negotiations of COP21, which reached the breakthrough 'Paris Agreement' to reduce global warming (see Chapter 2). Reaching the targets of this agreement has proven as intractable in France as elsewhere. In his first term, President Macron initiated a Citizens' Convention for the Climate (composed of 150 people), which resulted in 149 proposals for change but which, to its critics, were inadequately translated into the 2021 Climate and Resilience Law. Macron, as with many other national leaders, finds himself accused of sacrificing commitments to climate change mitigation and biodiversity preservation to the pressure of corporate interests (agricultural, business), all the while burdening individuals and communities with the costs of meeting net-zero targets (through home renovation, for example). This latter issue of the costs of energy transition was a political opportunity seized upon by the National Rally, in keeping with their sister parties elsewhere across the EU27, successfully tested in the elections of 2024, as seen above.

Insecurity and terror

More historically typical of the RN agenda was the issue of insecurity, defined as a breakdown of law and order in a context of rising antisocial and violent behaviour. By the 2000s this had already become a priority for Presidents Jacques Chirac (1995–2007) and Nicolas Sarkozy (2007–12). At the heart of the question then were France's outer-city environments, known as *les banlieues*, and the often dilapidated housing estates (*les cités*) that composed their neighbourhoods (*les quartiers*). These terms have all become synonymous in France with urban strife and high-profile incidents of police discrimination and violence, in a context of social and economic deprivation and high concentrations of ethnic minority populations. The literal meaning of the term *banlieue* denotes banishment outside city limits, to the wrong side of the tracks. In real life, these are typically areas of high-rise social housing with a concentration of ethnic minority populations and extremely high unemployment, predominantly but not only in urban areas. The 1995 acclaimed film *la Haine* (*Hate*) portrayed these facts of life in grim and pessimistic detail at a time of notorious uprisings in *banlieues* outside Paris and France's second largest city, Lyon, and the 2019 movie *Les Misérables* focused on the troubled state of relations between police and residents in one such Paris suburb.

As minister of the interior in 2002–04 and 2005–07, and then as president, Nicolas Sarkozy had already gained notoriety for his crude-speaking on the subject, drawing a link between immigration followed by faulty integration into society on the one hand, and law and order on the other, as expressed in his 2006 soundbite 'love France or leave it'. There followed a series of tough immigration laws alongside measures designed to stigmatize and penalize those deemed guilty of poorly integrating into French society (see also Chapters 2 and 5). The extremely serious riots of autumn 2005 in *banlieues* across France, sparked by the electrocution of two French youths fleeing the police in the Paris suburb of Clichy-sous-Bois (not because they had committed a crime but, rather, feared an identity check and its possible repercussions), suggested that such policies had missed the point. Public policy failures across the board were subsequently found to have incited the violence that followed the Clichy incident and gripped and shook the whole of France (tens of thousands of cars were burned, at least) for over a month. Most of the protagonists were found to have been motivated by frustrations bred by failures to fit into French society, and not a rejection of France on extremist or separatist grounds, religious or other.

But, as president, Sarkozy continued with the crackdown, targeting primarily foreign-born, naturalized French citizens deemed to be acting unpatriotically, French citizens deemed guilty of un-Republican behaviour (such as wearing the full Islamic face veil in public), and young offenders – branded as delinquents – from France's *banlieues*. The measures included curfews for those aged under 13 years, the extension of CCTV surveillance equipment throughout France, stiff penalties for 'outrage' committed against the French flag, and the gradual tightening of immigration policy, as seen in Chapter 2. This linking of crime to ethnic, racial and religious – specifically, Muslim – origins brought a staple discourse of the far right into the mainstream of French politics. Police discrimination against young men of visibly ethnic origin – i.e. skin colour, or dress – in the form of stop and search interventions are well known, as are tragically notorious instances of deaths of such individuals at the hands of the police. In 2021 a controversial 'Global Security' law was passed to attempt to join the dots between various security actors while preserving individual freedoms; some of its initial provisions were struck down by France's Constitutional Court precisely for their attacks on personal freedoms and privacy.

The arrival of Islamist terrorism in France gave fresh impetus to this dynamic. Internationally, the so-called 'war on terror' unleashed by the US and its allies following the 9/11 attacks on the US stigmatized Islamic and Muslim communities throughout the West. In Europe, governments found themselves incapable of preventing atrocities perpetrated by terrorists, some their own ('home-grown') citizens, radicalized to act in the name of other Muslims but espousing extremist, jihadist ideologies of hatred for the West and its wars and whose attacks rarely discriminated between their victims' faith or origins. France has suffered terribly from such attacks. The most notorious have been on a mass scale, including the killings on 7 January 2015 of 12 staff of *Charlie Hebdo*, a satirical magazine that had published cartoons mocking the prophet Mohammed, and the massacres of 130 people at multiple targets in Paris on the night of 13 November 2013 and of 86 people in Nice on 14 July 2016, the French national holiday. Hundreds more victims were injured in these attacks, to which must be added the toll of seemingly disconnected acts of terror carried out on individuals including Catholic priests, police officers and schoolteachers.

But subsequent trials have revealed patterns linking the tragedies, such as the radicalization of some perpetrators in France's own prison population; the ease of communications and operations between terrorists across borders and the internet; the psychiatric disturbances of some individuals; the failures and impossibilities of security and intelligence services to track all known suspects before they act; and the ongoing conflicts elsewhere in the world generating chances for individuals to serve extreme ideological causes such as Al Qaida, Daesh and ISIS. All of these developments have found space in French politics, repackaged by populist politicians as yet more reasons to fear others and close ranks.

Patriots, the people and the rest

French political history, as seen in Chapter 1, includes episodic appeals to the French people to revere an imagined past as an exclusive nation defined by racial purity and a traditional identity, and to scapegoat targets identified as threats to that utopia. Such appeals belong to the present as well as the past, featuring different targets and threats, but revolving around the same simple message that defines populist politics, namely: it's us, the people, against them, the outsiders and others. The French people are at the very heart of the republican regime: we saw above that in the French Constitution (Article 2) '[t]he principle of the Republic shall be: government of the people, by the people and for the people'. Furthermore, Article 3 pronounces that '[n]ational sovereignty shall vest in the people'. It goes on to specify that the people 'shall exercise it [sovereignty] through their representatives and by means of referendum'.

In today's France, these ideas of *the people* and their *sovereignty* seem to be gaining ground on the reality of *representative* democracy, at least in the form it took for the first half-century of the Fifth French Republic. In contemporary France, the RN is particularly vocal in its claim to speak for the people, and in its denunciation of their representatives to date as an incompetent 'elite'. This is despite the fact that the RN has, as seen above, exploited the institutions of that very elite (its parliament, access to state funding and broadcasting) to establish itself as a future party of government. In this, it is at the forefront of the trend in various European and Western countries to successfully call on the people to vote against the status quo and for political figures or projects that, in their language at least, reify the people, their sovereignty and their voice. The UK's decision in 2016 to 'take back control' and leave the EU (Brexit); the election of Donald Trump as US president in 2016 to 'Make America Great Again' and his re-election in 2024 on an even more pronounced version of that programme; the denigration by UK Prime Minister Johnson and US President Trump of domestic courts and both the national and international rule of law; and the successes at different points in time of anti-immigrant, nationalist parties and figures of varying extremes in Austria, Germany, Hungary, the Netherlands and Poland all testify to the strength of a trend in Europe where France enjoys the dubious status of a pioneer in terms of the popularity of its populist right, if not – just yet – accession to executive power.

We saw above that scepticism in France regarding the impact of its membership of the EU on French economy and society is nothing new, but in the hands of France's contemporary populist politicians it has found a permanent home, based on promises to reform the EU and to reduce France's commitment to it to an *à la carte* choice featuring heavily in their electoral manifestos (such as Marine Le Pen's in 2017 and 2022). Le Pen and others, including Jean-Luc Mélenchon on the radical left, have so far failed to make credible cases for leaving the EU altogether but are pushing at an open door: the French population has grown increasingly Eurosceptic, again along with most other EU populations, and as exposed in the narrow win of the 1992 Maastricht referendum and the loss of its 2005 successor. President Macron was bold enough in 2016 to tell the UK's BBC, in the context of the UK's Brexit convulsions, that, were he to put French EU membership to a vote by referendum, he could not be sure that he would win, and he discouraged fellow EU member states from considering further treaty reform. His predecessors Sarkozy and Hollande had avoided the risk by approving EU treaty changes via the parliamentary route instead, and Macron's caution did not deter him from campaigning for election on an intensely pro-EU platform (see Chapter 8).

Today's French populists increasingly see the EU and specifically its parliament, elected every five years by proportional representation, as a megaphone for their ideas and a forum for organizing themselves. Through their seats in the EP (when they occupy them, having a reputation for absenteeism), the RN has forged alliances with like-minded groups committed to a policy platform defined by its eco-nationalism and its anti-immigrant stance (they can point to the failures or unwillingness of sitting governments across Europe to control irregular and legal migration alike) with its sinister undertones of rejection of the 'other' as defined by religion (Islam; Judaism), and invoking the terrorist attacks discussed above to drive home their message of an existential battle between patriots – the people – and the rest.

Such tactics, however inconsistent or illogical, of demonization, othering and polarization have fallen on fertile ground in France. As we have seen above, France has a population with revolutionary genes and reference points. It has metamorphosed in its habits and loyalties along with the decline of traditional points in common (class, religion) and the rise of new technologies. It is spooked by scandal and wrongdoing in the political class. François Mitterrand's secret second family and even his connivence in the 1985 sinking by French secret agents of the Greenpeace ship *Rainbow Warrior*, protesting against French nuclear testing in the Pacific, may have been largely forgotten, but less so the sentencing of former presidents Jacques Chirac and Nicolas Sarkozy and former prime minister François Fillon for financial misconduct while in office. Cases of sexual misconduct in politics as in other spheres of life, far less well tolerated today, have also been exposed, creating a climate such that President Macron made the passing of a bill to clean up the ethics of French public life a priority of his term, but led a government far from immune from such misconduct. The French population witnesses or, worse, experiences the horror of terror attacks, the violence inflicted on and by the police at demonstrations infiltrated by extremists, the armed fights between rival football supporters, and attacks on individuals by gangs having convened and travelled to cause mayhem. It endures public services seemingly in retreat from swathes of the country in the name of cost-cutting, efficiency measures (see Chapters 4 and 5) and notes that the state alone is largely powerless to protect them from existential threats such as planetary collapse. Above all that, France lives in an era ripe for conspiracy theory, fake news, disinformation and lies. As the nation fragments, the populists in France gather strength.

Conclusions

It would appear, by way of conclusion, that France is far from immune from political developments characteristic of 21st-century Europe. We have seen that these include the challenge of climate change and the environment (protect it or protect voters from the costs of transition to net zero?) and the calls of largely young voters for direct action in response; the growing presence of the populist far right and their nationalist agendas; sceptical if not radical attitudes towards the EU's free-market economics and towards international trade, cooperation and interdependence in general; an increasingly disaffected and demoted middle class that has turned away from traditional parties and politics; the advent of new technologies to subvert the political process and open it to nefarious influence and interference (including hacking by foreign powers); and the struggles of the parties and politicians who have governed France for decades to command trust – or the truth. In our following chapter we turn to the institutions of French government and state to assess the extent of their resilience to such developments.

4

Government, Governance and the State

Introduction

Like other liberal democracies, contemporary France is governed by formal political offices and their incumbents, and by bureaucratic policy-making processes and the staff that service them. At the top is a dual executive composed of a president and prime minister; the power relationship between them is fixed by the constitution but variable in practice. The president is directly elected, commands his (as we have seen, there has yet to be a woman in this post) own staff, appoints the prime minister and chairs the government (the Council of Ministers). But the machinery and business of government is piloted by the prime minister (only two since 1958 have been women), who, unlike the president, is accountable to parliament. When French presidents have a supportive majority in parliament, as was the case for President Macron in his first term (2017–22), they can and do set policy direction across many domains. In Macron's case, this resulted in a reputation for a highly top-down or 'vertical' interpretation of his role, much derided by his critics and problematic for good governance. All presidents think ahead to their legacy but the days of Mitterrand's vanity 'great projects' (most emblematically, the Louvre Pyramid) are probably over, as presidential authority wanes in an age of changing attitudes to democracy, as seen in the previous chapter.

Beyond the institutions of government, France is characterized by a pervasive tradition that only a strong state can guarantee the republican ideals enshrined in the 1958 Constitution; this is the pact between the state and its citizens. Hence France, by tradition, is a *secular* state, designed to unite diverse faiths into one republican nation; it is a *centralized* state, concentrating power tightly in the core executive in Paris by means of an extensive administrative apparatus; France sustains a costly *social welfare* state, the policy expression of solidarity between citizens of the nation (old and young; employed and unemployed; rural, urban and suburban); and France takes its place in the international arena as a *nation*-state whose citizens are bound by their nationality – their Frenchness – and whose state is *sovereign* over its own decisions.

Contemporary developments such as European integration, the globalization of markets, the growing ethnic, religious and generational diversity and needs of the French, the pressures on public finances, particularly following the crises of the global financial system (2008–09), and the COVID-19 pandemic have placed this model under serious strain. Over time, these challenges, alongside political swings and cost-cutting exercises, have resulted in incremental changes to the redistribution of powers and competences between different levels of government (the region, the department and the *commune*); and to the supranational level of the EU. Public expectations of the French state are still high, and perceptions of repeated policy failures to meet them have created distrust on the part of the French electorate in the first decade of the 21st century. We saw in the previous chapter how the *gilets jaunes* movement was sparked by a sense of injustice that motorists were facing extra costs in rural areas, where they had no reasonable alternative to the car for reaching essential public services (or their place of work).

This chapter, first, tackles the subject of government in the narrow sense of France's central, Paris-based political institutions, which form a semi-presidential regime where political power is highly concentrated in the president of the Republic, the head of state. In this respect, France is still in the present day a *Gaullist* state, shaped around the preferences of its founder president, Charles de Gaulle. The 1958 Constitution has outlasted its early critics, and the semi-presidential regime has become a new form of parliamentary democracy in its own right, emulated elsewhere in the world. Yet in France itself semi-presidentialism can still have the air of a temporary, stop-gap measure, and the 2022 presidential candidate Jean-Luc Mélenchon, who came a very close third to Marine Le Pen, as seen in Chapter 3, is a strong promoter of a Sixth French Republic that would substantially restrict presidential power. The trend over time has been for presidential power to be consolidated in the letter of the constitution and for presidents to wield it even when they lack a supportive parliamentary majority. This was the case in President Macron's second term and it generated strong resistance to him, his government and their policy agenda, as we see below. A parallel trend is for declining interest or belief in the presidency itself, as seen in the rising abstention levels at presidential elections, and we explore the significance of these developments, alongside a discussion of the ways in which the French executive is scrutinized and held to account by parliamentary and legal institutions, as well as directly by the public in referenda.

Second, we expand our perspective to encompass the complex nexus of actors, processes and mechanisms that constitute the French policy-making environment at supranational, national, regional and local levels; this is best defined as governance. Here, our discussion seeks to establish the extent to which France can still, today, be classified as a state-centric model of administration, historically wary of so-called intermediaries between the state and the people such as civil society organizations and trades unions but where such organizations, especially associations (see below), have a legal footing, are funded by public money, and provide much solidarity between the French. We see that successive presidents and governments have themselves sought to enhance that solidarity by 'decentring' the state, to bring it and its representatives closer to the citizen, with mixed results. Third, we ask how far French public policy is upholding the 'indivisible republic' we discussed in Chapter 2, given the many decentralization reforms implemented since the 1980s that create opportunities for political competition, differentiation and power at various levels, especially the region. Finally, we assess the sovereignty of France's policy-making powers in the light of the obligations of France's EU membership, which have seen policy-making competences constitutionally transferred to, shared with and limited by EU authorities, a process of Europeanization that, as we saw in the previous chapter, has created a significant fault line in French politics. In conclusion, we review the most consequential of the trends defining French government, governance and state in the 21st century so far and assess the extent of the problems yet to be resolved.

The semi-presidential regime of the Fifth French Republic

'Semi-presidentialism' is the term coined specifically to describe the political system of the Fifth French Republic whereby a politically powerful president is grafted onto a Westminster-type parliamentary democracy, and where the executive branch of government is top-heavy. The origins of this regime lie in the circumstances of 1958. Faced with army rebellion in Algeria, the government of the Fourth Republic called upon Charles de Gaulle, who drafted a new constitution designed to restore stability and strength to the French Republic. This settlement was, therefore, negotiated in a very specific set of circumstances, namely the collapse of the political authority of the Fourth Republic under the weight of the doomed fight for *l'Algérie française* (see Chapter 1). These events provided de Gaulle with an opportunity to return to power and implement his ideas of government, which previously, immediately after World War II, had been rejected as too authoritarian. The result, argue some such as Nabila Ramdani (2023), is a system with militaristic overtones.

The 1958 Constitution was ratified overwhelmingly by referendum on 28 September 1958. It forms the framework for contemporary French government by acting as the fundamental law of the Republic. It draws its principles from the 1789 Declaration of the Rights of Man and the Citizen, the preamble of the 1946 Constitution, and the 2004 Charter of the Environment. The 1958 text defines the powers and roles of each of the central institutions of French government. It is also ambiguous and flexible and has been amended multiple times; France's Constitutional Council lists 25 amendments in total, ranging from the accommodation of EU law to the right of abortion. It was de Gaulle's own incumbency of the presidency for the first 11 years of the regime (1958–69) and his unconstitutional but successful amendment of 1962 providing for a *directly* elected presidency, that shaped, in practice, the power relations between the core institutions and, in particular, between president and prime minister.

Who's in charge? Power and political leadership in the French dual executive

The 1958 French constitution provides for simultaneous political leadership by both president and prime minister. In this system, a directly elected president coexists with a prime minister appointed by the president and who 'directs the actions of' a government (the Council of Ministers – Conseil des Ministres) chaired by the president. Both prime minister and government are responsible to parliament and, until 2008, the president was banned from the parliamentary chambers. Now, '[h]e may ... take the floor before parliament convened in Congress for this purpose' (1958 Constitution, Article 18), Congress referring to the joint session of both houses, held in the pomp and splendour of the Palace of Versailles. This is the separation of powers, French–style. When the president and prime minister both represent the majority in the National Assembly (the directly elected lower house) – usually, but not necessarily, this is when they both emanate from the majority party – power and powers are divided between them on the basis of a unique pact dependent on their personalities and the political circumstances of the time.

The stronger of the executive duo in terms of the overall policy-making agenda, and certainly in terms of public visibility, is the president, and all presidents have certainly seen this as the true spirit of the constitution. It is, in any case, the president who at all times retains the constitutional upper hand by having the right to call new elections (Article 12), appeal to the electorate via referendum (Article 11) or, in very extreme cases – the last resort – decreeing a state of emergency (Article 16). These powers are the levers by which the president can fulfil his duty of 'arbitration', laid out in Article 5 of the constitution, in order to ensure 'the proper functioning of the public authorities and the continuity of the state'.

Article 5 of the constitution also requires the president to 'be the guarantor of national independence, territorial integrity and due respect for Treaties' and thus it is France's presidents who are the international face and voice of France. All presidents of the Fifth Republic, with de Gaulle setting the precedent, have played an active diplomatic role. President Macron has emphasized this role, framing each of his presidential terms by his international outlook and taking a very active part, with varied success, in international crises such as the Russian war on Ukraine in 2022. This presidential power is known as the 'reserved domain' and, since the president is not accountable to government or parliament, French foreign policy is relatively insulated from democratic control (but see Chapter 8). The French president is moreover, in formal terms, the head of *state*. In all other EU countries this is a ceremonial role but in France it is a politically powerful role underpinned, we have seen, by the popular legitimacy of direct election. However, by the same token, French presidents can, and do, become extraordinarily unpopular during their mandate, with President Hollande's approval ratings plummeting as low as 4 per cent towards the end of his five-year term. In practice, a president's actual (as opposed to constitutional) power can be curtailed by a lack of party political support in the National Assembly. This happened five years into each of François Mitterrand's seven-year presidential terms, at the end of the National Assembly's five-year mandate, in 1986 and 1993. These were Mitterrand's mid-term elections, which he lost on both occasions, forcing him for the remaining two years of the presidential term to 'cohabit' with a prime minister and government nominally of his choosing but politically his opponents. The third period of cohabitation of this type to occur since 1958 forced President Jacques Chirac into cohabitation for five years with his Socialist prime minister Lionel Jospin (1997–2002). This blow was self-inflicted by the president, who ill-advisedly called and lost early elections only two years into his first (seven-year) term of office.

By the time of Chirac's re-election as president in 2002, the 1958 Constitution had been amended to reduce the presidential term from seven to five years and thus make cohabitation less likely; this shortened term is known as the *quinquennat*. Presidential elections are now held at five-yearly intervals and are immediately followed by legislative elections, the function of which is now to confirm the president in post by means of a parliamentary majority. Thus, in May 2017, Emmanuel Macron was elected president and the legislative elections the following month returned an absolute majority for his party, by now renamed as la République en marche! (LREM). Five years later, in May 2022 (see Chapter 3), Macron was re-elected as president but, in the legislative elections that followed, his party, renamed Renaissance and campaigning with allies under the coalition label Ensemble (Together), won only a relative majority of seats, making parliament a place of contestation for Macron's agenda in his second term, rather than a source of predictable support. This state of affairs was dramatically exacerbated when Macron called and lost snap parliamentary elections in 2024 (as seen in Chapter 3), following which France effectively entered a fourth period of cohabitation between President Macron and the man he appointed as prime minister, Michel Barnier, not from Ensemble but from the Republicans to their right. When Barnier's government fell after only three months, Macron appointed a successor from closer within his ranks: François Bayrou, whose MoDem party had supported Macron in his first term. Less uncomfortable than previous periods of cohabitation, this was nevertheless an appointment which did very little to shore up parliamentary support for the beleaguered president.

This electoral sequence thus links the president far more explicitly than previously to his parliamentary majority, and also raises the profile of the prime minister, whose job it is to manage this majority in order to support the presidential policy agenda. As the president's appointee, the prime minister more often than not serves the function of drawing any political poison (unpopularity; failed policy) away from the president into the prime ministerial office, culminating, if necessary, in the appointment by the president of a new, fresher prime minister destined to fulfil the same purpose. Such instrumentalization of the office of prime minister is not a constitutional right of the president but a practice that has become a norm of French political life.

The prime minister does play the vital role of running French government by heading the ministries and their political cabinets and coordinating the machinery of daily administrative life, with the lion's share of the nation's bureaucratic resources at their disposal. But even here the prime minister is rivalled by the president, who chairs the Council of Ministers and has the right to appoint his own staff in the Elysée Palace (the site of the presidential office). President Macron was known for surrounding himself with mainly men in his own image and for a permissive culture of lax management, from which in 2018 erupted the scandal of one of Macron's closest advisers, Alexandre Benalla, who was found guilty of assaulting a demonstrator while impersonating a police officer. The French dual executive may be top-heavy but it is certainly not above the law, and it is indeed subject to various forms of scrutiny from parliament, the courts and the media.

French parliament

The French parliament is a bicameral institution comprising the National Assembly and the Senate. The National Assembly is the lower house: it is a directly elected chamber, whose 577 members are called 'deputies' and who represent their constituencies. The upper house is known as the Senate and is there to represent France's subnational units of governance (see below) on the mainland and overseas, and including its diaspora across the world. Its 348 members are voted in for a six-year term by an electoral college composed of National Assembly deputies, senators and locally and regionally elected figures. Within this legislature, National Assembly deputies have the right to initiate legislation alongside that proposed by the government (with certain limitations regarding public finances), can propose amendments to government bills, and have control over the parliamentary agenda for two out of every four weeks they are in session. Fewer than half of successful legislative acts, however, emanate from parliament.

The Senate is there to scrutinize and vote on legislation, proposing amendments or even its own legislation as it sees fit; it examines public policy in public sessions and committees; it enjoys the legitimacy derived from the stability of its membership (longer terms than the Assemblée, and only half of the members renewed every three years); it has powers of patronage (its president nominates three of the nine members of the Constitutional Council, as does the president of the National Assembly – the president of the Republic nominates the remaining three); and it ranks highly in institutional protocol: the Senate's approval is also required of any constitutional reform and the leader of the Senate is second in line to the French president. When de Gaulle resigned from office in 1969, and again in 1974, when President Pompidou died in office, it was Senate leader Alain Poher who on both occasions served as interim president before new elections were held. However, the 1958 Constitution severely curtailed the power of the legislative branch as a whole, and the 65 years of the Fifth Republic's existence have confirmed this balance of power. The constitution confines parliamentary involvement to designated statutory domains, with all other areas being matters for government-issued regulation and decree.

Furthermore, the government can force parliament's hand by means of the 'blocked vote' or 'package vote' of Article 44-3 of the constitution, whereby deputies have to accept or reject an entire legislative package on the basis of government amendments. Just as significant, under the terms of Article 49-1 and 49-3, the government can call for a vote of confidence on its general policy programme or on specific finance bills respectively (see Figure 4.1). In the latter case, confidence is considered granted (without a vote) unless the deputies can, within 24 hours, muster a vote to the contrary, in which case the government would be defeated and required to offer its resignation. By late 2023, the provision had been invoked 101 times since 1958 by governments seeking to hurry along their legislative programme, or to bully an unstable majority to support government policy, but until December 2024 when a no-confidence vote brought down the government of Michel Barnier, the Assembly had not toppled a government under this provision for over 60 years. In Macron's second term alone, in the absence of an absolute parliamentary majority as seen earlier in this chapter, his prime minister Elisabeth Borne resorted to Article 49-3 on 15 different occasions between May 2022 and October 2023, most notoriously in March 2023 in order to force through legislation on pensions reform, particularly the raising of the retirement age, during which the government came within only nine votes of defeat. She did so in the face of sustained strikes and demonstrations outside parliament not only against the bill itself but specifically against the use of Article 49-3 (see Chapter 5 and Figure 4.1 below). In the National Assembly itself, debates were rancorous and ultimately ineffectual, and damaged parliament's reputation as an effective check on executive power.

The president's control of foreign policy and his prerogative to call national referenda on government proposals creates the potential for important matters of national policy to bypass parliament as a decision-making body. With regard to EU and foreign policy-making, the French constitution does confirm parliament's right of scrutiny and debate in these areas. In EU affairs, for example, the National Assembly in the 1990s and 2000s won the right to be consulted and informed, and to vote on resolutions on government policy, although these are not binding. The National Assembly or Senate delegations, despite their expertise, do not have the resources fully to expose or influence government policy towards the European

Figure 4.1: Handwritten sign on a shopfront in Savoie, 2023, calling for a rally against pensions reform and against the use of Article 49.3 (Author)

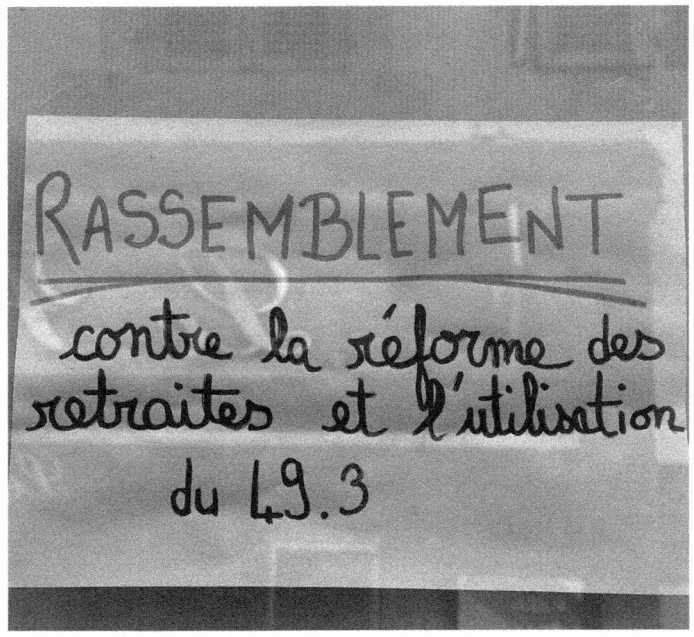

Union, despite their upgrading. The National Assembly has also won the right to longer sittings than was provided for in 1958, to a ministers' 'question time' and to a vote on social security budget bills. These alterations are best understood as attempts by successive governments to preserve the uneasy balance that lies at the heart of the design of French government, namely to preserve the prerogatives and power of the executive, and especially of the president, within the framework of a parliamentary democracy.

Referenda

This endeavour is complicated by provisions for popular votes by referenda that were written into the constitution at the outset and demand for which has risen in line with citizens' demands to have their voice better heard in the democratic process. During Macron's first mandate, one demand made by the *gilets jaunes* had been for a 'citizens' initiative' or 'popular' referendum (*referendum d'initiative citoyenne* – *RIC*) whereby if a citizens' proposal had sufficient popular report, parliament would be obliged to turn it into a bill that would then be put to the electorate by referendum. Article 11 of the constitution does allow the executive to initiate referenda on proposals that would affect the 'organisation of the public authorities'; on 'reforms relating to the economic, social or environmental policy of the Nation'; or which 'provide for authorization to ratify a treaty which, although not contrary to the constitution, would affect the functioning of the institutions'. The scope is therefore wide. The loss of France's last referendum, in 2005 on EU reform (see Chapter 3), shows how risky a manoeuvre it can be for a president (Article 88.5 still provides for a referendum in the case of treaties proposing further EU enlargement), but public demand for a better say in policy-making has not disappeared.

In 2008, Article 11 was amended to provide for a 'referendum of shared initiative' (*referendum d'initiative partagée* – *RIP*). This would need the support of one fifth of members of parliament (deputies and senators combined) and one tenth of registered voters (almost 5 million) and would only take place if the proposal is not then examined within six months in each of the Assembly and Senate. To date, six attempts have been made, all during Macron's presidency, but have not fully met the necessary criteria. On 4 October 2023, on the 65th anniversary of the Fifth Republic, President Macron suggested that the right to referendum of Article 11 could be expanded further still, perhaps to the hugely sensitive 'questions of society' such as the right to choose one's end of life, and immigration, and that the restrictions on holding an RIP could be loosened. Parliamentary support for such a constitutional amendment looked unlikely (constitutional amendments, under Article 89, require strong parliamentary backing) and Macron abandoned the idea.

The Constitutional Council

The evolution of the role of the Constitutional Council, created in 1958, is part of this broader picture in which the executive branch finds itself exposed to scrutiny that falls short of wholly transforming the original power balance between France's institutions of government. The Constitutional Council is composed of nine members for one nine-year mandate, plus former presidents of the Republic who sit (or not) *ex officio*. All members are political appointees: three members and the president of the council are appointed by the president of the Republic, the other six by the presidents of the National Assembly and Senate, as seen above. The council's function is to rule on the constitutionality of legislation before it is promulgated, to ensure that elections are conducted constitutionally, and to issue guidance; for example, if the president were to choose to trigger the emergency powers of Article 16.

The council is increasingly called upon by opposition deputies in the National Assembly (a minimum of 60 is required) as a way of raising public awareness of the nature of government legislation and, increasingly, the council finds itself engaged in matters of human rights and individual freedoms. Following a historic reform passed in 2010, for example, individuals involved in legal proceedings have the right, via the appeal courts, to challenge the constitutionality of legislation *after* it has come into force (Article 61-1). In these ways, the council can intervene in the policy process in a way unintended by Charles de Gaulle. He saw the council as a mechanism for exposing *parliamentary* forays into government prerogatives, and could not have imagined how it could harass the government instead. There is no appeal against a council decision, and its evolving role is to be seen as part of the process of the judicialization of French politics, and the taming of the French state.

The state and the Republic

One of the key features of French government that is not immediately obvious from the 1958 constitutional text is the centrality of the French 'state'. The meaning of 'the state' is not fixed, and it does not denote a finite set of discrete institutions, although at its core are administrative bodies, and at its head is the president of the Republic. Significantly, 'the state' has become equated in France with the nation itself and its historical continuity. It therefore follows that a weak state would undermine and potentially threaten the fabric of the nation, with potentially negative consequences for social harmony. Contemporary developments including European integration, the rising costs of the welfare state, the logic and dynamic of decentralized government, and the globalization of economic exchanges and of cultural opportunity and influence have all resulted in challenges to the institutions and norms of the French state. In many aspects of state activity, we find both conservative and reformist forces in contemporary France as it faces public policy challenges confronting all of Europe's liberal democracies, but within the constraints of this unique political and administrative culture.

The administrative state

At its simplest, the French administrative state or civil service (*la fonction publique*) is the machinery of government (*bureaux* and bureaucrats) that lies directly behind executive decision-making and brings decisions to life at the national and subnational levels. Its officials are *fonctionnaires* (functionaries) and the most senior of these are the *hauts fonctionnaires*, a very prestigious career label in France yesterday and today. The term implies both the notion of the British civil servant, working in the public interest, and also denotes the specialization and professionalization of functions. This is especially, but not only, the case in the higher echelons of the French bureaucracy, where, until a reform in 2022 that accelerated their merger, the state was organized into prestigious, distinct and respected 'great bodies' – *les grands corps* – each responsible for the main sectors of public policy (local government, infrastructure and public works, taxation, hospitals, education, diplomacy); this is France's policy-making elite.

The system is underpinned by the ideal of meritocracy, whereby the equality of opportunity provided by education and qualification should trump chance, luck and personality. This characteristic of French bureaucracy has fed into a society reputed to cling to a hierarchical social structure whereby pecking orders and fierce *esprits de corps* coexist with incontrovertible evidence that social class and distinctions are reinforced and reproduced by an education system typified by a strata of elitist and specialist establishments, particularly at the level of higher education (see Chapter 5). Some of the very 'old schools' do still exist today. One of the most iconic is the École polytechnique for public sector engineers, which is run on a military regime and whose students are salaried. Post-war reforms in turn created their own elitist channel for France's most ambitious and fortunate graduates. In particular, France's famed 'school for national administration' – l'ENA (l'École nationale d'administration) – was founded in 1945 precisely to professionalize the French civil service, and to produce generalist senior elites to go on and work in senior administrative bodies such as the Conseil d'État and Cour des Comptes (Council of State and Court of Auditors; see below), the French diplomatic corps, and the tax inspectorate and the prefectoral staff, who top the state at the local level (see below). L'ENA, in time, became a stepping stone in its own right for would-be politicians seeking the highest office. Most presidents and prime ministers of the Fifth Republic have been graduates (*énarques*) of this school, including President Macron. He, however, despite having himself taken this typical path, announced in 2019 the closure of l'ENA – or at least its transformation into a new body, the Institut National du Service Public (INSP) – as part of a broader vision of reconstructing the French state. The extent of discontent revealed by the *gilets jaunes* movement and the costs to the state of addressing COVID-19 were factors driving this particular round of change.

Deconcentration, diversity and reform

The French state is indeed hardly immune from the pressures that permeate Europe's liberal democracies and, in the 21st century, the French state has undergone change and reform. For example, state employees – not all of whom are *hauts fonctionnaires* but, rather, are public employees with a public service mission – have, since the 1980s, found themselves 'deconcentrated'. This refers to the ongoing process in France whereby state functions have been delegated to the 'field' or locality, and given more autonomy from the Paris-based government ministries for matters such as the maintenance of law and order, emergency and disaster relief, the arbitration of labour disputes, the implementation of EU policy on the ground, and the more prosaic but vital functions of tax collection and administration.

The presence of the state in the regions and localities of France nevertheless remains a powerful symbol of the historical role of the French state in forging the nation; immigrants seeking residents' permits, for example, must still appear in person at the *préfecture* of their *département* where the 'prefect' and his/her adjuncts are the gateway to the rights and duties of citizenship, and a historically key conduit between the state and its citizens. Similarly, no marriage is legal unless sealed in a ceremony conducted by the local mayor.

Marriage is a *civil* contract in France, and the mayor on these occasions (as with births and deaths) is quite literally the face of the state in even the smallest hamlet of mainland France or the most remote municipality in the overseas French territories. That, indeed, is the point: that the nation coheres across physical and cultural borders and boundaries by virtue of the uniformity of the state. In reality, variation (of service provision and delivery) is as much a feature of French administration as its fabled uniformity.

Indeed, recent decades have seen reforms designed specifically to accommodate the diversity that characterizes contemporary France. Elitist institutions, such as the former ENA's Paris-based feeder school known as Sciences Po (School of Political Science), have experimented with programmes designed to achieve what would be known elsewhere as 'widening access'. This involves admitting bright pupils from socially disadvantaged localities (and, by extension, backgrounds), by means of a differentiated admissions process (see Chapter 5). At the national level, attempts have been made to provide for a degree of administrative 'experimentation' in regions such as Corsica, while stopping short of ceding the degree of autonomy afforded to France's overseas territories, although the discussion remains open. The balance has proved virtually impossible to achieve – certainly in the high-profile case of Corsica, where separatist claims to regional identity are strong.

President Macron's immediate predecessors, Sarkozy and Hollande, each initiated a fresh round of state reform that ultimately amounted to efficiency measures that stopped short of a wholesale rethink of *what* the state should and should not be doing, as well as *how*. In Macron's first term, his prime minister Edouard Philippe launched a further review ('Public Action Programme 2022'), couched in terms of a transformation of France's public services including strategic aims such as accelerating France's transition to digitalized public services. It also foresaw further reductions in the number of people working for the state and other public bodies (including the hospital sector), an aim that exacerbated the impact of the COVID-19 pandemic. That crisis saw 'dysfunctions within the State, especially in the tense relations between the prefectures and the regional health authorities' (Cole and Pasquier, 2021: 141) and revealed the limits of the 'State as an arbiter of the public good' (Cole and Pasquier, 2021: 141). Digitization by definition, furthermore, interposes faceless technology between the state and its citizens and can exacerbate the distrust and discontent with the state as expressed in opinion polls and in direct action. These developments underscore the demand by citizens in France for ways of convening in solidarity, most notably in organizations with the legal status of associations, and particularly in times of crisis such as the coronavirus pandemic of 2020–22. Indeed, expressions of civil society are important elements of the French social fabric despite centuries of state suspicion of such 'intermediaries' between itself and its citizens.

Associations and civil society

Associations are very much part of French society, and a resource for government. They are non-profit-making organizations run mainly by volunteers for the benefit of their members, although some bigger associations also employ paid staff. They are defined in law as a body where two or more people come together to pool their knowledge or activity for a purpose other than profit. It is estimated that in 2022 there were roughly 1.4 million associations in France, run by over 12 million volunteers and 1.8 million paid workers. Most French people will belong to at least one association at any one time, and associations spring up whenever there is a cause to defend or an activity to organize. Associations usually ask their members for dues and, if the association registers with the local authorities, it is usually subsidized by public money (often minimal sums and subject to cuts when the public budget is squeezed) and is eligible to use local facilities such as the village hall. Associations are independent from local authorities but often work with them for the benefit of local people. Some associations are nationwide, often created in defence of the most vulnerable (the homeless, the poor, refugees and others otherwise excluded from mainstream society); most bring people together locally around shared sport and cultural activities, and many make important contributions to the life of the village, community or neighbourhood.

Historically, the French state has feared any form of group or gathering that could act as a rival magnet for popular loyalty. Church and workers' organizations were banned in the aftermath of the French Revolution: if people associated, they might have undermined the revolutionaries and tried to bring down the new regime. For more than 100 years, governments remained suspicious of groups that might have had 'subversive' goals – such as campaigning for better wages, or supporting the church. It was not until 1901 that the law gave them official recognition and access to resources – and keep an official eye on them. The expression 'la loi 1901' (the 1901 law) is often heard in France to refer to an officially registered association.

Today, associations play an important role in France, for the individual wanting to join in and be part of the local community to the activist trying passionately to influence government policy. The French authorities have come to rely on associations for the part they play in holding society together, and call on their expertise as partners in the policy-making process when making decisions about people's lives. This is part of a picture that normalizes France's statist model of policy-making along more pluralist lines, and which coincides with broader policy trends in favour of the liberalization of society whereby the rights of the individual or intermediary find themselves championed, if not pitted, against the historical dominance of the state.

The État de droit – *the rule of law and the judicialization of the French state*

There are strong historical reasons, as seen above, for the French state to be suspicious of what we call 'civil society', and notions of the public good trump individual or group interests in French republican theory. In comparative terms, the traditional French state is neither corporatist nor pluralist but uniquely statist. However, while state secrets (*le secret d'État*) for state-given reasons (*la raison d'État*) are hardly a thing of the past in France, they are more open to challenge and liable to exposure in the present-day context of rolling news (see Chapter 6), social media and the influence of legal norms and precedent imported from the European Union's legal corpus, known as its *acquis*. Indeed, individual or even group rights increasingly find themselves championed in contemporary France by organizations empowered to challenge the traditional pecking order of politics above the law. The most significant of these are the bodies at the highest echelons of France's unique system of administrative law – the administrative courts – which have instituted a French version of judicial review, and bodies with independent regulatory powers, as in many other European countries. The administrative courts are part of France's dual justice system, where administrative cases are hived off from what is known as 'ordinary' justice, meaning civil and criminal law. The state, in other words, prosecutes the state, protected from the judicial branch of government. The Conseil d'Etat (Council of State) is the most prestigious of these bodies. It is at the summit of France's unique system of administrative courts and tribunals and it runs in parallel to the civil justice system, hearing final appeals. The court rules on the legality of state administration, acting as court of appeal for administrative law; it also, nevertheless, acts as the government's legal adviser. All government bills and decrees are submitted to the Council of State for opinion before going before parliament; the council's decision is non-binding but influential due to the legitimacy conferred by the body's status.

The Cour des Comptes (Court of Auditors), for its part, oversees the efficiency of public spending and ensures its transparency by means of audit and the certification of accounts. Its members are administrative judges and can sit for life. The Défenseur des droits (defender of rights, or ombudsman) is an independent administrative authority with constitutional status, unlike the previous 'Mediator of the Republic', and is a presidential appointment. Article 71-1 of the constitution states that '[t]he Defender of Rights shall ensure the due respect of all rights and freedoms by state administrations, territorial communities, public legal entities, as well as by all bodies carrying out a public service mission'. Independent administrative or public authorities are numerous, and provide regulatory oversight of public policy domains and issues such as the freedom of the press, audio-visual policy, and transparency in public life. Finally, French governments make frequent recourse to ad hoc consultative committees (usually known as *commissions*) for the provision of expertise and advice, presumably to legitimize subsequent policy. President Sarkozy instructed his prime minister, François Fillon, to establish a rash of these in 2007–08, on institutional reform, the teaching profession and economic growth. President Macron for his part favours 'councils' (*conseils*) to advise him, including a 'National Council for Refoundation' that he established following his re-election in 2022, derided by his critics as a gimmick. Alongside all of these evolutions sits the so-called *grande affaire* (big idea) of the 1980s, which has most directly transformed the lives of France's *administrés* (its 'administered' citizens), namely the ongoing process of political decentralization. This, too, has proved complicated, and change has been incremental.

Decentralization, local and regional democracy

Local and regional government in France is complicated by any standards, with a bewildering range of bodies, actors, powers, resources and duties, most overlapping by design. Nearly 2 million (approximately one third) of France's public servants work at one of the local levels, and roughly half a million elected representatives exercise decision-making power in the name of local populations. Arguably, this situation is also a perfect reflection of the complexity of a country with as strong a tradition of both *pays* (see Chapter 2) and *État*. The 1958 French constitution tells us that France is an 'indivisible' republic and also that, since 2002, it has been organized 'on a decentralized basis'. This apparent contradiction means, in practice, that the drive in France since the early 1980s to disperse power, resources and political responsibility across the French territory into regions, towns and villages has its limits. Namely, France is very unlikely ever to become a federal or a multinational state.

The 'big idea': 25 years of decentralization

Decentralization in France has been a piecemeal process answering to no single institutional or ideological blueprint. Today, it is both irreversible and incomplete, with underlying twin trends of ever-present central steering and acknowledgement in principle of the 'right to difference' of France's territorial units (Cole and Pasquier, 2021). This principle of loosening the grip of Paris over the entirety of the French territory, at home and overseas, was uncontroversial from the first decade of the Fifth Republic. However, it was not until the 1980s that the idea took shape in the form of the 'big idea' of President François Mitterrand's first seven-year term, from 1981 to 1988. The timing was not coincidental: the generation of the social 'revolution' of May 1968 was coming of age; key members of the French Socialist Party, by now in power, had long supported the idea;

it fitted with Mitterrand's agenda of modernizing and liberalizing French systems and society; and it was played out in a specific context of higher EU spending at regional level, for which more flexible structures and responses were required. There were to be limits, nonetheless: not too much *liberté* in comparison with equality and solidarity: this was not a liberal but, rather, a social state agenda.

A key characteristic of the 1980s decentralization legislation was that decision-making – executive power – would be transferred to locally elected authorities at a variety of local levels, none of which would be hierarchically answerable or superior to any other, and all of which would coexist in the shadow of central state oversight. Functions – called 'competences' – were also transferred *en bloc*, along with certain revenue-raising powers (such as car tax), block grants and some staff and buildings. Over time, the decentralization agenda has altered to account for new imperatives and objectives in keeping with the broader political context. So, in the 1990s, new legislation was linked to the drive to trim the fat off the state and, in response to an EU-wide governance drive, to take decisions at the smallest possible unit of government. The French state still invests heavily, nonetheless (for example in trains or in policing), and the traditional officers of the state on the ground locally (the *préfets*, seen above) are still there to advise, guide and approve *post facto* decisions taken by elected authorities at the local level. During the COVID-19 pandemic, Macron looked first to the *préfets* to roll out a national response, before permitting some local differentiation in conjunction with France's mayors. These mayors, we saw above, officiate for the state, and are also officials elected by his or her peers. At the same time, the scope of local authorities to raise revenue and exercise autonomy has grown, as has the scope for gaps to appear (in wealth, in creativity) between parts of France, in a context of population drift to large cities, as seen in Chapter 2.

Moreover, a new layer of representative government was created by the 1980s laws. This was the region, which, along with France's largest cities, has gained over time from the decentralization agenda. Regions, for example, are important actors in the raising and spending of EU funds, in partnership with the state. A definite trend also exists in contemporary France towards the so-called rationalization of local decision-making. This takes the form of incentives for authorities to group together in ever larger structures, both in urban and rural settings. At the same time, the French state has acknowledged persistent demands for ever-greater scope for local democracy and political participation. Voting at regional level, for example, is by proportional representation (but stacked to favour the winner), and proposals for local referenda were included in the decentralization legislation of 2002 in the form of a law on 'democracy and proximity'. But reforms brought in by successive governments are said to lack transparency, let alone meaningful participation of stakeholders, such as in the case of President Hollande's 2014 and 2015 reforms, which reduced the total number of regions from 26 to 18 (including Corsica and five overseas territories – see Chapter 2) and enhanced their status (see below), and which 'conferred a new legal status on the French metropolitan councils in the large cities' (Cole and Pasquier, 2021: 133). Under this reform, the city or *metropole* of Lyon, for example, now has a special status, which it describes as providing for public policy that is more efficient, prompt and coherent. Emmanuel Macron for his part has simultaneously pursued forms of tighter financial control over local spending and shown a willingness to support greater differentiation and experimentation in local governance, in limited cases (such as Alsace and Corsica).

Decentralization brought the political competition characteristic of national-level politics into local government, which, in turn, links the local back into national politics. Local and state interests in France have, in any case, never been remote, given the strong and enduring tradition of the *cumul des mandats*, whereby office-holders could accumulate more than one position, most usually mayor and National Assembly deputy – or even mayor and government minister. These are relationships intended to benefit both political careers and local authorities – particularly the big towns and cities – which stand to gain by virtue of being an important political stake for a national-level politician. However, the practice came to be seen as incompatible with evolving standards of democratic transparency and efficiency and in 2014 a law was passed that banned the combining of a local executive function with an elected parliamentary role (at either the national or European levels). The debate on the pros and cons of this aspect of French governance is far from closed, with Macron and others professing a desire to extend the practice. Local elections, finally, increasingly function as second-order, mid-term judgements on national government. The municipal elections of 2014 were a case in point when the Socialist Party, in power nationally, lost significant local control to both the opposition UMP and the FN. In the regional elections of 2021, abstention was a record high of almost 66 per cent in the second round, and left President Macron's party – a movement without local roots, as we saw in Chapter 3 – without control of any of France's regions.

Local power in practice

The coexistence in France of state presence and local politics is played out on a map that has changed remarkably little over the centuries, with many boundaries and local administrative entities – such as the *commune*, the smallest administrative entity but the biggest in importance for the daily lives of most French citizens – having their origins in pre-revolutionary times. The 1789 Revolution and the first Napoleonic Empire subsequently marked out an administrative map of France that remains remarkably intact still today.

The department (le département)

The provinces of the *ancien régime* were abolished in the revolutionary years and replaced by the *département*. There are 96 *départements* in mainland France today, plus five overseas *départements* that are also regions in their own right, namely Guadeloupe, Martinique, French Guyana and Reunion Island and, most recently, Mayotte (see Chapter 2). Each *département* is neutrally named, usually after a predominant geographical feature such as a river (for example, the Seine and Marne, Bas Rhin, Haut Rhin or Dordogne departments), a mountain range (for example, the Pyrénées Atlantiques, the Pyrénées Orientales and the Alpes de Haute-Provence departments) or a historical area such as Savoie. Each department has a unique number that still features in postcodes and, until 2009, prominently on car number plates.

French people profess attachment and loyalty to their *département*. It is also the core unit around which the state organizes its local services, and it has a symbolic value as a reminder of France's surge into modernity in the early 19th century. Thus, periodic proposals to scrap the *département* on the grounds of the costly duplication of administrative functions have, to date, failed to find sufficient support. Napoleon Bonaparte created the prefectoral system and, until the decentralization laws of the 1980s, the *préfet* was the chief executive officer of the *département*, a role now held by the elected president of the departmental council (known as le Conseil général). The *préfet* retains responsibility for policing at departmental level, and oversees policy decided by the elected council. The departmental council's main policy functions (having benefited from the lion's share of 'competencies' transferred in the 1980s decentralization legislation) are to promote solidarity and 'territorial cohesion' via social services (support for children, disabled and elderly people, and dispensing certain welfare benefits), roads and the upkeep of secondary schools.

The commune (la commune) and intercommunal relations

Contemporary France is divided into nearly 35,000 *communes*, of which all but 200 or so are in mainland France. The vast majority of these *communes* are small and rural in nature, around half of the total have populations of under 500 inhabitants and approximately 90 per cent have fewer than 3,500 inhabitants. At the same time, Paris is a *commune* in its own right, as are other of France's major cities that are the driving force of dynamism in the French economy. The *commune* (also called *municipalité*) has historical resonance, predating the French Revolution, which deposed the priest and installed in his place the mayor, the best-known of France's elected officials (who also represents the state, as seen above). France's mayors have their own association and are voices whose value President Macron belatedly discovered in the throes of the nationwide *gilets jaunes* protests.

The mayor's elected function is to decide on what should happen in his/her *commune* with regard to a wide range of aspects of daily life, such as the maintenance of roads and of primary school premises, the planning of land use and the organization of cultural events and facilities. Here, the mayor has their own resources – mostly raised by local taxes, one of which (*la taxe d'habitation* or residency tax was abolished on primary residences during Macron's presidency) – and is supported by a team of councillors. This team is the *conseil municipal* (municipal council) and is directly elected every six years; the team elects the mayor. In small communes, teams typically represent different local interests rather than traditional party politics. In villages with fewer than 100 inhabitants, the total number of seats on the council will be seven (in contrast to *communes* of over 300,000 inhabitants, which have 69 councillors, or Paris with 163), and the system in practice is complicated. The mayor will put forward his or her list of candidates, and there may or may not be an opposing list. The mayor's own list might contain the names of people who oppose him or her, officially at least, but who cannot put together their full list of people; these are neighbours. The list might have more names than there are seats on the council. Voters can add names to the list if they want to vote for someone who does not feature on the list; this is called *panachage*. Voters can also cross out names on the list, on their own ballot paper. EU residents are entitled to vote in these local elections, and stand for election as council members but not for mayor. Gender parity laws initially applied only to larger *communes* of 1,000 inhabitants, where lists must be composed of alternating male and female candidates. In 2021 the requirement for parity was extended to smaller councils, but with provisions for flexibility to ensure a full council membership. At the level of the *commune*, despite these provisions, men still dominate: in 2021, only 20 per cent of mayors were women.

Since the *commune* is far from being the most rational unit of administration in terms of cost and infrastructure, a strong trend in French governance has been towards the organization of intercommunal structures with the authority to raise revenues and deliver services (such as waste management). Thus, France in 2021 was home to 1,258 EPCIs, or public intercommunal cooperation establishments, which shared powers between communes, and strong arguments for more intercommunality are prominent in debates on reform, as are those arguing for ever more regional power.

The region

France's 18 regions were the last administrative units to benefit from the powers of decentralized government. They are disparate in terms of their population, resources and dynamism. French regions are not intended to resonate with old historical identities, and certainly not with the regional provinces and parliaments of the *ancien régime*, which were early casualties of the French Revolution. They were given no new electoral constituencies under the decentralization laws, and electoral turnout is notoriously low by French standards. The French term '*la province*' is, nevertheless, an extremely common way for French speakers to designate those parts of France that are not Paris or its 'island', and to refer to regions such as Alsace (subsumed in the 2014 reform into a larger 'Great East' region but subsequently reformed by the merger of its two former departments and redesignated as the 'European territory' (*collectivité*) of Alsace); and Brittany (which escaped change in 2014), home to flourishing local cultural identities, including local dialects.

The prime function of the French region is to boost and organize economic growth, innovation and development. They are outward-facing, towards the EU and beyond. For the purpose of attracting tourist revenues, French regions certainly capitalize on what they claim are their local specialities, especially the gastronomic. The Paris-centred Île-de-France, and the Lyon-centred Rhône-Alpes are by far the richest regions in mainland France, and are critical to the French economy overall. The region works in close partnership and in contractual arrangements with the French state in core economic sectors such as the provision of higher education, professional training and transport and it is a key actor in the raising and expenditure of European Union funds.

The region is run by a directly elected regional council (*le conseil régional*), whose president is indirectly elected by the councillors and who, like his/her counterpart in the *département*, coexists with the state's representative – in this case the regional *préfet*, whose main role is to facilitate the coordination of national government and regional council policy. Coexisting, finally, with all these layers of government are the complex and dynamic relations that exist between France's domestic institutions, offices and structures and those of the European Union.

France in Europe, Europe in France

The impact on France of its EU membership has been highly significant. It can be argued that the leading role taken by France in the beginnings of European integration is a textbook case of the 'European rescue of the nation state', as per Alan Milward's powerful thesis (2000). In the 1950s, France was a founder member of the first communities (the European Coal and Steel Community – the ECSC, and the European Economic Community – the EEC) that symbolized the French commitment to modernity in matters of economic and social policy. In the 1960s, President de Gaulle's insistence on a Common Agricultural Policy was the *sine qua non* of the survival of French agriculture and its millions of *paysans*, albeit with a new, industrial-look dimension. Again, in the mid-1980s, the European Community offered France a genuine alternative to President Mitterrand's failed 'socialist experiment' for the modernization of its public sector, and the internationalization of its economy in overall terms. In the early 1990s, the Maastricht Treaty extended the level playing field between France and the now-united Germany to include monetary policy, and secured German commitment to, one day, shouldering its part of the burden of defending Europe along the lines of France's strong preference for a *Europe puissance*: a regional power with its own military capability (see Chapter 8). But we saw in the previous chapter that reconciling the costs and benefits of membership is politically fraught. De Gaulle in his time sought to replace the new Communities with a looser model of cooperation on core issues including defence – with a secretariat based in Paris. His successors, including Emmanuel Macron, have shown some impatience with the collective decision-making rules of the EU and a willingness to turn to complementary arrangements such as today's European Political Community (EPC), a forum that includes the UK since its departure from the EU and other non-EU member states. French presidents, and Macron is far from an exception, are typically portrayed outside France, with some justification, as stuck in the Gaullist mode of thinking about Europe: that France should lead, and others follow.

A Europeanized France?

In the present day, interaction between French and EU-level institutions occurs on a permanent, continuous basis, and is just as much part of France's structures of governance as is the interface between the state and France's local authorities. As EU member states voluntarily relinquish control over more and more policy domains where there are shared incentives to tackle problems jointly,

France inevitably finds that public policy processes are subject to the pressures and norms of this 'Europeanization'. Thus EU law (its treaty provisions, plus secondary legislation) has primacy over domestic French law (as it does over the law of all its 27 member states) and takes direct effect. However, the Conseil d'État (for administrative law) and the Appeals Court (Cour de Cassation) for criminal and civil law took several decades to acknowledge and adjust to this fact of European Community life, and for decades France lagged behind its EU partners in the matter of transposing secondary EU legislation into national law. On the other hand, France is known for its well-coordinated routines for the formulation of French proposals to the European Commission (see Lequesne, 1993), for its formidable negotiating tactics at decision-making time in Brussels, and for the authority that the French president enjoys over his government colleagues and parliamentary scrutiny provisions in European affairs, as seen above.

These features of French government all constitute strengths when it comes to the so-called 'uploading' of French policy preferences to the EU level, such as, historically, in matters of the Common Agricultural Policy, the world trade in 'cultural products' (such as films; see Chapter 6) and the limits to the deregulation of public services. On the other hand, the same features have created a domestic climate in which failures to win support at EU level for other French preferences (in defence, in competition policy, in trade, in the governance of the single currency) have contributed to rising Euroscepticism in a nation where concerns revolve around a number of specific ways in which France's commitment to EU membership (and leadership) challenges the capacity of the French state to honour its republican pact with the citizens of France as outlined at the outset of this chapter.

There is a *sovereignty* problem: the French constitution states in Article 3 that 'French sovereignty belongs to the people'. But France's nationalist politicians (see Chapter 3) argue that this is undermined by the constitutional provisions (Article 88-1) recognizing that France exercises certain 'competences' collectively with its fellow EU member states (including where it has no veto). President Macron maintains that France can only retain its national sovereignty if it commits to building *European* sovereignty, redefined as the capacity to act – in digital technologies, in energy and food production, for example – independently of unwelcome external parties (countries and corporations). This is a battle line in French politics, as seen in Chapter 3.

There is also a *citizenship* problem. The Maastricht Treaty of 1993 included provisions for 'EU citizenship' (as seen in Chapter 2). Under the terms of the treaty, EU nationals have certain rights in any member state of the EU, including the right to vote and stand for election in local and European Parliament elections but not, in France, to stand for mayor or deputy mayor. Thanks to this development, the French people are, indeed, no longer exclusively sovereign over their own affairs: a Dutch municipal councillor in rural Normandy, for example, has just as much decision-making power as his or her French counterpart. Furthermore, the measure exposes a long-lived reality of French political life, namely that the French body politic is composed of more than one *nation*. Not only may EU nationals now reside in France with virtually identical rights to their French neighbours, but *their* rights contrast starkly with the lesser rights accorded to France's resident *non-EU* nationals (such as first-generation Maghrebin immigrants; see Chapter 2).

Finally, there is a *liberalism* problem. France proclaims that it is a 'social Republic', as we explore in the following chapter. An important aspect of this ideal is that the state has a duty to protect its citizens, particularly in their guise as workers, from the excesses of the capitalist economy. But since the EU's single market initiative of the mid-1980s, and the staged transition to Economic and Monetary Union (EMU) in the late 1990s, the scope for state intervention at the national level in competition, industrial or monetary policy is strictly regulated (see Chapter 7). EMU requires member states to adhere to strict financial discipline in the form of low inflation and public deficit targets. These 'Maastricht criteria' have become associated in France with austerity measures or, more accurately, cutbacks in state spending (on state employee pensions, for example). In practice, developments such as EMU have provided tactical opportunities for successive French governments of both left and right to scale back the public ownership of economic and industrial resources, making way for privatization deals of considerable financial benefit to the state finances (see Chapter 7). These developments have been controversial in a country where the notion of 'public service' is closely associated with state activity as seen above, and where support for economic liberalism, as espoused by Emmanuel Macron, is still politically suspect. An additional dimension of this problem lies in the clash we find in French political discourse between the values of 'Anglo-Saxon'-style capitalism in comparison with what French governments call the 'European' social model, which claims to 'humanize' market forces better to balance the interests of capital and labour. French governments are periodically accused of economic patriotism when they seek to intervene in market decisions deemed detrimental to home-grown enterprise (see Chapter 7). Similarly, French leaders have had some success in 'uploading' national preferences into EU-level policy; the 1997 Amsterdam Treaty, for example, bears the French stamp in its recognition that 'general interest' services play a role in promoting social and territorial cohesion, and accordingly may qualify for state aid.

French politicians used to justify the sacrifices involved in adjusting to 'Europe' by arguing that EU membership bolstered France's identity as a modernized post-war nation-state, that French leadership of the EU fulfilled France's ambitions to be a world power of global significance, and that European integration buffered France from the forces of globalization. These messages have lost traction in the face of evidence to the contrary but President Macron came to power convinced that European cooperation was a crucial element of France's future, and conducted France's EU policy accordingly in a Gaullist style, as we see in Chapter 8.

Conclusions

We have seen that the capacity of the French government and state to deliver its republican pact with the citizens is under pressure. The legitimacy of the French presidency, the very linchpin of the Fifth Republic's semi-presidential system, is in the balance, as successive presidents have found their authority countered by the institutional checks and balances built into the system, from parliament to France's mayors, and defied by the resistance of groups outside the core institutions taking to the street to express their protest. French people express low levels of trust or confidence in the political class and there are demands for more direct democracy; local and regional democracy does not seem to have drained such demands of their intensity. Where the face of the French state is concerned, successive reforms have been piecemeal and incremental and have resulted in a *mille-feuille* of territorial administration that typically interposes layers of bureaucracy and digital processes between it and the citizen. Controlling costs and organizing itself to confront the climate emergency only increase the difficulty of the state's primary task of serving its citizens in an increasingly complex French society.

5

Society and Identity

Introduction

The constitution of 1958 states that 'France shall be a *social* republic' (emphasis added), and maintaining a socially cohesive national identity is a goal of French politicians across the political spectrum. In question is the state's ability to implement the principle of solidarity (*fraternité*), which, alongside *liberté* (liberty) and *égalité* (equality), constitutes the famous motto of the French Republic. The first vehicle for solidarity is the welfare state, especially what is known in France as *la sécu* (*la sécurité sociale*) – the social security system that delivers health care and most social benefits. This took shape over the decade between 1944 and 1954, to foster national solidarity after the traumas and destruction of World War II, and is a key pillar of contemporary French society. A second instrument is the state education system, and particularly its schools. Shaped by centuries of political upheaval, the school system is designed to socialize children and young adults into the ways of the French Republic, win their loyalty to the nation and overcome inequalities of class and social background through the implementation of meritocratic and democratic ideals. A key aspect of this vision forms a third pillar of French society, namely its secular identity, known as *la laïcité*. Since the French Revolution of 1789, and especially since the 1905 law separating church and state, education in French state schools has been characterized by the rigorous exclusion of religion from school premises. This includes a ban in state schools on the wearing by a pupil in a state school of any item of clothing deemed by the school authorities to constitute a conspicuous religious symbol. *Laïcité* extends beyond the school into public places and services where, without a doubt, the wearing of Muslim clothing, especially by women, is heavily stigmatized (see also Chapter 3).

In 21st-century France, the secular state, the welfare state and the state education system are all creaking under the strain of adapting to sociological, demographic and economic change in a society where vested interests defend themselves with vigour, where expectations of the state remain high, as seen in the previous chapter, and where public policy is anchored by the revolutionary ideal of universalism. Universalism, in the French context, is a political philosophy whereby individuals are deemed to enjoy innate and natural characteristics that transcend differences, of gender, for example, or nationality for that matter. This ambitious perspective translates into the notional equality of all citizens, enshrined in Article 1 of the constitution as a commitment to the equal treatment of all (by the state in particular), whatever their identity in terms of origins, race or religion. The same article also indicates that the law should 'favour' the equal treatment in law of women seeking electoral office or other 'social and professional responsibilities' and we will see below that the fight to secure equality in terms of gender and also sexuality – and resistance to that struggle – have grown in significance in recent years.

From this perspective of equality, what many Anglo-Saxon and Nordic countries understand as minorities (cultures, religions, ethnicities) are not recognized as such by French public policy; neither, accordingly, is there a tradition of group or community rights, and this is a running sore in contemporary France. From the abstract perspective of universalism derives the idea that the French Republic is blind to difference and cannot, therefore, discriminate. In reality, discrimination on ethnic and religious grounds – particularly Islam, in the context of heightened tensions over what the French call 'political Islam', and Islamist terrorism, as seen in previous chapters – has come to characterize and blight daily lives. Some inhabitants of France live as second- if not third-class citizens. This is especially true for those perceived as foreign because of the colour of their skin or their accented French, and/or those living in housing that is dilapidated and neglected by public authorities, and/or those whose status is irregular, such as undocumented migrants or asylum-seekers. This is a situation that undermines the fabric of

French society and creates distrust in the state and government, as seen in Chapters 3 and 4.

In this chapter, we first review the social structures that typify contemporary France – matters of family, gender, sexuality and age – and consider how the state has responded to an evolving population in all these regards. Under this heading, we consider the French welfare state (and especially *la sécurité sociale*), which is reputed to offer some of the best health care in the world but at the cost of crippling public finances, in particular due to high consumption rates of medicines and medical services, and where reform is particularly unpopular and contentious, as in the case of pensions reform in 2023. We review the legislation designed to account for the growing diversity of French society with regard to marriage and the family in traditional and non-traditional forms, including rights around procreation, and conflicts in this domain; and we explore the broader debates that frame and contest these developments. These include discourses on women and gender in an age where the #MeToo movement against sexual violence and abuses of power has had real resonance but where violence against women and feminicide itself still find themselves headline news; and where in 2018 numerous famous French women including the actor Catherine Deneuve signed a notorious public letter defending the right to be 'importuned' and rejecting feminism that expresses 'hatred of men' (*Le Monde*, 2018).

We then examine the realities of France's secular identity, framed by the concept known as *la laïcité*. *La laïcité* is declared but not defined or guaranteed in Article 1 of the constitution; and all religions and faiths in France coexist within the boundaries of this secular state. *La laïcité* therefore refers to the constitutional and legal framework that separates religious affairs from public life in contemporary France. This system is supposed to guarantee freedom of expression and of conscience and deliver equality of treatment. By separating the private and public realms in the matter of religious belief, this radical interpretation of secularism has, for its opponents, in practice allowed for discrimination on ethnic grounds – for example, by targeting the wearing of the 'headscarf' (*le foulard* or *le voile*) by young Muslim women attending state schools; of the burqa in the street; and of the burkini on the beach; and it can certainly be construed as an attack on personal freedoms (*liberté*) and individual autonomy. The agenda of *la laïcité* is complex, in other words, especially at its intersection with ethnicity and gender, and has, ironically, given its definition as the separation of religion from politics and state, become a highly sensitive political issue.

Finally, we investigate the education system. This is designed to improve an individual's opportunity to lead a life that is both fulfilled (or 'examined', to borrow from French philosopher Jean-Paul Sartre's existentialist vocabulary) and economically productive, and to knit a peaceful, thriving, prosperous, democratic and French society. In this sphere, too, France has a history of strong state intervention whereby the state has sought to integrate children into a single, French nation with a strong republican and secular identity; we saw in Chapter 1 that the Third Republic sought to stamp out the use of regional languages, starting in school. Today, French schools accommodate and support such linguistic diversity. Primary school education in France has been free, compulsory and secular since the end of the 19th century but, by the middle of the 20th century, schooling beyond the age of 14 was still, by and large, confined to a social elite. Now, the French education system has 'democratized' itself to the point where a very large majority (approximately 80 per cent) of all 18-year-old French pupils take their *baccalauréat*, which is subsequently their entry ticket to higher education. At this point in the system, the impact that social origins and individual aspirations still have on young people's opportunities and professional chances in today's France are at their most obvious, taking the form of a parallel network of higher education establishments that still, to a large extent, train and reproduce a social and political elite.

State secondary schools and the curriculum, moreover, have themselves been subjected to repeated reforms and to close public attention in response to developments including pupil under-performance by international standards, growing antisocial behaviour (*les incivilités*), and evidence of declining trust in and respect for the very role of the school – including its teachers – in inculcating the values of the Republic. At one extreme of this tendency are to be found the horrific murders in 2020 and 2023 of state school teachers Samuel Paty and Dominique Bernard by individuals radicalized into extremism and, in the case of Paty, the involvement of school pupils and their parents in the chain of events leading up to his death.

In all of these matters of health and wealth – physical, material and psychological – the picture is as complex as we would expect from a

West European country, especially one with such a large population: we saw in Chapter 2 that France is the second largest EU country in population terms, with nearly 68 million people living on the French mainland (including Corsica). Despite its aspirations to national solidarity and equality of treatment, French society is just as typified as its European counterparts by the individualism that is so characteristic of a mass consumer society where materialism is becoming ever more entrenched, by the social inequalities and inequities of imperfect social policy, and by the tensions between equality on the one hand and equity on the other. We bring the chapter to a close, accordingly, by identifying the trends in contemporary French debate that shape the debate and policy on French society and identity.

Social structures and social policy

France, along with other European nations, has experienced the gradual breakdown of traditional social structures and norms that

Figure 5.1: A plea for solidarity: Place Bellecour, Lyon, April 2024, *Ensemble bordel!* This roughly translates as 'Let's bloody well stick together' (Author)

took root in the 19th century in relation to religion and class, age and gender. These structures once forged a society that was deeply conservative, Catholic and with a strongly Mediterranean and rural character. Only 50 years ago, these identities regulated individual choice and behaviours to a higher degree than in many comparable West European countries. In contrast, France today is a society that is extremely open to influences from the rest of the world, making it diverse and cosmopolitan. In terms of individual morality, furthermore, France in the present day is a markedly more liberal country than at any time in its recent past, with more children born out of marriage than inside it, and alternatives to marriage both popular and state-sanctioned. At the same time, however, Catholicism has found a new prominence, repackaged less as a matter of religious practice or allegiance to the Catholic Church (itself tarnished by repeated revelations of historic child abuse, sexual crimes and cover-ups) than as an expression of conservative beliefs and attitudes, especially regarding matters of family values seen by some as under attack from 'woke' developments including the right to 'gay marriage' and new forms of parenthood, as seen below.

Family and friends

The family is still central to France's social fabric, and a sense of family matters to the French, but its shape and composition continue to evolve. In 2020, over 66 per cent of families were still traditionally nuclear, although this figure is declining. In the same year, 'recomposed' families (la famille recomposée), where a couple lives with at least one child born before the couple formed, accounted for just under 10 per cent of all families, with single-parent households making up one quarter of all families, and on the rise. Large families (la famille nombreuse) of three children or more (where at least one is under 18) make up just over one fifth of all families (21 per cent) and this figure has been stable for at least a decade. Around 20 per cent of French couples live in a 'free union' (union libre), and the number of couples choosing the official alternative to marriage, the Pacs (pacte civil de solidarité – civil solidarity pact) has risen steadily since its beginnings in 1999: in 2022, 237,000 marriages took place between heterosexual couples and 7,000 between couples of the same sex; in the same year, 182,000 Pacs were concluded between couples of the opposite sex, and 10,000 between same-sex couples. Around half of French marriages end in divorce (records since 2016 are as yet inaccurate following a 'modernization' of the process for filing divorce); and people are waiting until their thirties to marry for the first time.

The *Pacs* is in fact open to any two individuals of any sex wishing to give their relationship (their 'life in common') a legal footing. The rights of a couple who are in a civil partnership are, however, less than those of a married couple and, since a change in the law in 2013, couples of the same sex can indeed marry. This development encountered significant opposition from those believing heterosexual marriage to be the bedrock of society if not civilization, and essential for a child's development. Some mayors initially refused to conduct same-sex weddings on the grounds of their 'conscience', and opposition was vocal both inside parliament and in public. The movement against it took the name of *la manif pour tous* (protest/demonstration for all), in direct reference to *le mariage pour tous* (marriage for all), as the extension of marriage to same-sex partners was known colloquially. The implications of same-sex marriage for parenthood were core to the arguments of its opponents but today same-sex couples do have the right to adopt children in France and in 2021, finally, women in same-sex couples, as well as single women, were allowed access to 'medically assisted procreation' in the same way as women in heterosexual unions.

Gender and sexuality

Family structures and relationships in France are therefore closely linked to questions of gender and sexuality, and those issues do not exist in a French vacuum. On the contrary, they are shaped by trends and ideas that cross borders via social media, on-demand, English-speaking TV series (see Chapter 6) and rolling news from around the world. The notion, for example, that powerful men will have their 'mistresses', as illustrated most notoriously by the open secret revealed on his death in 1996 that former President Mitterrand had maintained a second family for much of his 14-year presidency; or by former President Hollande's much-mocked scooter expeditions across Paris to see his then girlfriend, finds itself challenged in a France where the current president is married to a woman (Brigitte

Macron) 26 years his senior and where awareness of sexual abuse (and abuses of power in general) is acute. In France, cases of historical and contemporary sexual abuse in the Catholic Church, in politics, in sporting federations and in entertainment are, as elsewhere, being brought into the light and punished, and the fight against feminicide is prominent. The #MeToo movement resonated in France, where women encouraged each other to #Balancetonporc – denounce your (male) abuser (your 'pig'); the opposing claim to the 'right to be seduced' is part of this discussion too, as is the disquiet expressed in other countries too about trial by media of the accused, as information and emotions circulate and swirl at a speed that outpaces the legal system itself.

The terminology of women's 'liberation', or 'battle of the sexes', in any case arguably misses important points about traditional notions of femininity and sexuality in France, especially where feminist discourses have been fragmented by differing interpretations of French republicanism. Some of the most vociferous opponents of the parity reforms of 1999–2000, for example, were feminists who believed that any form of affirmative action for women undermines the universalist principle of equal treatment for all citizens, irrespective of their gender or any self-defined social identities. Structural gender-bias against women has however been gradually addressed. The constitution itself was amended in 1999 and again in 2008 to include a commitment in Article 1 to 'the equal access of women and men' to 'elective offices and posts as well as to positions of professional and social responsibility'; there is an evolving legislative framework; and there has been official encouragement to drop certain customs such as designating women (*madame* or *mademoiselle*) but not men (*monsieur*) by their marital status.

It is also the case that France has seen a decline in other patriarchal structures inherited from different times in the country's past. The feudal rule of primogeniture – where the first-born son inherited all a family's wealth – was swept away in the wake of the French Revolution; but the Napoleonic code of 1804, and the enduring influence of the Catholic Church in the 19th century, nevertheless fostered structures that, in practice, subordinated wives to their husbands. These are now past history, at least in principle. Since the 1970s, women have had access to abortion and contraception, and no longer need their husband's permission to get divorced or open a bank account. In 2024 the constitution was amended to enshrine in it (Article 34) women's right to abortion. The stigma of divorce itself is definitely fading, as separation by mutual consent has been made faster and easier. The very notion of an 'illegitimate' child has disappeared and, along with it, much of the former stigma, and children no longer need to bear their father's surname. But the *implementation* of change is another matter: political parties found ways to circumvent or defy parity rules, paying fines rather than complying, and French administrative offices can still casually apply old norms with impunity: the residency card (*carte de séjour*) for an immigrant married woman may still feature her husband's surname, while the reverse is not true, and a remarried widow who has never changed her name can still expect, bizarrely, to see her late husband's surname feature on official documentation.

France's openness to social and cultural influences from elsewhere has invited into France ongoing debates about many dimensions of inclusivity and diversity that are familiar to US or UK populations. Fights for LGBTQ+, transgender and non-binary rights, and the notion of gender theory itself find themselves contested in France by those seeing such developments as 'woke' and alien imports, and French schools and universities have found themselves caught up in the so-called culture wars seen in the US and the UK around free speech on university campuses and in the curriculum itself. All of these developments intersect with broader discourses of diversity, raising the question of how the state should respond in a high-risk social policy environment. The management of the population's health and well-being from cradle to grave further illustrates these vexed aspects of the quest for solidarity and inclusion.

Social security: health, wealth and the limits of solidarity

La sécurité sociale, or *la sécu* for short, is the overarching system that since 1945 has delivered welfare to the French population. It has been in overall deficit since the start of the 21st century, with its sickness (*maladie*) branch particularly badly hit by the COVID-19 pandemic. Its other branches provide cover for work-based accidents, for old age (pensions), for the family and for 'autonomy' – assistance to the elderly and less abled. Health care provision and these other key welfare benefits are principally resourced by what are known as 'social contributions', in a system of social insurance. Unemployment benefit (which has its own structures distinct from *la sécu* and was created in 1951) also operates along similar lines. The 'social contributions' (known as *les charges sociales*) are made by workers and their employers from their pay packets and payrolls respectively, and through occupational 'regimes' that, in turn, are run by workers' and employers' representative bodies known as the 'social partners' and negotiated with the state. In 2024, proposed reforms to the unemployment benefit system looked set to pitch the parties against each other in a process skewed in any case towards the power of the state.

This is solidarity in action, but it is flawed. 'Social contributions' are both inadequate to meet welfare costs, and costly to employers, themselves under pressure to control their costs and make profits. The assumptions on which the welfare state was created in the post-war *trente glorieuses* (particularly, full employment) no longer apply, and welfare dependency is expensive, as in most European countries. In particular, the *solidarity* it aims to create between the generations, and between workers and the unemployed, is no longer sufficient to provide for the aged, the chronically ill or the long-term unemployed, who are as much part of the fabric of contemporary French society as the welfare state itself. The state, accordingly, has had to step in and, unsurprisingly, is engaged in a war on cost. In terms of revenue, payslips show deductions in the form of generalized income taxes such as the CSG (*la contribution sociale généralisée* – general social contribution). This tax removes up to almost 10 per cent of an individual's income (including salaries, pensions and investments) and now accounts for one quarter of *sécu* spending. Similarly, the CRDS – the 'contribution to the repayment of the social debt' was designed specifically to 'reabsorb' the *sécu*'s deficit. In today's France, similarly, unemployment benefit is firmly linked to job-seeking, and today's workers can no longer fund today's pensioners in the pay-as-you-go schemes of the past. Raising the retirement age, creating new taxes as seen earlier in this chapter and, more generally, urging higher levels of personal responsibility (for job-seeking, for sickness prevention) are the challenges currently facing French society and its policy makers, if the French social model of welfare is to survive into the second quarter of the 21st century and beyond. But, since the welfare state is a pillar of French republican identity itself, attempts at reform are fraught with political danger.

Health and health care

The French population is healthy by international standards, falling into line over time with norms such as reducing people's dependence on alcohol and tobacco, and avoiding the health risks and costs associated with the habits. The Loi Evin of 1991 targeted the smoking of tobacco and the drinking of alcohol, placing limits on packaging, pricing and advertising, and attempting to separate smokers from non-smokers in communal areas such as restaurants. It was however not uncommon to find smokers enjoying their cigarettes directly under a 'no smoking' sign on the wall, and it took another decade at least for the anti-smoking measures to take meaningful effect. A quarter of the population, however, is estimated to still smoke, and tobacco is still the biggest cause of preventable deaths in France. Alcohol consumption remains more socially acceptable, and France is estimated to have the sixth highest consumption levels in the 34 OECD countries; it is a significant contributing factor to mortality and morbidity. Road deaths were dramatically reduced (from an annual tally of over 10,000 up to the 1990s, then steadily declining to around 3,000 annually) by measures including the introduction in 2002 of speed cameras onto French roads (these radars were among the infrastructure attacked by the *gilets jaunes* in their protests against burdens on motorists, as seen in previous chapters). France has a high rate of cannabis use compared to other European countries, despite being illegal, and it has not escaped the effects of the illegal trade afflicting much of Europe in hard drugs such as cocaine, including violent gang crime in cities, notably Marseille. Nor is France immune from the obesity-related diseases associated with other national cultures, now increasingly affecting France's young people. Its ageing population suffers from rates of Alzheimer's and cancer that are broadly similar to those of its European neighbours, and cancer is the number one cause of early death in France, ahead of cardiovascular disease.

In its health care provision, *la sécu* has traditionally placed a high premium on the patient's right to access and consume prescription drugs, services and specialisms based on the right to choose between a range of alternatives and, if so desired, to replicate this choosing until satisfied (but not necessarily cured). This emphasis on choice and on consumption has created a health care system that is renowned for being humane, high-quality and patient-centred, focused on prevention and access to doctors and medicine, but at the cost of duplication, wastage and high cost. Cost-cutting measures have been inflicted on the health care sector and during Macron's presidencies there was much disquiet at cuts inflicted on the hospital sector in particular and at the ongoing restricted number of university places for medical training. When the COVID-19 pandemic hit, understaffing and difficult working conditions in France's hospitals were exposed and exacerbated, and when the decision was taken in August 2021 to require frontline health and care workers to be fully vaccinated against the virus or be suspended, the extent of the mistrust between health care workers and the state in the form of anti-vaccine sentiment was laid bare.

Most health care professionals in France such as general practitioners (GPs), are known as 'liberal professionals', meaning that they charge for their services at rates (mostly) set by the state. Accordingly, most individuals (patients) are expected to take out medical insurance policies with private but non-profit-making organizations (called *les mutuelles*) to cover the shortfall between the total cost of this health care provision and the amount that the state will reimburse; those on low incomes or meeting certain other criteria can expect 100 per cent of their costs to be covered. In addition, and in recent years, the state has clamped down: medical professionals are no longer allowed to dispense medicines that are either not known to work or known not to work; or, rather, the state will no longer refund the costs of such drugs if a 'generic' drug is proven to work better. Patients must now, in most cases, make a small, non-refundable contribution towards prescription charges, and ambulance and hospital transport (up to €50 per annum), as well as a non-refundable payment of €1 per visit to the doctor and towards blood tests and X-rays (again, to an annual total of €50). The existence of 'medical deserts' – swathes of the country, urban as well as rural, blighted by insufficient numbers of GPs and specialists – reflects the difficulties of attracting French-trained medical students into this branch of the profession where workloads are high and working conditions strenuous. It also mirrors a more widespread, complex 'desertification' process driven by multiple demographic, economic and social trends.

Pensions and old age

Systematic state provision for old age in the form of pensions postdates the French health and unemployment benefits systems but is run along similar, social insurance lines to those regimes. Crucially, France operates a pay-as-you-go system, whereby today's workers (in the form of social contributions and taxation) provide for today's retirees and where private pensions are far from the norm, and the activity rate (in the job market) for those aged over 55 (*les seniors*) has typically been below the EU average (see Chapter 7), with clear evidence of discrimination against older workers. Just as critical, France is an ageing society like its EU counterparts. It is estimated that if by 2070 the French population reaches 76.5 million, as predicted on current demographic trends, almost all the growth would be accounted for by people aged 65 or over and particularly those 75 and above. France's high life expectancy is part of this picture, with the average lifespan of those born in 2018 expected to be 85.3 years for women and 79.4 years for men (see also Chapter 2).

State pensions provision is the product of a mix of general and occupational (complementary) pensions on the one hand, and means-tested, universal benefits drawn from general taxation on the other, especially where an individual's employment-linked contributions are minimal or non-existent. Over 13 per cent of France's GDP currently goes into its state pensions, an above-average figure in EU terms. Thus, high unemployment brings the state ever further into a system that is already even more politicized than the health system, and reform here has been incremental, politically painful, and slow. A specific challenge has been the discrepancy between provision in the private and public sectors, with many state employees enjoying generous pensions after only relatively short, and not necessarily physically arduous, working lives. Successive governments have chipped away at such privileges. The Balladur reforms of the early 2000s, for example, began to align the length of pensionable service in the public sector with that of the private sector (40 years of contributions) and to discourage early retirement. Sarkozy's governments successfully dismantled the 'special regimes' enjoyed by a small minority of public sector workers, not all of whom worked in physically demanding occupations, and passed legislation raising the minimum retirement age from 60 to 62 (the right to retire at 60 being one of the reforms enacted during François Mitterrand's presidency and which has acquired symbolic significance in France). The depth of feeling in France about the workers' rights to a decent, respectful pension came to a head in 2023, when President Macron restarted the pensions reform he had signalled when first elected in 2017 but which was interrupted by the pandemic. At the core of the reform and opposition to it was the proposal to raise the minimum retirement age from 62 to 64. To its critics, the bill was poorly conceived and short-termist in its perspective; the president insisted that the system was unsustainable without change. The president and government lost control of the debate in parliament, where debates broke down in failed attempts to agree amendments to the bill; across the country, protests and demonstrations were extensive, protracted and often violent. The government resorted to forcing the measure through parliament using the unpopular confidence vote tactic (seen in Chapter 4) and the bill came into force in September 2023 (but in the 2024 legislative elections the left-wing bloc called for its repeal).

This was a bitter pill to swallow for many in France and did nothing to enhance the reputation of Macron's presidency or the political process more broadly, or to allay fears about the broader questions of care for the elderly in France and of dignity in dying. As in other countries, the COVID-19 pandemic revealed existing problems in France's system of care homes for the dependent elderly (les Ehpads – *établissements d'hébergement pour les personnes âgées dépendantes*), particularly where these were run for profit at the expense of their residents, as in the scandal of the Orpea group of homes. Also in question regarding old age and sickness was the right or not to end one's own life in dignity, a sensitive issue on which the government, in 2023, began to legislate, in favour of assisted dying.

Precarity and exclusion

Those reforms fit into a French political environment of shifting priorities in matters in response to poverty, exclusion (from society – the opposite, therefore, of *solidarité*), and 'precarity' – living hand-to-mouth on either benefits and/or short-term, low-paid employment contracts. 'Exclusion' refers to people with little or no social protection, usually marginalized. Poverty, exclusion and precarity are socially visible and politically charged questions, and they include the 'withouts' (*sans*). These are people lacking the basic credentials to thrive in French society such as the homeless or *les sans papiers* (undocumented migrants), some of whom have lived and worked in France for years, some who are seeking to survive as asylum-seekers or hoping to reach other destinations such as the UK via France. French governments find themselves lobbied by civil society groups campaigning on behalf of the disadvantaged. Such actions invariably occur in the name of solidarity, making it impossible for the state to look away without being seen to undermine a very pillar of society. Provisions do exist, including a ban on landlords evicting tenants during the winter months; emergency health cover for undocumented migrants (under threat in the 2023 immigration bill but finally left untouched), and episodic proposals (including in that same immigration bill) to regularize undocumented workers in certain sectors. But state responses, as in the matter of health, pensions and education reform, are typically incremental, symbolic or short-termist, increasingly subject to political whims and competition.

A secular state in a diverse society

In the same way as welfare spending in France must increasingly account for the diversity of French society, even at the expense of universalist ideals, the secularism at the heart of French society and identity is challenged by a society that is ethnically and religiously diverse. Individuals in France enjoy the freedom of expression and the right to practise their faith without persecution or discrimination, providing they do so in the private sphere, such as the family home. French history, we saw in Chapter 1, featured periods of extreme religious persecution and discrimination, and freedom from these is an important ideal and pillar of French republican society. Religion may not structure society and individual behaviour as it did in the 19th or even 20th centuries, and while it is formally absent from politics, it is never far from the surface of political debate (when President Macron invited France's chief rabbi to the Elysée Palace in December 2023 and permitted the lighting of a candle to mark the start of the Jewish festival of Hanukkah, he was swiftly accused of betraying the secular principle).

Religion

There is no established church in France, by virtue of a process that began with the French Revolution and culminated in the 1905 law separating church and state. From 1801 until 1905, Napoleon's Concordat with the Catholic Church had ensured that the French state paid the salaries of Catholic clergy while appropriating their property and controlling their activities, and it recognized Catholicism as France's first religion. The 1905 law formally separated church and state and overturned the Concordat regime, with the exception of the *départements* of Haut-Rhin, Bas-Rhin and Moselle, which, in 1905, were part of Germany; here, today, religion still plays a bigger part in school and university curricula than anywhere else in France.

The majority of French people today declare themselves to be Catholics – although this does not necessarily extend to attending church (fewer than 10 per cent of all Catholics are estimated to attend church on a regular basis). At the end of the 20th century, Mendras and Cole (1991: 67) showed how a 'fundamentally Catholic mentality' continued to shape French society in the form, for example, of demand for places at Catholic schools, and the ongoing emphasis on the family as the key social structure of French society. We have seen above the fading but not disappearance of these echoes. There is also a clear bias in French society that testifies to the symbiosis of the Catholic Church and state for many centuries. Thus, the holiday calendar in France revolves around Christian holidays (Easter, Christmas and many others: France has more public holidays than most other EU countries thanks to Christian festivals, and every day of the year is associated with a Christian saint's day). When schools and other public bodies venture to accommodate other religions in their lunch menus or Christmas-time celebrations, it is a contentious matter. Visitors to rural France cannot help but notice the statues and shrines to the Virgin Mary on the outskirts of French villages, along with listings of the times that Mass and Holy Communion take place in the village's Catholic church. Moreover, the French state subsidizes private Catholic schools that contract to teach the national curriculum.

Indeed, over 20 per cent of French children at secondary level are educated in private schools; the figure is 13 per cent in the primary sector. Most of these private schools are Catholic schools, and virtually all are 'under contract' with the state to teach the same curriculum as state schools and to subsidize – but select – its pupils. This can be an attractive option to parents who are losing faith in the state system, but its impact is to weaken the social fabric of the education system. Other faiths can also benefit from such provisions (which have strong public support), and several hundred Jewish schools in mainland France do so. One of the few Muslim schools (the Lycée Averroès in Lille) was also operating under contract until December 2023, when the *préfet* (see Chapter 4) suspended it on alleged grounds of religious curriculum content. Traditionally, finally, time has been set aside in the school week (usually Wednesdays) for children in state education to take religious – Catholic – instruction outside the school. Nevertheless, the large majority of French school-age children are therefore educated in state schools in France, where the principle of *laïcité* is applied with increasing rigour. No significant or systematic accommodation is made for any cultural or religious practices or beliefs (unlike in the UK, for example), and there is no religious education or instruction.

In today's France, there is also strong competition to the Catholic Church in the form of other religions and belief systems, and this includes atheism. France has more Muslims than any other EU country (figures vary and are usually between 3 and 8 million); Judaism is the country's third most followed religion, and Protestantism is fourth. Paris is said to have both Europe's largest Muslim and Jewish populations (Kuper, 2023). Buddhism and Scientology have their followers too, but the state reserves and practises the right to outlaw cults (*sectes*) it deems dangerous to public order by dint of 'brainwashing'. The French state has for many years sustained an institutionalized dialogue with the Jewish and Muslim religious communities. In the case of the Conseil français du culte musulman (the French Muslim Council), the state's interlocutor for 20 years, President Macron announced in 2021 that the relationship was at an end, the state preferring henceforth to speak to the Forum of Islam in France. To date, however, the overriding state response to such religious pluralism has been to stiffen the law on *laïcité*, primarily at the expense, it is argued by critics, of Islam and its French followers.

Bans: religions or cultures under stress?

In 2004, a law was passed in France that banned the wearing of 'ostensible religious insignia' in state schools; these 'insignia' include Jewish skullcaps, Christian crosses and the Muslim headscarf (*le foulard*) worn by many practising Muslim young women. The 'problem' of young girls wearing headscarves in school had been an issue for at least a decade before the law was passed and, up until that point, head teachers were given the discretion to decide whether or not such symbols were disruptive of class discipline or being worn defiantly, in which case the child would be obliged to remove the item. When former President Jacques Chirac began the process of hardening the rule that led to the 2004 law, he said it was because *la laïcité* was 'non-negotiable'. This was in the international context of the international so-called 'war on terror', and strong domestic support for Jean-Marie Le Pen, leader of France's National Front party that opposed any formal tolerance of minority ethnic and religious behaviours and practices (see Chapter 3). The law, in practice, still left it up to head teachers and their staff to interpret what constituted defiant behaviour; some have allowed the *foulard* or *bandana*, which leave the neck and ears visible, but others have not; most have banned the *hijab*, which hides the hair, ears and neck from view. The trend is for ever-tightening rules for schoolwear: by 2023 the *abaya* (a long tunic or dress) had also been banned, and some schools were even experimenting with the wearing of school uniforms – a preference typically expressed by ultra-conservative politicians.

In 2009 President Nicholas Sarkozy extended the debate regarding such symbols of religious affiliation out of the school to include the wearing of religious clothing in public. The *niqab*, he said 'was not welcome' on French soil, and he supported a parliamentary enquiry into its significance in French society. This, in turn, led to a 2010 law outlawing the wearing of the item in public. The *niqab* is usually referred to in English as the *burqa*, but they are not exactly the same: the *niqab* has a gap for the eyes between the headscarf and the fabric covering the rest of the face, whereas the *burqa* – associated with the Taliban regime in Afghanistan – hides the eyes too, behind a fabric mesh, and are worn in public by a tiny minority of France's Muslim women. Sarkozy's argument referred to this latter form of veil and claimed that this was not an item of religious clothing but a cultural practice that forced women to compromise their freedom, dignity and identity behind the '*grille*' of their clothing. This was an opportunity for President Sarkozy to make explicit the distinction between the respect for all *religions* that is the basis of *laïcité à la française* and the tolerance of different *cultures* – which, for Sarkozy and his successors, clearly had its limits (in this case, when cultural habits are deemed degrading to women). *Liberté* – in this example, apparently derived from a subjective interpretation of what constitutes a woman's freedom – has trumped *égalité* (the freedom for *all* to dress how they like) and has challenged French Muslims to define the line dividing culture from religion.

The so-called 'headscarves affair', the 2004 and 2010 laws, and subsequent developments have seen *la laïcité* become ever more politicized. Those on the left, seeing in the practices of *laïcité* discrimination against Muslims, are accused of *islamo-gauchisme* (overly sympathizing with Islam and questions of identity, in 'woke' style), and those defending those views in France's higher education establishments have found themselves in the eye of a storm. Those on the far right still espousing ideas of an exclusionary definition of national identity and Frenchness find in *la laïcité* a convenient weapon for driving those beliefs ever closer into the political mainstream. These developments all point to the difficulties France experiences in reconciling the realities of its multicultural and multifaith society with its theoretically universalist principles. France does not define itself as multicultural and, by the application to everyday life of philosophies such as *la laïcité*, attempts to downplay the differences between people, at least in public life. This, in turn, has led to serious problems of social integration and unrest in France (as seen in Chapters 2 and 3) and to ongoing reform in the education system, the pillar of society designed to flatten out, if not equalize, differences of origin of social, ethnic and religious kinds.

Education, class and opportunity

French state schools are not only a battleground for the expression of personal autonomy over and above religious beliefs; they also shape life chances. They are expected to do this in the manner of a social elevator (known as the *ascenseur social*) that moves in one direction only: from the bottom to the top. French children, on average, stay at school for longer than their counterparts in any other OECD country (nearly 17 years in full-time education) and France spends very slightly more of its GDP (around 6 per cent) on its overall education budget (including higher education) than the OECD average. Many French children from the age of two months attend a state day nursery (*crèche*) and both child-minders (*les assistantes maternelles*) and after-school care (*la halte-garderie*) are similarly regulated by the state. Virtually 100 per cent of all three-year-olds go to nursery school (*la maternelle*) and stay in full-time education until they are 17 or 18. In 2023, 80 per cent of the cohort achieved the high-school leaving examination, the *baccalauréat*, in comparison with only 20 per cent in 1970 and 5 per cent in 1950. Pass rates at the *baccalauréat* are high: over 83 per cent of entrants passed the exam in 2007, 83.5 per cent in 2008, nearly 86 per cent in 2009, 85.4 per cent in 2010 and 90 per cent in 2023. Yet school failure and dropping-out are common (as they are in the early years of university education, where over 50 per cent of students still fail or leave after their first year); over 8 per cent of young people aged 18–24 left school in France in 2019 with no qualification whatsoever; unemployment rates in France for those aged between 16 and 24 are persistently high; qualifications are gradually being devalued on the job market; and, unsurprisingly, reform of the French education system is politically challenging.

Democratization

The state education system in France today is based on the principle of equality of access, treatment and opportunity for all children. It underwent a rapid democratization and massification process from the 1950s onwards but, inevitably, the system is far from perfect. Historically, education in France was based on a clear hierarchy of social classes, and structures of hierarchy and elitism still characterize education in France today, albeit in more subtle and changeable forms. The Ferry laws of 1881 and 1882 dictated that primary school should be universal, obligatory, free and secular; indeed, the teachers of the Third Republic constituted an important and vociferous source of support for the regime and its republican ideals. The Catholic Church, however, was still allowed to teach at secondary level; and secondary level education itself was still reserved to a small elite. The secondary *lycée* establishment and its leaving examination, the *baccalauréat*, were founded under the Napoleonic regime in 1802 specifically to train elites, along military lines, for the state bureaucracy; entry to both the *lycée* and the teaching profession itself was reserved largely to the wealthy middle classes, irrespective of merit.

Part of France's post-1945 transformation included a succession of attempts by the government to democratize education. Fees for secondary school had been abolished in the 1930s but entry to the prestigious *lycées* and their *baccalauréat* was academically difficult, and most children ended their formal, primary education aged 14 (with or without a leaving certificate – *le certificat d'études primaires* (CEP) – a passport to employment and, possibly, a career), at which point they were available to work for their family or, perhaps, find work in training as an apprentice. The late Harvard academic Laurence Wylie's sociological account of living in France with his family in Provence in 1951 provides an excellent account of the high stakes of the CEP, as well as a summary of the contents and grading system of the exam itself (Wylie, 1964: 91–7).

The Berthouin reforms of 1959 extended compulsory education to the age of 16 and channelled all 11-year-olds into 'secondary' schools (*les collèges*); this was a concerted drive to raise the educational standards of the whole population. In 1975, the Haby reforms transformed the *collège* into what it is today, by and large. This is known in the UK as the 'comprehensive system', and in France as *le collège unique*. It is intended to standardize all pupils' experience of secondary education, and thereby raise the chances of equal access for all to the *lycée*, aged around 15, and thereafter to higher education. By means of the *collège unique*, moreover, children should *not* 'know their place' in society but, rather, see themselves as equal, and be treated as such. But a combination of the historical hierarchies inherent in French society and its education system on the one hand (where the teacher knows best) and the diversity of French society on the other has undermined the egalitarian ambitions of these reforms, and the *collège unique* is once again in the firing line of critics of the French school system. Many factors dictate and structure different outcomes for different children through the state school system, where early choices (of subject, stream and so on) can seriously narrow subsequent career prospects. Public policy, here, seeks a balance between the pursuit of equality, and the goal of equity (fairness), by compensating for the social factors that make school failure more likely.

Although success in France's meritocratic system is in theory confined only by ability, in reality it is also conditioned by more structural factors. These include gender as well as, crucially, a child's origins and identity in regional, social and ethnic terms, which form the child's cultural 'baggage' or 'capital' that, in turn, influences their ability to access the resources made available to them. In reality, schools can reproduce these inequalities and fail to lift their charges beyond the ground floor and, if a child fails at school (there is even a specific term for this experience – *l'échec scolaire*), they are likely to fail in society and find themselves excluded (from jobs, housing, health and wealth), or at least marginalized from it. Failure at school and failure to get the 'right' qualifications matter greatly in a national job market where qualifications definitely trump experience, and where jobs and careers were until recently still thought to be for life. On paper, this may well be a fair system, but it struggles to accommodate inequalities of birth and early childhood, which can be left to mutate into a second-class educational and career trajectory – or long-term unemployment. French society is less structured by class than it was in its past but, as in other countries, subtle and not so subtle distinctions apply and affect everyday lives in real ways.

Of such factors, gender is perhaps the least significant, since girls are as numerous and successful as boys right through school and into higher education, although girls are over-represented in so-called 'soft' subjects (such as literature) at the *baccalauréat*, and their glass ceiling comes later in professional and domestic environments where gender stereotyping can work against them. More pertinent than gender is the matter of a child's social origins, defined by class. Class means different things in different societies; in France, it is very closely correlated with occupation. Class consciousness is historically high – particularly among the working classes, whose identity was transmitted throughout the 20th century by the French Communist Party, now virtually defunct. But other occupations in France have developed strong class identities. We saw in Chapter 2 that farmers, and especially *paysans*, carry a cachet of their own; so do *artisans*, for example craftsmen and women in regulated professions (from bakery to builders) for whom the *artisan* label is a badge of status and, probably, quality. Similarly, independent professionals and the wealthier, leisured classes once known as the *bourgeoisie* have their place in the French social pecking order.

The decades after World War II in France (as seen in Chapter 1) brought about a rapid decline, first of the *paysans* and then of industrial workers as distinct classes. In their place came the rise of a new class, the *cadres*, white-collar workers with managerial responsibilities in large organizations in the public and private sectors. These were the architects of France's post-war socio-economic transformation and the bedrock of what is today, in France, a sprawling middle class that extends from white-collar salaried workers (*les employés*) to include senior managers and civil servants, and large-scale agricultural owners. As in other European countries, it is predominantly the middle classes that worry about the loss of distinction and the devaluation of their status – in particular, on the job market. This is a prominent political and social issue in contemporary France. Accordingly, strategies to maximize their children's opportunities in the school system are commonplace, and map on to hierarchies in schools that perpetuate and compound differences arising from children's social origins, as well as their innate abilities and motivations.

So, for example, not all *baccalauréats* are equal; neither, more to the point, are *lycées*, and attempts by parents to get around the rule of attending the closest school are commonplace. Reforms enacted during the Macron presidency aimed to update the *baccalauréat* to meet evolving needs, as understood in Macron's modernizing agenda. The differentiation in the main ('general') *baccalauréat* pathway between literature, science or economics was removed in favour of a core curriculum (including French and philosophy for all, still) plus 12 specialist subjects from which students could choose three. Alongside that pathway is the 'technological' *baccalauréat*, which includes subjects relating to the tertiary and industrial sectors of the economy but is still designed to encourage students to continue their studies further; a 'professional' *baccalauréat* would be a logical route for a young person seeking primarily to enter skilled work on leaving school. Of the various pathways, the majority of French students take the general, followed by the *bac pro* and then the *bac technologique*. Who takes the 'general' *baccalauréat*? Among the children of *cadres* or 'higher intellectual professions' (such as doctors and lawyers), three quarters head to the general *baccalauréat*, compared with approximately one quarter of children of blue-collar workers (Dabet, Epiphane and

Personnaz, 2024), and the discrepancies between social origins and educational attainment grow with each year of further study.

Meritocracy and elites

Indeed, this scrambling to preserve the middle-class privileges of social and cultural 'capital' or resources perpetuates itself into higher education. Although more young people have entered higher education over the decades, the figures mask disparities according to the parents' profession: by five years of higher education after the *baccalauréat*, roughly five times more students are from parents who are *cadres* as opposed to *ouvriers* (Dabet, Epiphane and Personnaz, 2024). The French higher education system, moreover, offers very distinct routes to very different career outcomes, where a student's social and cultural background and confidence are at a premium. The public university system itself (there are approximately 70 French universities) is based on the principle of access for all young people who have passed their *baccalauréat* exam, however well or badly, who pay minimal tuition fees. It therefore provides a public service that is underfunded and which in the international marketplace of higher education puts it at a competitive disadvantage, particularly in terms of its attractivity to overseas students. The universities are chronically overcrowded, and failure after one year is commonplace. During President Macron's first mandate, an online system was introduced – *parcoursup* – to streamline students' choices and universities' decisions but both the process and the criteria by which students were offered places were deemed to lack transparency and to resemble selection by any other name.

In contrast, the French state heavily funds what are known as its *grandes écoles*, of which there are over 200. *Grandes écoles* are selective by design and exist explicitly to train elites; historically, these were confined to the teaching, military and engineering professions. In today's France, however, many *grandes écoles* specialize in business and management studies, and, since 1945, the 'National School of Administration' – l'École nationale de l'administration (l'ENA) – has become a virtually indispensable rung on the ladder to high office in politics, government or the state bureaucracy, until abolished by President Macron (seen in Chapter 4) as part of his drive to, as he saw it, bring France into the 21st century of flexible skill sets and careers. These schools, particularly the best of them, are renowned for their strong *esprit de corps*, which translates in their working lives into powerful alumni networks of influence and patronage (see Chapter 7).

Notions of elites and elitism are nothing new in France. From the nobility of the *ancien régime* to the lawyers of the French Revolution, the military and bureaucratic leaders of Napoleon's empire, and the political and intellectual elites of post-war France, France has maintained an innate sense of social hierarchy that can be experienced in everyday life in France. The entry ticket to the *grandes écoles* (a system with strict hierarchies of its own) is itself high, although most *grandes écoles* operate a system of means-tested grants for poorer pupils. The prestigious, Paris-based Political Science Institute (Sciences Po), the feeder school for the former ENA, has for many years implemented a form of positive discrimination in favour of pupils from unconventional and disadvantaged neighbourhoods, who are allowed to bypass the competitive entry exam. Results suggest the experiment is a success, and it has gained momentum, spreading to other establishments. The barrier separating universities and *grandes écoles* is also gradually becoming more permeable, with movement from one to the other a possibility. In general, however, the degree of cramming required to pass the competitive entry exams (usually in special preparatory classes that last up to two years after the *baccalauréat* – *les classes préparatoires aux grandes écoles* – CPGE or *classe prépa*) works against students for whom the 'school canon' of Franco-French literature, history and language jars with their own ethnic and cultural backgrounds, and for whom intensive cramming and studying aged between 17 and 20 may simply not be an option.

French education reform is politically sensitive and the past decades are littered with piecemeal attempts and a succession of ministers at the helm of the education ministry (three during President Hollande's five years, three by Macron's sixth year in office). But the themes tackled by reform are constant: how to address rising levels of violence and 'incivility' among school pupils? When certain students defied the call for a minute's silence to honour the memory of the schoolteacher Samuel Paty assassinated in 2020 for having offended Muslim pupils in class (see above), this issue saw the cold light of day. How can opportunities be improved for pupils from minority ethnic or disadvantaged social groups? How to respond to what is widely seen as a decline in deference and in respect for authority in the family, and its repercussions on society at large? How can the employment prospects for children from ethnic minorities, proven to be worse than those of other young people in France, be improved? And how can reform be conducted in a field – education – where beliefs in the abstract principles of French republicanism are high, and where interests are entrenched, thanks to a system that prizes so highly the 'right' qualification (as a teacher, for example) as a passport that remains valid for the rest of one's working life no matter, often, how one performs (attempts to peg teachers' career prospects more closely their performance have been disruptive and often disturbing)? These issues take us back to the general questions addressed in the course of this chapter.

Conclusions

All EU member state governments find themselves under pressure to trim the size and the cost of the state. Welfare and education provisions are not immune from this exercise. In France, the task is complicated by the framework of historical and political battles that constitute today's French republican culture. French governments find themselves under the obligation to translate its historical traditions and its commitment to universalism into everyday policies. In the case of social policy, this means the encouragement of solidarity between citizens, on the understanding that the state will treat its citizens equally while respecting and protecting their differences. Among political and intellectual elites there is considerable attachment to this interpretation of republicanism and in particular to the notion that it constitutes a 'model' of society that is admirable, exceptional and exportable. Others in France have lost faith in this model in their own country, as shown in changing political behaviours (seen in Chapter 3). Indeed, citizens and politicians alike in France are confronted with the stark realities of the differences, diversity and discrimination that characterize French society and identity, just as much any abstract notion of the 'universal' citizen. Social contributions (the practice of solidarity) fall short of funding welfare provision. The hardening of *laïcité* legislation has brought culture and ethnicity into a relationship between state and society that is supposed to govern religion only. The meritocratic and egalitarian principles underlying the state education system have allowed inequalities to take root and distort individuals' experience of society at crucially formative stages of their life. The scaffolding of *égalité, fraternité, liberté* is therefore showing its age as French society continues to evolve in line with trends examined above, and with regard to its cultural practices and lifestyle preferences, as we see in the following chapter.

6

Culture and Leisure

Introduction

Contemporary France is renowned for its culture and famed for its *art de vivre*. French art, literature, cinema, fashion, film, cuisine, wine, photography and theatre have all enjoyed periods of epic and global status. French ideas are the backbone of much contemporary philosophy, and the French language has historically been deployed by French governments as a vehicle for challenging the 'Anglo-American' (Hayward, 2007) orthodoxies of the world. French kings and presidents from the *ancien régime* to the present day have conducted themselves as arbiters of taste and fashion, and the state has always spent heavily on culture, even in lean times. France's hosting of the men's Rugby World Cup in 2023 and the Summer Olympics and Paralympics in 2024 fit into this national image. The grandest buildings of Paris, new and old, and the châteaux of the Loire Valley, to cite only a few examples, are permanent reminders that, in the history of France, appearances matter, and heritage (known as *le patrimoine*) has pedigree. Cultural diplomacy – the promotion of French culture and language across the world – is an important dimension of French foreign policy, and France is known for its cultural 'wars' waged in defence of home-grown French cultural assets such as Roquefort cheese, champagne and art-house cinema. France champions these cultural 'products' against alternatives – often Anglo-American in origin – deemed inferior, homogenized or both. But there is a taste in France for America and to quote Philippe Roger (2005: 451), himself relating an anecdote, '[w]earing Nikes doesn't stop you from wanting to screw America'.

Typically, these battles end in triumphs for quantity and quotas, and are matters of trade and competition as much as tradition.

Indeed, French culture is indisputably a commercial affair: culture sells. The manufacture and export of the famous, luxury, so-called 'Paris' goods – such as perfume, and *haute couture* from the small, extravagant fashion houses of Chanel, Dior, Givenchy and others – are just as important for the French economy as for national pride. Moreover, as seen in Chapter 2, France is the world's most visited country, with over 80 million international tourist visits in 2022, and tourist spending in total accounting for roughly 3 per cent of France's GDP; it would appear that Paris receives the most tourists per year than any other city on earth. Disneyland Paris is the most popular of all French tourist attractions, with about twice as many visitors annually (15 million in 2022) as the Louvre (see Table 6.1 below). The aesthetics of French design fuel lucrative French business in fields as diverse as fashion and automobile construction. History and heritage are economic commodities, as are France's architecture, gastronomy and natural attractions. French cultural successes in film, literature and art owe as much to the market and its demand for entertainment and popularity, and to the exceptions to trade regulations that are made for 'cultural products', as they do to norms of art, taste and refinement.

Alongside its glamorous international image and its exports, French culture has a role to play in fostering the social cohesion examined in Chapter 5. Facilitating people's access to culture, not only as consumer or observer but as participant and creator, has historically been seen by the French state as an important and legitimate aim of public policy, with finances to match. Culture in this respect is understood as a vehicle for civic education: learning how to be a citizen by sharing the practice of what it means to be a civilized human. Here can also be found the darker side of culture when it is coopted into broader battles – culture wars – around identity, belonging and inclusion, as seen in previous chapters. As a colonial power, furthermore, France sought to 'civilize' native populations overseas by cultural means including language (as well as religion), and its model for the integration of its minorities in France today still echoes the traditional goal of assimilation, by immigrants, of the dominant national culture, principally but not only expressed through the French language (as seen in previous chapters). Thus, nation-building in France has at times involved the systematic repression of regional languages and identities, and sustained state spending on and intervention in cultural matters.

But culture is also entertainment, leisure and lifestyles that are not all about the state, and here most recently we see trends unsurprisingly shaped by digital technologies; these include the blurring of the distinction between news and entertainment via social media and rolling TV news channels chasing audiences, hits and likes, and ongoing struggles by French authorities to regulate the tech giants – both their ethics and their contributions to public finances. The facts here suggest that culture is both more prominent in French society, and more democratically enjoyed, than at any other time in France's history. The take-up of digital technologies and the accompanying decline in traditional TV watching across the population has narrowed the gap in cultural practices between generations, locations and social class, although differences do still exist in terms of daily practices, and even definitions of culture itself.

Indeed, in the present day, French culture is closely linked to the diversity of France's population (as seen in Chapter 2). Ethnicity is as vital a source of cultural creation in France as is youth, or the expression of differences such as gender, sexuality and lifestyle, or the quest for tourist revenue. Much that is iconic for the tourist visitor to France, especially in Paris, is typically bound up with traditional images of France. But it is only part of the variety that makes up French cultural identity and, in this respect, is as authentic as the literary canons, regional country cooking and ethnic music forms. Cultural life in France is as much a local as national affair, moreover, and the state periodically intervenes to ensure that this is so. From a cultural perspective, there is no one 'real France', just as we saw in Chapter 2 that there is no *France profonde* beyond nostalgic imaginations and sentiment. It would be an exaggeration to claim that there are significant sub- or counter-cultures in today's France but there are diverse ways of speaking (and even writing) French, especially among the young (as in most cultures), and a strong demand for and creation of music other than the traditional French *variété* (pop) or *chanson* (lyrical song), by way of example. Franco-Malian female singer Aya Nakamura has global reach but was a controversial pick for the 2024 Paris Olympic Games opening ceremony (where she was brilliantly choreographed alongside an all-male, overwhelmingly if not all white, awkwardly dancing Republic Guard brass band); to her critics, she was too 'diverse' (and the ceremony was, notably, closed by Céline Dion, a far less challenging pick for those critics). French national and local authorities, by and large, attempt to support 'cultural diversity' at home, but critics – in the fields of contemporary literature, for example – argue that anti-establishment voices on France's cultural scenes are left out in the cold.

In what follows, first, we explore the politics of culture in contemporary France: culture is definitely political and has been for as long as modern France has existed. This revolves around the role of the state, especially in fostering, regulating, promoting and protecting cultural norms and 'commodities' at home and abroad. We emphasize the examples of language and cinema to illustrate our arguments: in each case, French governments have sought to protect and promote their assets in equal measure, and their motives have been commercial as much as political. Cultural politics and policy, finally, are products of their time and, in today's France, reckonings with the recent past (as seen in Chapter 1) and the near future (the growing impact of digital developments including artificial intelligence) are relevant to current thinking. We then, second, survey the cultural practices, behaviours and aspirations of the French, and surmise here that notions of lifestyle are as much part of the image that France projects as its claims to 'exceptional' creativity and heritage, and that the French amuse themselves in ways broadly similar to their counterparts in the UK, the US and beyond. In our conclusions, we emphasize the complexity that lies behind the dominant, stereotypical images of French culture: virtually all aspects of French cultural life have a market and often international dimension, for example, and tales of 'decline' are apocryphal. In France, the past – 'history' – has commercial value, as does the 'heritage' business in many countries; but it also constitutes what Sonntag (2008) has aptly called a 'prison wall' that is perceived by policy makers as risky and costly to cross. Culture – its practice, its value, its significance – is closely linked to the evolution of society at large.

The politics of French culture

Culture may well have intrinsic value, but for centuries in France it has also served a variety of political purposes. All presidents of

Table 6.1: But is it culture?

Ranking	Site	Number of visitors (million) in 2017
1	Disneyland Paris	14.8
2	Louvre Museum, Paris	8.0
3	Château de Versailles	7.7
4	Eiffel Tower, Paris	6.2
5	Georges Pompidou Centre, Paris	3.3
6	Musée d'Orsay, Paris	3.1
7	Cité des Sciences et de l'Industrie, Paris	2.4
8	Le Puy du Fou (Vendée)	2.2
9	La Cité médiévale (Carcassonne)	2.1
10	Le Parc Astérix (Paris region)	2.0

Source: INSEE, 2019

the Fifth Republic, drawing on their considerable powers, have sought to make their mark on the cultural face of France, and to bequeath to the nation their very own cultural legacy. Are these vanity projects or expensive gifts to the nation? Dating from the very beginning of the Fifth Republic in 1958, the principal cultural agendas pursued by French presidents have been threefold. First is the promotion of France's *heritage*. Heritage has intrinsic value – in commemorating (and glorifying) the past, which, in turn, is designed to unify French society, and commercial value – in terms of tourist receipts. André Malraux, friend of de Gaulle and first minister of culture of the Fifth Republic, referred to this agenda as 'making accessible the key works of humanity, and especially those of France, to the greatest possible number of French people'. When demonstrators deface the Arc de Triomphe or terrorists strike near the Eiffel Tower, they have the hubris of this heritage in their sights, and we see below that enthusiasm for heritage has waned faster than all other forms of cultural enjoyment in France.

A second agenda is to foster creativity and cultural production – '*la création*' – by encouraging and supporting creativity in its own right, and as an 'industry', such as the cinema. This Malraux defined as 'giving preferential treatment to the creation of works of art and of the spirit which enriches our cultural heritage' (thus defining culture rather narrowly). The third broad policy goal is closely linked to, but potentially in contradiction of, the two previous goals: the more nebulous notion of 'democratization': making more culture more accessible to more (types of) people; we saw just now that the internet has done some of the state's work for it here. Indeed, equal access to culture has been a constitutional right for the French since 1946 and is supported by initiatives such President Sarkozy's free entry to France's national museums' permanent collections for those aged under 26 from France and other European Union (EU) countries and their teachers, or President Macron's digital 'Culture Pass' that credits young people from age 15 with a sum to spend on culture (in practice, principally on books, cinema, concerts and musical instruments). Tax breaks exist to encourage the private funding of cultural creation, and to attract foreign production companies to make films in France, hence showcasing France's natural assets.

State and nation

The city of Paris itself offers an exemplary chronology of presidential cultural politics in the form of eye-catching architectural projects, in some cases housing cultural treasures, known as *les grands projets*. Georges Pompidou's cultural centre in the heart of Paris (called the Pompidou Centre or Beaubourg) is one of the top five most visited 'cultural sites' in France (as seen in Table 6.1). François Mitterrand (president 1981–95) was the most ambitious of all: the Pyramide du Louvre; la grande Arche de la Défense; the Opéra Bastille and the Bibliothèque française (the national library building in the 13th *arrondissement* in Paris) all symbolize this aspect of Mitterrand's presidential agenda for culture, and were celebrated in style on the occasion of the 1989 bicentenary celebrations of the French Republic – itself a conspicuous cultural event. The Paris hosting of the 2024 Summer Olympics was a further opportunity to showcase the present-day city and had been preceded since 2021 by the

Cultural Olympiad, aiming to reconcile the 'emotions' of sport and culture in a pluridisciplinary artistic programme.

Paris can be derided as a 'museum city' that reeks of national nostalgia for the past. Many of its monuments, such as the Arc de Triomphe, are testaments to past victories, but the city has moved with the times (Kuper, 2024). The Pyramide du Louvre and the Pompidou Centre in particular were, to their opponents, deemed shockingly modern and transgressive of traditional norms of taste, and the grande Arche de la Défense could not be more different from the Arc de Triomphe. The Louvre, for its part, projected itself into the future in 2012 with the opening of a regional Louvre in Lens, northern France, and, more daringly, in 2017, the Louvre Abu Dhabi in the United Arab Emirates. The Pompidou Centre has its own sister museum in Metz, Lorraine.

Alongside his *grands projets*, François Mitterrand supported a policy of *le tout culturel* (translatable as 'everything is cultural' or, to its critics, perhaps, 'anything goes'). This was the 'democratization' plank of cultural policy under Mitterrand and it was, by and large, the work of the minister for culture appointed by Mitterrand to his first government in 1981, Jack Lang, whose legacy is significant. It was also part of a policy to encourage *la création* and, thereby, to boost the economic and business benefits of cultural activity, demonstrating not only how closely these different aspects of the politics of culture are intertwined but also how tightly connected culture can be with broader political agendas. Looseley has pointed out, for example, how these 1980s attempts to get 'beyond high culture' (1995: 113) were part of a much broader Socialist Party manifesto of social reform that prioritized the recognition of the 'right to difference', working with those marginalized by society, and the fight against racism. The decentralization agenda of that decade (see Chapter 4) was also reflected in cultural policy.

In today's France, the annual *fête de la musique* – launched by Lang in the mid-1980s – takes over the streets throughout France in June and has proved popular, as has the *fête du cinéma* of September each year, when cinema tickets are available at bargain prices, and the joys of cinema-going are advertised using state funds. Just as popular are the *Paris Plage* summer event, when a stretch of the Seine in Paris is turned into a summer resort with sand and palm trees; the *nuits blanches* or 'all night' openings in cities across France every October;

and, more formally perhaps, the September *journées européennes du patrimoine* (European heritage days, an initiative credited to Jack Lang when culture minister in 1984).

Language policy

Thus, the French state has a history of aiming to steer the image, production and consumption of French culture, both in France and internationally. Its legislation on the use of the French language at home exemplifies these efforts and their limitations. For centuries, language policy has been used as a tool to attempt to unify the French around a common language by means, at different times, of repression or regulation seeking to protect and/or promote the use of French within France's boundaries. Even today, the status of France's regional languages is contentious: only since 2008 have regional languages been identified in the French Constitution as part of France's 'heritage', but not in the preamble of the Constitution itself, as supporters would have wished.

The move in 1539 from Latin to French for official purposes (the Villers-Cotterêts ordinance) was an early example of the use of language as a tool of cultural policy, and the 1992 amendment to the constitution of the Fifth Republic to add to Article 2 the declaration that '[t]he Language of the Republic shall be French' is a more recent example of French governments turning to the law – here, the highest law in the land – to control the pace and impact of social change and, just as significant, to shore up the usage of French at home and abroad. The Académie française to this day continues a centuries-old tradition of codifying and standardizing the language, particularly in its written form, and acting as watchdog over its 'purity'. This amounts to proposals for amending, or stiffening, rules of grammar and vocabulary in line with social developments such as feminism and the openness of French society to foreign terms. In practice, language regulates itself and respects the law far less than it subjects itself to fashion and trends. Hence, it is now commonplace for grammatically masculine nouns designating professions (judge, mayor, professor) to be feminized (ungrammatically, strictly speaking) when referring to female post-holders (*madame* la *juge*, la *maire*, la *professeure*), or for so-called inclusive writing (meaning that it includes all grammatical markers of gender) to be adopted by organizations throughout France, for example when hiring, to indicate commitment to gender neutrality.

Indeed, the laws of the mid-1990s in France – which placed quotas on the quantity of French-language music to be broadcast in prime time on France's music radio stations, and which imposed the use of French in several professional and public settings – were justified in terms of the importance of the French language as a source of cultural creativity (artists must not be stifled by being forced to write/sing in English in order to sell records). French-language music has flourished and been exported, especially rap, as has non-lyrical electronic music known as the 'French Touch', francophone 'world music', especially African and raï, and French music sung in English. By virtue of the law, in addition, French(-speaking) citizens have the right not to be forced to struggle with other languages just to go about their business. By way of example, all adverts featuring foreign-language slogans used the world over (the McDonald's 'I'm Lovin' It', by way of example) must carry a French-language translation (*C'est tout ce que j'aime* – It's got everything I like/love). Such legislation can be seen as a means of promoting citizens' right to expect their native language to be sufficient to carry them through their daily lives. In reality, the use (and misuse) of English in French, consumer-facing public spaces is prominent and ubiquitous (see Figure 6.1).

But the agenda of language policy is complex: it promotes uniformity (all must speak French) at the same time as acknowledging the value of diversity (there is more than one language – English – in the world: there is French). Thus, plurilingualism has, for several years, been part of language policy in France, namely the obligation in the school curriculum for children to learn at least one foreign language from a relatively early age. At the international level, the corollary of the policy of plurilingualism is a sustained campaign of support for cultural and linguistic diversity. President Macron – arguably France's most prominently fluent English-speaker – has for his part attempted a critical 'reprojection' of the French language (Ahearn, 2022) in an attempt to divorce it from its historical connotations of colonialism and of misguided attempts to maintain strategic influence in French-speaking countries; in the case of the 1994 Rwandan civil war, the limits of this approach were stark (see Chapter 8). Macron's policy culminated in the 2023 opening of the International City of the French Language (la Cité internationale

Figure 6.1: English, everywhere (Author)

de la langue française), a project designed to promote the French language as a vehicle for 'cultural exchange, dialogue and diversity', in Villers-Cotterêts, a place that is symbolic, as seen above, of the adoption in the 16th century of French as France's official language (Macron, 2023b).

The promotion of cultural diversity: broadcasting and la Francophonie

French language policy is indeed a key dimension of France's cultural and public diplomacy (see also Chapter 8), where it serves the same twin objectives as domestically, namely to *protect* the French language (as a means of preserving a key aspect of French culture) and to *promote* its use – in this case, in other countries worldwide, as well as in key international organizations such as the EU, the World Trade Organization (WTO) and the United Nations (UN). The challenge for France is to strike a balance between its *voice* being heard (and that voice being in keeping with the times) and the use of its *language* in order to do so.

Broadcasting in English is, inevitably, part of the answer, and in 2007 former President Chirac launched a heavily state-sponsored CNN à la française, France 24, which broadcasts in English and Arabic, as well as French. This was to complement the all-French-language television channel TV5 Monde, created in 1984, which is supposed to be the voice of the entire French-speaking world but which is heavily financed by France. The Franco-German television station Arte, created in 1992, broadcasts Franco-German content, mainly arts and documentaries, in French and German, and RFI (Radio France Internationale) is France's flagship radio broadcaster, in French, throughout the world, grouped with France 24 in France Médias Monde. The battle to be heard, in French, is far from won. This pursuit of global French influence by cultural means also includes a strong French state presence across the world in the form of an extensive network of embassies, consulates and cultural institutes; a broader system of 'outreach', where cultural activities are part of a range of means by which France assists other countries and populations (also see Chapter 8); and the support and promotion of prized aspects of French culture, such as its gastronomy (the 'gastronomic meal of the French' has since 2010 been included in UNESCO's list of the Intangible Cultural Heritage of Humanity), its international sporting presence and its cinema.

French cultural diplomacy also relies heavily on the weight of France in the institutions of *la Francophonie* – the organization of countries 'having French in common' and whose mission is to promote cultural diversity, democratization, human rights, sustainable development and conflict resolution across the world. La Francophonie, established in 1970, was not originally initiated by France but, rather, by some of its former colonies seeking mutually beneficial relations with France. La Francophonie has institutions (it is properly known as the OIF – l'Organisation internationale de la Francophonie/the International Francophone Organization), headquartered in Paris and very heavily subsidized by France; it has a charter; it organizes summits; and it has around 88 members, associate members and observers. It puts the number of people speaking French worldwide at around 321 million (Francophonie.org, 2024) of whom 255 use it on a daily basis. The majority of these do not speak French as their first language and Vaïsse (2009) already pointed to the decline in number of French language learners across the world. There has also been an ongoing, steady drop in use of French in international organizations, including the EU and the UN. The OIF's mission also embraces the worldwide promotion of linguistic and cultural diversity, and France relies on its francophone allies in other international bodies, such as the UN, for support in this quest, with some success including the 2001 UNESCO Universal Declaration on Cultural Diversity and its October 2005 Convention on the Protection and Promotion of the Diversity of Cultural Expressions.

Trading in the cultural exception: French cinema

French support for international cultural diversity, however, is best understood in the context of the so-called 'exceptionalism' of culture, French and otherwise, when it comes to international trade. This linguistic see-saw between what is a French 'cultural exception', to be protected and defended, and what is a proof of diversity, to be celebrated, promoted and traded, is ongoing. When in her acceptance speech the Cannes 2023 film festival Palme d'Or winner, director Justine Triet (for *Anatomy of a Fall*), accused President Macron's government of giving into neoliberal, market pressures at the expense of the 'French cultural exception' of cinema, she was underlining this tension between cinema as culture and cinema as business (and making a broader critique of French politics). An important aspect of French cultural diplomacy is the French pressure brought to bear within key international organizations, especially the EU (and through it the WTO) and the UN, to exempt from market liberalization what have become known as 'cultural products' in the audio-visual field, namely film and cinema. (Foodstuffs specific to given *terroirs* – such as Camembert cheese, quality French wines or champagne – benefit from a similarly regulated trade regime by virtue of the labels of and designations of quality; these restrictions are not limited to French produce.) The rationale behind such rules is that, without them, such 'products' – which in France are deemed to have intrinsic cultural or artistic value – would be crushed by mass-produced competitors. They are, therefore, exceptions to the rules of international trade, different to commodities of other kinds.

In an environment marked by English-speaking global forces, 'Anglo-American' norms of entertainment, and a taste for America in France (which is the largest European market for McDonald's in revenue terms, serving what its critics call *la malbouffe* – junk food – to growing numbers of French customers, as well as the thriving tourist trade), the right to protect and promote cultural 'industries' and 'products' (such as film) with subsidies and quotas is strongly supported across the political spectrum in France. The case of French cinema demonstrates French support for the regulation of culture both as a traded commodity and as a vector of the diversity that should, ideally, characterize global humanity.

During the Fourth French Republic in the 1940s, French politicians made themselves unpopular at home by agreeing to restrict the number of French films shown *in France*, let alone the numbers exported to the US. This was in order to free up screen time and space for Hollywood imports that had been halted during the war years; these were the Blum–Brynes agreements of 1944, and they remind us that the regulation of cinematic trade does not necessarily operate exclusively in France's favour, as common mythology might suggest. The US was in the ascendant in Europe following World War II and was physically present in France in the shape of military personnel and cultural programmes (in the context of the Marshall Plan – the European Recovery Programme) and also via the import of material comforts designed for the mass market. American cinema and Coca-Cola not only became symbols of real commercial threats to the nascent post-agricultural markets of Fourth Republic France (see Chapter 1) but also represented a potentially more insidious reminder of the power of the market to win hearts and minds, and of the ease with which the US was dominating both these market and cultural forces. A form of cultural rivalry continues to characterize the Franco-US relationship, and this mingling of trade, culture and identity is its context.

In France, cinema is referred to as the 'seventh art', and there is little disagreement at the political level that cinema is, indeed, an art form in its own right. Former President Jacques Chirac called it a 'national treasure' that underpinned the French nation's 'vitality', and the term *la cinéphélie* – cinephilia – is commonplace in discussion of French cinema and cinema-going. The French *nouvelle vague* or new wave that characterized French cinema of the 1950s, and the equally familiar notion of *cinéma d'auteur* – authors' or directors' (as opposed to producers') movies – are just as symbolic of the emphasis in France on the artist as a creator, with the freedom (from market pressures) to create. At the same time, cinema in France, as elsewhere, is a 'cultural industry' embedded in market structures that, left to their own devices, would ignore this intrinsic – 'exceptional' – aspect of the value of cinema.

On the basis of international agreements and conventions permitting state intervention in the market for film, the French state has therefore, over the years, developed a complex system of support for home-grown and European cinematic production. Significant mechanisms regulating the market in France today were created in the Vichy period, in particular the state-run CNC (the National Centre for Cinema and the Animated Image – le Centre national du cinéma et de l'image animée). This agency still oversees the mechanisms for collecting and redistributing revenue, and it plays a role in selecting candidates for support. A similarly entrenched device to support French cinema is the 'ticket tax' of 10.72 per cent (5 per cent in overseas France) levied on cinema box office takings that are channelled back into film production. In 2022, this brought in €117.9 million; because of the COVID-19 crisis this was significantly less than the 2019 figure of €154.4 million. Blockbuster US films thereby fund French (co-)produced cinema. Further sources of revenue have been constructed over the years in keeping with technological and other developments (both opportunities and threats), including the co-funding (worth around one third of all cinema funding) of film and television productions by TV channels, principally the subscription cable TV channel Canal +, and more recent taxes on streamed, on-demand content providers including Netflix and YouTube. These resources are distributed back to the film industry on an equal basis (however successful or not at the box office) providing the film is at least majority French-produced, as certified by the CNC (CNC, 2023).

Besides the national level, French regional authorities may and do choose to subsidize film productions to raise their profile and support the local economy. Finally, the EU's MEDIA programme is an additional source of support to cinema in France; the EU's 1989 'TV sans frontières' directive permits the imposition of quotas by national governments; and the EU's Audiovisual Media Services 2021 Directive allows France to require subscription on-demand streaming platforms to reinvest up to a quarter of their takings in the production of 'European works and works of original French expression'; in practice, to TV series rather than cinema.

French cinema has undoubtedly benefited from these mechanisms, with a significant number of international co-productions, but the system of aids and subsidies is not without their political critics in France. Cinema-going is still popular in France (see below), which is home to over 6,000 screens, the most in Europe, and there is room in the French market for cinema both as art and as entertainment, both of which are popular. French companies produce their own blockbuster-type movies (such as the comedy *Bienvenue chez les Ch'tis* (*Welcome to the Sticks*), which was a huge box office hit in 2008, and *Astérix et Obélix: l'Empire du Milieu* (*the Middle Kingdom*) in 2023), alongside its more traditional *cinéma d'auteur* and historical epics, and France certainly has its own international movie stars from across the generations, including (the now disgraced) Gérard Depardieu, Catherine Deneuve, Juliette Binoche, Audrey Tatou (of *Amélie* fame), Vincent Cassel (*la Haine*) and Marion Cotillard (Oscar winner in 2008 for her part as Edith Piaf, herself a French cultural icon, in the French film, *La Vie en Rose (la Môme)*. French multiplex screens in France's big cities have sustained cinema-going as a cultural practice among the French (see below), particularly in *la banlieue*, as have state-sponsored initiatives such as the annual Cinema Festival (*la fête du cinema*; see above). US films are popular in France, particularly among the young (as are US television series; see below). In 2007, nearly 50 per cent of all box office entries in France were for US-made films, as against 37 per cent for French films. The top US films that year, ranked by box office takings, were *Ratatouille* and *Spider-Man 3*, outranking the most popular French (co-produced) films *la Môme* and *French Taxi 4*. In 2023, 40 per cent of cinema tickets were sold for French films, 42 per cent for American movies and 13 per cent for non-French European films (CNC, 2023).

Finally, French government support has been extended to foreign producers seeking to make their films in France. Notoriously, the rules on what constitutes a 'French' film are tortuous and controversial. Tax breaks are given for private investors in film, and Unifrance, a state body, plays the role of promoter and distributor of French cinema abroad. Cinema in France remains an important cultural and commercial asset, but the regulation of trade in this 'commodity' continues to divide France not only from its US trading partner but also from EU partners and the EU's market liberalization regimes. French people, today, show themselves to be as open to US-style influences in cinema and other aspects of popular culture as was the case over half a century ago. French cinema and French culture at large are certainly not dead but they are open to challenge (and opportunity) from transnational, technological developments such as on-demand, streamed entertainment and from the evolutions of French society itself.

Culture, leisure and entertainment

The spread of leisure was a defining feature of 20th-century France, and the 21st century is not set to change this. As far back as 1936, the Popular Front government famously introduced a limited working week (40 hours) and the principle of paid holidays (known as *les congés payés*: then limited to 12 days; now five weeks). Subsequently, the practices of sport for pleasure and holidays away from the home took root. In the late 1990s, just as famously, the Socialist government of Prime Minister Lionel Jospin introduced legislation to bring about the 'reduction of working time' (known as *la réduction du temps de travail* – RTT) by capping the working week at 35 hours. These provisions have subsequently been eroded (see Chapter 7), but they have meant that a new generation of workers, especially in white-collar and professional occupations, have developed new leisure habits (such as taking mini-breaks, already growing in popularity thanks to the dramatic growth of cheap air travel from the 1990s). The baby boom generation (born between 1945 and 1954) in France are among the most avid consumers of art and culture, particularly in their traditional forms, including attending classical music concerts and visiting museums; as this generation dies out, those pursuits may well decline (see below). The spread of the television into people's homes in the second half of the 20th century for its part further 'sensitized' people (Looseley 1995: 35) to the notion of leisure and pleasure, and the social uprising of May 1968 (see Chapter 1) raised expectations regarding an individual's right to self-expression and pleasure, irrespective of the state and its strictures. As schooling and literacy spread, moreover, so did the taste for and consumption of culture; and we saw earlier that the 1946 Constitution referred to culture as a right for all.

Accordingly, successive governments of the Fifth Republic, best symbolized by Jack Lang in the early 1980s, as seen above, sought to 'democratize' culture through the encouragement of diverse modes of cultural expression and creation. The decentralization agendas of the early 1980s and late 1990s, moreover (see Chapter 4), included provisions for greater powers at local and regional levels over cultural matters. In any case, as Dubois points out (2008: 25), watching television 'is immune from official cultural action'. People's cultural practices, in other words, have a habit of escaping the state, and new technologies are an important aspect of this. Nevertheless, the state remains vigilant, especially where technology is perceived to encroach upon core cultural values or goals, but keeping up with technology and balancing different interests is challenging.

Thus, the liberalization and privatization of the television and radio airwaves that occurred in the 1980s and 1990s in France was accompanied by the language laws seen above, and by a stiffening of the powers of the regulator to oversee the activities of both state and market regarding the media, in the name of pluralism and freedom. Commercial advertising was banned from France's public television channels after a watershed of 8pm (but restrictions have since gradually eased, in a fast-moving sector); 2009 saw the proposal of highly controversial legislation and a new administrative authority, with the remit of cracking down on internet piracy, especially illegal downloads. Some of these measures were subsequently deemed contrary to civil liberties by the country's Constitutional Council. Similarly, in 2010, the French government aired proposals to tax the advertising revenue of Google and other internet search engines to help fund France's creative industries. In 2023, a government proposal to tax the turnover of music streaming platforms such as Deezer and Spotify for the benefit of French musical creation was forced through parliament.

From a different perspective, one of Jack Lang's most memorable legacies is the 'single book price', which forbids retailers from discounting the cost of books to the customer, thereby forcing retailers to compete on quality and choice rather than price. This applies to Amazon.fr, as well as to bookshops and other stores. The consequences for the reading public are positive: a visitor who may only be passing through France en route to elsewhere will find that airport and train station outlets are well-stocked with a wide range of books, including many foreign titles in French translation. Those with longer to stay will discover rich pickings in independent book shops as well as the large FNAC stores in big towns, and even in the out-of-town hypermarkets and budget stores. Books are expensive in France, but many publishers produce good-value paperback editions of popular fiction and non-fiction titles (*les livres de poche*). If the content matters more than the cover, then book-buying – and so, perhaps, reading – is an entirely affordable exercise. To buy books – and *bandes dessinées* ('drawn strips' – akin to comics, close to graphic novels and extensively read by adults) – and to read is also to be part of a national passion for literature: the annual *rentrée littéraire* in September, with its array of new titles and prizes, is a cultural phenomenon in France. Critics argue with some justification that non-establishment figures such as self-styled rogue Michel Houellebecq and writers from France's ethnic minorities are frozen out of this scene, although Houellebecq's winning of the 2010 Prix Goncourt, France's most prestigious literary prize, suggested evidence to the contrary.

Culture and entertainment in daily lives

In this context, what are the cultural practices of the French? The French government has since the 1970s commissioned surveys every decade to measure the extent to which the French population participates in leisure activities and 'cultural life' (Lombardo and Wolff, 2020–22). The 2018 survey provided an overview of evolutions since the start of the survey 50 years previously and was accompanied by a survey of how the French defined and thought about culture in the first place. When asked to spontaneously evoke what they thought of as culture, respondents most of all mentioned learning and knowledge, literature and reading, and music and dance. There was a consensus that heritage, art, travel, science and cookery were culture, but that TV reality shows, TV series, video games and theme parks were *not* (only younger people aged 15–24 were more inclusive of 'mediated' forms of culture such as the press, the TV and video games). Only a small minority (5 per cent) spontaneously considered built heritage (monuments, chateaux) to be culture, and only 14 per cent evoked cultural places such as museums, although 84 per cent of respondents identified these as cultural when asked. Common practices such as playing video games or playing sport were typically identified less as culture than as entertainment and leisure. Based on this study, the French understand culture more broadly than the versions promoted by official institutions including school; they distinguish culture from entertainment but on the basis of a flexible, dynamic understanding of what culture represents today.

In terms of the actual daily cultural practices of the French, the 2018 survey set out to measure 'the participation of the population in leisure and cultural life' (Lombardo and Wolff, 2020–22) and to look at the long-term trends of the previous 50 years in these regards. They identified six main tendencies. The first was the growing significance of culture in people's daily lives, especially listening to music and enjoying audio-visual content (including the TV). Second, and since the previous survey in 2008, there had been, unsurprisingly, a steep rise in the use of digital platforms for these pleasures; this was especially true for the 75 per cent of 15–24 year olds who listened to music, watched videos online, played video games and engaged with social media. French society is thus not immune from the tendency of technology to tempt people into fundamentally individual and passive pursuits. However, third, more French people also went out to enjoy themselves, and not just the young, who consistently, over the decades, have spent their leisure time outside of the home; cinema-going, for example, had grown in the over-40 age group. Fourth, the 2018 survey saw the closing of some regional and social differences in French cultural practices, in part due to the spread of digital access to culture, although the gaps (of class and location for example) also lessened for live events. Despite this, education and occupation were still somewhat relevant markers for the importance of certain traditional cultural practices such as the enjoyment of heritage. The fifth trend was that the young generation stood out for the extent of its engagement (the majority of the age group) with digital media, including as an 'inescapable source of information' (p.14); in contrast, sixth and finally, the baby boom generation was distinctive in their range of practices including reading, and engagement with traditional culture such as heritage and classical music, leading the researchers to wonder whether, as this generation dies out, so too will those forms of daily culture.

Entertainment, information and infotainment

These trends therefore map onto developments in information and communications technologies that are bigger than the French case alone. In the case of the television, for example, decades of state-regulated public broadcasting in France have given way to the liberalization of choice and the creeping privatization of provision and rise in subscription services. Where France initially had just three private TV channels (TF1, M6 and the subscription channel Canal + – the latter's proceeds providing one finance stream for France's film production industry, as seen above), there are now almost 30 channels available on terrestrial TV alone, and many more offered in bundles with a household's other internet services.

The watching of streamed TV series on Netflix and competitor platforms is highly popular in France, as we saw above, pushing out the more traditional viewing of full-length films. These series are predominantly imports, especially from the UK and US (including royal or aristocratic dramas such as the UK's *The Crown* and *Downton Abbey*); in keeping with France's language policy as seen above, these are not subtitled but dubbed into French. France has also successfully produced and exported its own TV series such as the police drama *Spiral* (*l'Engrenage*), the detective series *Lupin* and the film industry drama *Dix Pourcent* (*Call My Agent*). These French productions have brought French actors (Omar Sy, Camille Cottin) into the mainstream of the global entertainment business.

French television remains an important source of news for the French, with flagship news programmes on the state channel France 2, for example. However, it has also evolved to accommodate the rolling, 24-hours news cycle available through the internet and by satellite, familiar the world over, complete with its polemical and politicized approaches to news. In France, BFMTV (since 2005) and CNews (a newcomer, arriving in 2017 and owned by infamous French billionaire Vincent Bolloré, major shareholder in Vivendi, the self-proclaimed 'world leader in content, media and communications') have become the most popular of such channels, with CNews notorious for espousing highly conservative views. French broadcasting must by law allow political figures (such as election candidates) strictly equal airtime but this does not prevent prime-time opinionated discussion hosted (on CNews) by figures such as Eric Zemmour, extreme far right candidate in the 2022 French presidential election (as seen in Chapter 3).

The print media, for its part, continues to decline in popularity in France: only around one quarter of the population read a daily newspaper on a daily basis. The recurrent financial difficulties of the national daily titles, notably the left-wing *Libération* but also *Le Monde*, have demonstrated the slowing demand for highbrow content as well as the challenges of maintaining editorial independence in a landscape of media ownership concentration (right-wing daily *Le Figaro*, for example, is owned by French industry giant Dassault). The origins of the print media in France are in literature and politics, where it functioned as the mouthpiece for public intellectuals. These titles still make considerable space for opinion and tribunes but have to compete with other platforms making space for often vociferous exchanges of views and opinions, including the print and audio-visual channels owned by or close to Bolloré. These include the CNews TV channel as seen above, as well as the weekly *Journal du Dimanche* newspaper.

The decline of France's traditional national press is particularly notable when compared with the investigative journalism of, for example, the weekly (and illustrated) *Paris Match* (briefly owned by Bolloré before passing in 2024 into the ownership of another of France's richest individuals, Bernard Arnault), or *Mediapart,* an independent, online title co-founded by former *Le Monde* editor Edwy Plenel. Weekly news magazines of different political leanings such as *le Nouvel observateur* on the left and the more conservative *le Point* and *l'Express* are also relatively popular, as is France's regional press, with over 100 titles including *Ouest France*, the country's most widely read daily title, and the satirical, national, weekly titles *le Canard enchaîné* and *Charlie Hebdo* (the latter being the target of the deadly January 2015 terror attack that killed 12 of its writers and cartoonists for its satirical coverage of Islam). One of France's leading national dailies remains the sports paper *l'Équipe* (with a circulation of around 300,000). As elsewhere in Europe, the print media is under pressure from free newspapers, distributed in large cities, as well as from online media offering free content. In addition, France has a history of tight union and state control over the printing and distribution of its newspapers, and vested interests here have arguably hampered reform.

Spectating or taking part?

Culture is not only passively consumed in France: sport, and *la vie associative* at the local level (see Chapter 4), are among the most popular ways of participating in the cultural opportunities on offer in France. The smallest village in rural France habitually runs a range of cultural activities through its associations, with only minimal support from state bodies such as the mayor. Similarly, France's peasant traditions (see Chapter 2) live on in the form of enthusiasm for predominantly rural traditions such as markets and festivals, and in support for *artisan* products of all kinds. Gastronomy, for its part, remains popular in France in the form of dining out, and as a more intellectual interest in the whole subject of food, eating and cooking. This interest, moreover, links France's agricultural tradition with the international prowess of its chefs and food-writers, past and present, aided by the popularity of TV chefs, as in many other countries, and still measured in part by the award (or loss) of the famous – some would say infamous – Michelin Guide stars.

Such activity is not confined to rural areas: the annual, national, grassroots music festival occurs in June in towns and cities across France, and Paris leads the way with its summer 'beach' and 'white nights'. Paris is also the site for France's annual Agricultural Salon, a showcase for French agricultural produce (30 per cent of the French, according to the 2018 survey mentioned above, think of 'agriculture' when they think of culture) and business, and May 2010 saw the country come to Paris in an initiative aptly named 'Nature Capital'. For several days, the iconic Avenue des Champs Elysées was covered in miniature plots of plants and crops, and flanked by farm animals in a heavily subsided effort to remind the French of their rural roots – and of the importance of agriculture to the French economy (see Chapter 7).

Just as French agriculture and gastronomy bridge the worlds of popular culture and cultural diplomacy, so is sport an important dimension of France's international presence, and also a popular pastime among the French population. Around 16 million French people are members of sports federations: amateur sport clubs whose membership is regulated by the state. The democratization of sport during the 20th century was also very much the doing of the state, including during the Vichy years, when some of today's structures were established by means of the 1940 Sports Charter. Sporting activity is embedded in school life through 'discovery' classes, including physical activity, that take children at subsidized rates to the sea, snow and countryside; skiing in France, moreover, is very much a staple winter activity of the middle classes. State employees are among the personnel that coach and train amateur sportsmen and women, and local communities are generally well-equipped in sports infrastructure.

Participation in sport also extends to enthusiastic support for France's flagship annual sporting event, the men's Tour de France (the women's version exists and is gathering strength). This extraordinary event is about far more than professional, elite, male cyclists enduring extremes of suffering as they speed through France on an epic three-week journey, averaging over 150 miles per day at speeds of up to 50 miles per hour. Originating in the early 20th century, the Tour showcases the country in its glorious diversity, revealing it to the French themselves as well as to the world at large, thanks to commercial sponsorship and worldwide media coverage. The Tour is anything but a spectator sport: fans line the route, often perilously close to the riders, sometimes with tragic consequences for rider, spectator (or stray pet). The point is to be part of the drama, and the event is supposed to be conducted very much in the public eye in a country where cycling is seen as an indigenous sport and is a top amateur sport among the French population, along with rugby, tennis and football (soccer).

France also lays claim to having launched the modern Olympic movement in the late 19th century and, during the Fifth Republic, strenuous efforts and resources have been put into training elite athletes for such prestigious, international championships. France sees itself as a choice host for such events; it has hosted the Winter Olympics on three occasions (1924, 1968 and 1992, and may again in 2030, a contentious ambition when France's mountain ranges are suffering badly from climate change – see Chapter 2). France lost out to China (2008) and the UK (2012) in its bids to host the Summer

Games and was finally successful in 2024, but in an environment marked by acute security concerns and questions over the cost and sustainability of such mega-events. In the event, and on their own terms, these were successful games for the host. France reached its official goal of finishing within the top five countries in the medal table (it came fifth, and eighth in the Paralympics). The showcasing of beautiful Paris landmarks at many of the sporting venues, and the smooth running of the games counterbalanced voices critical of the costs, the disruption and the exuberant cultural diversity represented by the opening ceremony staged on the Seine, in pouring rain for three hours, on 26 July 2024

France did host and win the 1998 football World Cup, and much was made of the success of its so-called rainbow team, which included famous players from France's ethnic minorities, such as striker Zinédine Zidane. This team, it was suggested, was repainting the French flag: no longer blue, white and red (*bleu, blanc, rouge*), but *noir, blanc et beur* (black, white and *beur* – the word used to denote the children, born in France, of France's North African, postcolonial population). This notion of the team positively representing an evolving French national identity was shattered a decade later when the French team failed to move beyond the first stage of the 2010 World Cup, hosted by South Africa. This loss was compounded by sex scandals concerning certain players; rifts between players, manager and coach; and unfavourable comment (including from politicians) on the presence in the team of players from the suburbs who were said to have imported unpatriotic values and behaviours into the squad, with disastrous consequences for the team's performance. Predictably, President Sarkozy ordered an official enquiry into the *débâcle*. The ignominy of South Africa 2010 served to demonstrate both the fragile connection between French sporting and national identities and the importance that is attached in France, as in many other countries, to the role of sport in consolidating state, society and the nation.

The cultural canon in question

France's many cultural achievements and practices – spanning traditional arts, popular culture and everyday icons of French taste, design and aesthetics – have been integral to the process of 'inventing the nation', to use Baycroft's term (2008). Being French, the argument goes, implies buying into myths about what does and does not represent the 'Frenchness' of the French nation; conversely, challenging those myths is to contest the nation and one's place in it. Subsequently, and to a considerable extent, we can speak of a canon of cultural references that young people are assumed to acquire at school, and which they then must convert into cultural capital if they are to progress in society and the market economy (see Chapter 5 and Ramdani, 2023). These references span French history and geography, as well as culture per se, and include a very proper mastery of the French language in its written and spoken forms, where form itself is of paramount importance: arguments must have a recognizable shape, however well-informed their content.

But these are norms that may well be at odds with young people's reality, and one aspect of cultural life in contemporary France is the coexistence of competing claims to represent the 'real' France in any number of art forms, including, for example, music, film and urban culture, as well as specifically youth and suburban vernaculars and varieties of the French language. Opening the canon to a more representative inclusion of French-speaking voices from overseas France and la Francophonie, and, more generally, to a critical questioning of France's past as an oppressive colonial power is a gradual, ongoing process, as is the inclusion of French-speaking voices in international accolades. Only in 2021, for example, was France's prestigious literary Goncourt prize awarded for the first time to a black writer from sub-Saharan Africa (Senegal), Mohamed Mbougar Sarr for his book *The Most Secret Memory of Men*. In the same year, the International Booker Prize for literature went for the first time to a French novelist, David Diop for *At Night All Blood Is Black*, also the first winner of African (also Senegalese) heritage. The following year, 2022, female French author Annie Ernaux won the Nobel Prize in Literature for her lifetime body of work, praised by the organization 'for the courage and clinical acuity with which she uncovers the roots, estrangements and collective restraints of personal memory'. Other best-selling authors such as Edouard Louis or Constance Debré express their otherness and alienation from the domestic French establishment.

Indeed, the French intellectual tradition itself has a history of resistance and opposition to the norms of the day, especially political and religious. From the centuries-old café culture, still in evidence in France today, to France's world-renowned thinkers, writers, philosophers, psychoanalysts and sociologists, the tradition prizes spirited argument and public expressions of (exquisitely formed) opinion. In today's televised and internet age, intellectuals engage in public spectacle as much as anything else, and the contemporary philosopher Bernard-Henri Lévy is the living embodiment of the celebrity French intellectual, derided by his critics as all looks and no substance and passionately *engagé* – committed to his cause. But author Michel Houellebecq (see above), notoriously media-shy, arguably has more influence through the global reach of the translated editions of his books.

Thinkers including Emile Zola, Jean-Paul Sartre, Simone de Beauvoir and Raymond Aron were the celebrity minds of their day, equally politically 'engaged': for or against anti-Semitism, Marxism (famously, in the Cold War years), the US, globalization, neoliberalism and so on. Despite the developments seen above, the intellectual realm today remains largely the preserve of a mainly white, elitist establishment still enthralled by the Académie française itself, whose members – all leading minds in their field – are dubbed 'the Immortals'. More prosaically, nevertheless, the argument as a form of communication, the propensity to abstract thought, and the potential robustness of verbal exchanges between 'ordinary' French people today remain a noticeable and characteristic dimension of the French psyche, inculcated from a very early age, and perpetuated thereafter by education and experience. To be French, perhaps, is to argue.

Conclusions

Culture in France, we have seen, links into numerous political agendas, principally in matters of foreign policy, education, sport, health and, crucially, the economy. The state finds it near impossible not to intervene – governments habitually fight hard to maintain the budget of the Ministry of Culture – given the critical links between culture broadly defined, on the one hand, and national identity, cohesion and image on the other. We have also seen how embedded culture is into France's economic fortunes and, importantly, into people's daily lives. But culture as a vector of French identity and social cohesion is vulnerable to critics of change who experience loss and nostalgia (for imagined past traditions; for dominant norms); and to critics of stasis for the repressive dimensions of a respect for traditional forms and stories of the past. French culture, moreover, is not immune to the reform of the state – and, in particular, to ongoing processes of cost-cutting and the elimination of duplication and waste. In the domestic sphere, as in the global marketplace, French culture, increasingly, must make itself heard, pay its way and compete.

7

Economy and Business

Introduction

France has a diverse, open and internationalized economy that in 2023, with a gross domestic product (GDP) of US$3.03 trillion (World Bank Group, 2024), was ranked as the seventh largest in the world. It is classified as a highly developed and high-income country, one of the 30 richest in the world: with a GDP per capita in 2022 of US$55,064, the French economy sits above both the EU27 and Organisation for Economic Co-operation and Development (OECD) averages (OECD, 2023). Since 1 January 2002 France has used the euro single currency, and its economy is second in size only to Germany in the 19-country Eurozone. It is home to multinational companies and prestigious products of worldwide renown, was the top destination in Europe for foreign direct investment (FDI) in 2022 (ahead of the UK and Germany, and growing, unlike them), and invests heavily abroad, in turn. France boasts an agricultural sector that makes France the fifth largest exporter of foodstuffs and food products in the world, and it is equally renowned for its industrial strengths. In particular, the French economy generates much high-tech activity and scientific know-how in the fields of transport (infrastructure and equipment), defence, aeronautics, aerospace, automotives, pharmaceuticals and nuclear energy. Its carbon emissions, at 4.03 tonnes per capita in 2022, are well below the OECD average (7.78), and plans for a green transition away from fossil fuel dependence are in place.

Traditionally characterized by state intervention in the market, broadly known as *dirigisme*, a tightly regulated labour market (including a nominal 35-hour working week and a national minimum wage), conflictual industrial relations, and a seam of pervasive scepticism towards capitalism, big business, entrepreneurship, the profit motive *and* globalization, the French economy has typically defied classification, styling itself as a 'model' in its own right. Yet this is decreasingly the case. President Macron's vision of France's future as a 'start-up' and 'tech' nation set the tone for how he wished to liberate – as he saw it – the French economy from the past, in order to face the momentous challenges of the near future; his early decision to slash France's wealth tax was a serious misstep towards these goals. The limitations of state intervention in the economy had already been exposed in 1983 when President Mitterrand's experiment with 'socialism in one country' (see Chapter 1) ended with a definitive turn towards ever closer economic European integration piloted by Jacques Delors, first inside the French government and subsequently as European Commission president (see below). France is a member of the key global institutions charged with overseeing the global economy – namely, the WTO, the G7 group of highly industrialized nations, the G20 and, above all, the European Union (EU), and France regularly seeks to influence global agendas via such institutions. Indeed, the EU's single market and single currency provide the framework for the French quest for competitiveness, and for the bulk of its trade flows with EU partners and with the rest of the world. The EU also functions as a platform from which France seeks to influence the rules of international trade – especially, but by no means exclusively, with regard to the protection from trade liberalization of agriculture and 'cultural products' (see also Chapter 6).

In contrast with its industrial heritage, moreover, France today is, by any standards, predominantly a service economy, with world-class provision in tourism (accounting in 2021 for 3 per cent of the country's GDP, a loss of one percentage point compared to pre-COVID-19 figures); a financial market with ambitions to rival the city of London, particularly post-Brexit; a banking sector of acquisitive and global dimensions; and four fifths of the workforce employed in the service sector. Furthermore, France is located centrally and accessibly in Europe, and invests heavily in its transportation and telecommunications infrastructures. Its population is relatively healthy, educated, productive and long-lived (as seen in Chapter 5) and, seen from outside, appears to enjoy an enviable quality of life. These are key business strengths by any international standard.

Inevitably, the situation underlying these aggregate figures is far more complex. Some of these traditional pillars of the French economy are showing signs of weakness. French agricultural export competitivity, for example, has declined in the 21st century (from the world's second-largest exporter after the US in the early 2000s), and France's overall trading deficit since the 2000s points to structural problems of competitivity. France was absent from the list of countries that rapidly produced vaccines to combat the COVID-19 pandemic, at some cost to its national pride: it was the prestigious Pasteur Institute in France that in 1983 had first identified the HIV Aids virus, and France is home to Sanofi-Aventis, now a global health care and pharmaceutical company. Government debt has been stubbornly above 100 per cent of GDP since 2011 (in 2023, nearing the sum of €3 trillion), which keeps France on a tightrope with regard to its global credit ratings, and this figure, as for household debt, has risen faster in France than elsewhere in Europe. France's public deficit regularly exceeds the EU's target threshold of 3 per cent of GDP (it was closer to 5 per cent in 2022), with government spending routinely amounting to over 50 per cent of GDP. Parliamentary negotiations in October 2024 on the annual budget were particularly fraught as France's then prime minister, Michel Barnier (see Chapter 3), wrestled with both a hung parliament and worsening public finances. Around one fifth of the country's work force is employed by the state (including the hospital sector) and GDP growth was already sluggish before the global economic crisis struck in 2008, since when it has rarely climbed above 2 per cent and has, along with many other countries, been struck hard in the 2020s, first by the COVID-19 pandemic restrictions and then by the impact of the Russian war in Ukraine from 2022 onwards.

Following that conflict, moreover, living costs in France rose sharply and compounded underlying inequalities of income and purchasing power, and the accompanying fears and realities of *déclassement* – the loss or downgrading of one's socio-economic footing – that were unsurprisingly at the top of French voters' concerns in an economy where low wages are typical. Unemployment in France was by 2023 showing signs of falling on average from its historically and persistently high rates: in 2022, 6.10 per cent of the working population aged between 25 and 75 was unemployed, the lowest rate for some time. Long-term unemployment has also fallen from a rate of over 40 per cent in 2010 and, on this indicator, France performs better than the EU27 average. But those aged 55–64 – known as *les seniors* – have in France typically faced discrimination and exclusion from the job market, as seen in Chapter 5, and youth unemployment (those aged 18–24) remains high by comparative standards: at 17.7 per cent in 2023, it dwarfed the G7 average of 9.6 per cent and significantly exceeded the OECD average of 10.7 per cent. Compared to other European countries, the gap was less stark but still significant (an EU27 average of 14.5 per cent).

Relations between capital and labour are typically strained in France, despite a relatively low rate of unionization, with the number of individual days per 1,000 employees lost to strike action in 2022 (99) up 71 per cent on the previous year. These dynamics have been fuelled by France's rapid deindustrialization since the 1980s that Jérôme Fourquet and Jean-Laurent Cassely (2021) refer to as France's metamorphosis. This phenomenon is a political headache of the first order, not only because of the impact of factory closures on the lives of individuals and their communities (and thus on social cohesion) but also because of the national vulnerability it generates at a time of severe geopolitical turbulence. In his 2024 new year wishes to the French nation, President Macron spoke of retooling ('rearming') the French economy to meet domestic and international challenges, and his wider ambition of ensuring 'economic sovereignty' (meaning capacity and resilience) at the European if not national level ran through both his presidential terms.

This interplay of the French economy with its membership of the EU is a key factor shaping the French economy and its business environment. It has also fuelled a growing scepticism towards the costs of EU membership that, as we saw in Chapter 3, has contributed to an angry polarization of French politics. As the EU has developed, in particular via the construction of its single market since the mid-1980s and its Economic and Monetary Union (EMU) since the 2000s, the French economy has evolved to keep pace, notably liberalizing competition across numerous sectors from agriculture to transport, and integrating its economy into the global marketplace (particularly for goods). For France, these changes were the economic price to pay for the political gains of a close relationship with a reunified Germany and for the greater global influence arising from being part of such a large regional grouping, and this trade-off drives an ongoing French quest for influence over the EU's direction. President Macron's commitment to French leadership of the EU featured prominently in his 2017 election campaign and during his presidencies he had some successes, notably his role in securing the EU's unprecedented post-COVID-19 recovery plan (NextGenerationEU). Economic planning, we shall see, is in the French DNA.

In the remainder of this chapter we first return to the idea of a French model of political economy. For many years, France was deemed exceptional both for the way it framed its political economy in the terms of its republican ethos (as seen in previous chapters), in policy as well as rhetorical terms, and for the role of the state in piloting or directing the economy towards these goals – a process broadly known as *dirigisme*. It is also notorious for conflictual relations between labour and capital. We look at the specifics of these characteristics, from state planning, patronage and regulation to the place of organized labour in often explosive dialogues over the economy, the business environment and the workplace. We see that, over time, the trend has been broadly towards less not more regulation of both market forces and the labour market itself, with consequences for the social cohesion and equality nominally at the heart of the French republican economic model. This trend is due in no small part to the transformations brought about by the costs, constraints and opportunities of France's EU membership whereby France's economy has in particular been tightly bound to that of its neighbour, Germany, and into which President Macron has put his faith when facing the grand challenges of the present and future, from averting climate catastrophe to harnessing advanced technology. We devote the second part of the chapter to this uneasy balance between the domestic and European dimensions of France's economy.

A French model of political economy?

Systematic, intensive and widespread state intervention was characteristic of the Fourth Republic (1946–58), when the rebuilding of the French economy after World War II was of paramount importance (see Chapter 1). During these years, the state became best known for its 'national champions' – companies strategically favoured by the state in sectors from banking to transport and its system of 'indicative planning' of the economy. This denoted a data-rich set of rolling plans for production and output, especially relating to agriculture and industry (see Chapter 1). We also saw that state intervention was a hallmark of Charles de Gaulle's presidency (1959–69), when economic interventionism was equally designed to boost national independence and greatness, or at least give the impression that it was. This recent past has meant that the tradition of state interventionism in the French economy has become entrenched, mythologized and embedded in contemporary norms of political discourse and policy-making. It in fact harks back even further, to the days of the *ancien régime* in the 17th century under King Louis XIV, when ministers such as Jean-Baptiste Colbert invested in large-scale, industrial infrastructure projects (including the building of roads and towns) in order to shape modern France and its destiny, and from whom the doctrine of *colbertisme* – the notion of state interventionism in the economy that is virtually synonymous with the more commonplace term *dirigisme* – is derived. The French state may, in the current day, be in retreat from the market in the face of powerful global forces that defy or escape state control – such as the globalization of technology, and EU rules, as we see below – but it still maintains a robust language of activism, in some cases backed up by action, and especially in industrial policy. President Macron's new year address to the French nation for 2024 was a case in point, highlighting his commitment to *agir* (taking action). Most or all national leaders make similar promises to be proactive but, in the French case, the rhetoric is redolent of specific ways in which the French state has typically piloted the economy, both strategically and operationally.

From public ownership to (part-)privatization

State ownership of industrial and other enterprises such as utilities and infrastructure was long a preferred means of providing the public service that is deemed essential for delivering 'social cohesion' in France (as seen in Chapter 5), ensuring the security of energy supply (such as in the nuclear industry) and providing employment. Since the symbolic nationalizations of the post-war years and the full-scale nationalization programme undertaken by Socialist governments in the early 1980s (see Chapter 1), the French state has subsequently sold off many of its assets as a means of reducing public debt, providing firms with more competitive autonomy on the global market and complying with EU and international regulations for a liberalized global economy. Privatization remains a politically sensitive term in itself but has nonetheless been encouraged, for example via the 2019 PACTE law for the 'growth and transformation of business enterprise', which aimed to raise funds to lower the national debt and support innovation.

The French state still involves itself politically in commercial decisions taken by its large national corporations in the case of mergers, acquisitions and, especially, takeovers, real or threatened, by non-French or, especially, non-European rivals. Successes include the 2000 BNP–Paribas merger in banking; the 2004 acquisition of French pharmaceutical firm Aventis by its French rival Sanofi, fending off the rival bid by Swiss firm Novartis; Danone (a multinational food business) being protected in 2005 from a possible, hostile Pepsi-Co bid; and Macron's 2018 reform of the SNCF (rail transport) that stopped short of privatization but opened the state-held company to competition and ended the special provisions for job security for new recruits (Milner, 2021: 175). Less successful interventions include the 2006 merger of Arcelor (steel) with Indian company Mittal in the face of opposition from French and other European politicians, and the failure to prevent the 2021 bid by Véolia (waste and water) to buy French firm Engie's stake in rival Suez. State interests in such cases typically include the protection of jobs over and above the more amorphous quest for national prestige associated with France's *dirigiste* phase. In an increasingly unstable geopolitical environment, however, and couched in the political terms of 'retooling' the French economy and shoring up its 'sovereignty', state ownership of economic assets is still seen in France as a legitimate policy tool, despite its impact on public finances. By 2023, for example, the state had regained control of 100 per cent of the capital of the electricity company EDF. This ability of the French state to interfere in the market is facilitated by the tight webs of political patronage characterizing the French economy (but constrained, as we shall see below, by its deep integration in the EU).

Mixing politics and business

Political patronage refers to the network of elites running public enterprises on the one hand and, on the other, the close links between those elites and other business organizations across the economy, including the media. The mainstream element of this latter sector is long known for its deference to political figures, their lives and scandals, but political patronage of the press in France today sees both deference and its opposite, namely sensationalist, personalist and extremist political coverage.

These networks and relationships have long 'operated as a coordinating mechanism of French capitalism' (Clift, 2009: 158), giving rise to a 'system of cross-shareholdings and overlapping board memberships of large French firms' known as *noyaux durs* or 'hard cores' (Clift, 2009: 158). Many of those running France's top 40 publicly quoted companies (on the exchange known as the CAC-40) still come from the tiny number of elite *grandes écoles* seen in Chapter 5 (especially Polytechnique and the former ENA, now INSP), from the French senior public service and from ministerial cabinets where they pursued a political career, and they even include former ministers and presidents themselves among their number. Almost all of the CAC-40 leaders in 2023 graduated from France's most elite *grandes écoles*; the number of women leading CAC-40 companies remained in single figures (the number of women in executive board roles across the listed companies has been boosted by parity requirements but is still unequal and uneven); and the list counted relatively few foreign nationals. To his opponents, President Macron's ties to wealthy business individuals in key sectors from the media to energy, as well as his government's recourse to international business consultancies are constraints on his motivation and capacity to effect the transformational changes he politically professes to champion (including the green transition). A more general embrace in France of *le mécenat*, whereby private funds and sponsorship shore up state funding, for example in leading cultural institutions, is a further illustration of the dynamic webs of influence characterizing the French political economy.

Rules, codes, dialogue and decrees

The French model of political economy is also known for its highly codified and regulated nature. Rules are embedded in the numerous legal codes governing or touching the economic sphere, such as labour law (the Code du Travail) and business law (the Code du Commerce). These codes provide French governments with the scope to tightly regulate – or seek to deregulate – many aspects of the market economy. Examples of such codification include, significantly, the length of the working week, the nature of employment contracts and industrial relations practices. Also covered are matters such as rules on Sunday trading and other retail practices, and restrictions on the total number of practitioners allowed to exercise certain professions, such as taxi drivers or pharmacists.

Successive governments and presidents have pulled the levers of regulation and deregulation to suit their political visions of the economy and their interpretation of the correct balance between the broader goals of French republicanism explored in previous chapters (egalitarianism and social cohesion, for example) on the one hand and economic competitiveness on the other. The Socialist-led government (1997–2002) of Lionel Jospin was best known for its passing of legislation reducing the working week from 39 to 35 hours without a reduction in pay (the Aubry laws, after the name of the minister responsible, Martine Aubry). The law stands but has since been relaxed such that, under certain conditions, workplace agreements can favour and enable longer working hours. Jospin's government was succeeded by that of President Sarkozy, which introduced a raft of measures designed to create more flexibility in the labour market. These included the August 2007 'TEPA' law to promote work (*le travail*), employment (*l'emploi*) and purchasing power (*le pouvoir d'achat*) and which allowed for controversial tax cuts – on inheritance, for example – and the 2008 law to 'Modernize the Economy' in order to 'liberalize competition' within the domestic market and make the French economy more competitive. This was based on the findings of a committee that reported in January 2008 and which was headed by a writer, intellectual and former political adviser to President Mitterrand, Jacques Attali. The report recommended at least 300 measures to free up the economy, only a small number of which were adopted. Among the measures rejected were the opening up of professions, such as taxis, where supply is restricted by law (hence the virtual impossibility of hailing a taxi on Paris streets; Uber had a ready market for rides). Other measures included the consolidation of the attractiveness of France's biggest and richest region, the Île de France, and the abolition, from 2010, of the *taxe professionnelle*, a tax raised on businesses at the local level for the purposes of funding training and education.

Additional reforms were introduced in the first three years of Sarkozy's presidency with the explicit intent to 'modernize' the French economy, principally by relaxing the business environment with relation to regulation, codification and taxation. The overriding aims of the programme, other than the broad objective of exhorting the work ethic, were to facilitate entrepreneurship; to encourage the growth of France's dense network of medium-sized enterprises (which account for over four fifths of employment in France), which would then be more active on the export market; and to concentrate resources in 'centres of excellence' (*pôles de competitivité*) clustered around France's most dynamic regions (including the richest of France's regions as seen above, the Paris-centred Île de France, and the country's second-largest economic centre, focused on Lyon and the Rhône Valley in the south-east of France).

Sarkozy's Socialist successor, François Hollande (2012–2017), campaigned on a platform of socio-economic change that named big finance as his 'adversary', included pledges to raise taxation rates for the very rich, and promised to renegotiate the EU Treaty on Stability, Coordination and Governance in the Economic and Monetary Union (TSCG), signed during Sarkozy's mandate and designed to tackle EU member state deficits and debts. In the difficult circumstances of the Greek debt crisis of 2015, which threatened the very existence of the single currency union, Hollande in fact allowed for the approval of the TSCG as it stood, and struggled to win support for any wholescale reorientation of EU socio-economic policy. It was during his presidency, moreover, that France passed laws designed to further deregulate aspects of the French economy in the aim of encouraging competitiveness.

One such law was piloted by Emmanuel Macron, appointed minister for the economy, industry and digitalization by Hollande in 2014. The 2015 law for Growth, Activity and Equality of Economic Opportunity became known as the Macron Law and is remembered for certain flagship reforms such as the deregulation of the coach industry and further relaxations of evening and Sunday trading. It was followed in 2016 by a law (remembered as la loi Travail or la loi El Khomri after the minister who introduced it) specifically designed to loosen the Code du Travail to continue this work of the 'liberation' of France's workforce. Both laws encountered opposition from workers and the El Khomri law was not implemented by the time of the 2017 election that brought Macron to the presidency, but it 'prepared the way' for further reforms (Milner, 2021: 168). Immediately following his election as president in 2017, Emmanuel Macron ruled by decree – a method favoured by former President Charles de Gaulle in the post-war provisional government, and therefore highly symbolic of the authority of the French state – to pursue this path of economic reform and modernization as he saw it. In January 2024, moreover, and following a change of prime minister, President Macron indicated his desire for a Macron Law II to continue this ambition to transform France's economy without, he argued, destroying its social foundations.

Underlying this balancing act is a sense, in France, that there is – or used to be, more to the point – a uniquely French model of political economy that is somehow less ruthless and more moral and humane than the neoliberal norms castigated by successive French presidents as 'Anglo-Saxon'-style, *laissez-faire* capitalism. At the level of corporate governance, especially regarding France's big employers, this translates into an expectation that bosses will refer to the 'social interest' as well as the profit motive and/or shareholders when taking strategic decisions, where social interest refers to a firm's duty of care to its workers and, beyond them, to the social fabric of France as a whole. This is part and parcel of the republican ideal of social cohesion (Chapter 5). We saw that, as recently as 1981, the French president – François Mitterrand – was elected on an explicit manifesto to 'break with capitalism', an experiment that we saw lasted barely two years and whose failure created a fault line in the Socialist Party that has never repaired. There have typically been high levels of support in France for increased and tighter regulation of global flows of capital, and the so-called 'alter-globalization' ('other' globalization) movement shaped the political agenda at home in France by circumscribing what can be said in economic policy-making, Culpepper noting the 'discursive illegitimacy' of the free market (2006: 45–6). Political language about the French model had, indeed, early into the 21st century, come to centre on the pros and cons of globalization, with reference to specific consequences – such as the 'outsourcing' of labour, known in French as *la délocalisation* – whereby French employers are seen as tempted to offload their labour (and, especially, manufacturing) costs abroad at the expense of the local workforce.

Increasingly, however, the drive for international competitive advantage has 'forced French companies to provide value for shareholders' (Maclean, 2008: 157). Such perspectives are behind high-profile cases in France of 'boss-napping' and lock-ins (albeit not new phenomena in France) and other forms of protest against strategic decisions made by companies to close or downsize factories, lay off workers and/or move production overseas: in the case of Air France, workers were themselves put on trial in 2016 for physical violence against management executives. Evidence has also been forthcoming in recent decades over harsh working conditions in certain of France's flagship sectors including tourism and travel. Journalist Florence Aubenas (2010) gives first-hand accounts of the harsh working conditions she encountered when undertaking a cleaning contract with holiday and transport companies in northern France. In the tech sector, too, the shocking tragedy of multiple workplace suicides that occurred during a restructuring in 2008–09 at France Telecom (now the mobile phone operator and broadband provider Orange) eventually culminated in the conviction of the company's CEO and other executives in trials that for the first time recognized the 'institutional harassment' endemic in its corporate culture and working conditions. These cases were a shock to a country that has prided itself on the social gains made for its industrial workers over the course of the 20th century (see Chapter 1) including paid holidays, a minimum wage and a welfare safety net (see Chapter 5) and, in more recent years, a legal right to negotiate the ability to disconnect from electronic workplace communication (especially email) after working hours.

In France, dialogue, negotiation and bargaining are as much part of the business environment as regulation and legislation, and the 'social partners' in France – representatives of labour and capital – have traditionally been co-opted by the state as part of the policy-making process. They also, crucially, share responsibility with the state for administering much of France's social security system – specifically, unemployment and other social benefits and pensions. This system is known as tripartism and has been a keystone of the post-war quest in France for a cohesive society, as seen in previous chapters. As with other dimensions of the French socio-economic model, the system is finding itself transformed by changes in the economic and business climate, including the fading of class consciousness, which, for decades, sustained conflictual relations between the partners, and fragmented the labour movement from within.

French industrial relations and the social partners

Trade unionism in France, for its part, emerged in the late 19th century from a history of banned associations and, over the past hundred years, the movement has reflected the many political, ideological and religious divisions in French society, and has been shaped in particular by the strong forces of post-war communism and socialism. It taps into strong emotions relating to the 'social gains' – improvements to working conditions – made by labour, and by the political left, over the course of nearly a century. Unions have, as a rule, proved themselves more effective at disruption, and at getting their voice heard by government, than at building their membership, or at representing the diversity of employees in the workplace; or even, at times, at negotiating good conditions for 'outsiders' or new entrants to the labour force such as women or immigrant labour.

The first decade of the 21st century saw significant reforms to French industrial relations, and to the business environment in general. These were accelerated following the election of President Nicolas Sarkozy in May 2007. Sarkozy had campaigned on an explicit platform of reforming French working practices, and rehabilitating the work ethic per se, as seen above, and had openly lauded the UK's flexible labour market as a source of inspiration for French reforms. Where critics saw an ideologically driven intent to concentrate power into the hands of capital, especially big business – by loosening regulations, for example, on hiring and firing – the picture is more nuanced. Many of the structural rigidities of the French labour market, upheld by powerful unions to uphold hard-won workers' rights, have contributed to high levels of unemployment, particularly among the inexperienced young, and especially when they are poorly qualified. Symbolically, so-called 'McJobs' in France divide opinion – do they offer employment to people who otherwise would be out of work (McDonald's itself provides jobs in many of France's run-down suburbs, as does Disneyland Paris) or do they seek to undermine reasonable working conditions?

Other developments have included the employers – capital – seeking greater autonomy from the state, particularly in the early

2000s after employers' organizations failed to prevent legislation introducing the 35-hour week; new unions seeking independence from the old organizations and their rules; and old unions changing their spots. The state itself has begun to legislate to force unions to earn their right to speak and disrupt in the name of workers by insisting that unions are more representative – and, therefore, legitimate – at the level of the firm; and firm-level negotiations are spreading, taking their place alongside the national and industry-wide bargains that have long been the norm in France. Thus, the old rulebook – whereby the state authorized a small number of unions to sign agreements on behalf of the entire workforce, irrespective of how representative they were or how low their membership levels were – is being ripped up. 'Minimum service' agreements, moreover, have been imposed upon public service providers, in transport, for example, as a way of preventing France from grinding to a halt when public transport workers take to the street; and on the key issues for state, labour and capital in the 21st century – unemployment, *la précarité*, pensions reform and the updating of working practices such as the 35-hour working week – the state has increasingly turned to legislation and regulation to affect change and reform, a process that has met with significant unrest.

One such reform in 2005–06, to introduce more flexibility for employers when hiring a young person in their first job, was so badly handled by the government of the day that mass protests were held on the streets, and the government bill was effectively withdrawn. This episode neither improved job prospects for young people as intended (by encouraging employers to open more positions, on the condition that they had more control over the hiring and firing) nor satisfied employers themselves. In the matter of pensions, reform by 2010 was underway to extend pensionable service in both the private and public sectors and the general retirement age was raised from 60 to 62 years, as seen in the previous chapter. Social unrest around pensions exploded during Macron's second term (see also Chapters 3 and 5) when his government forced through parliament a highly unpopular bill to raise the retirement age again, from 62 to 64. During his presidency, labour market reforms also included reducing access to comparatively generous unemployment benefits, improving employment prospects for *les seniors* and, overall, aiming for full employment. The challenge of balancing republican values, traditional French business practices and international competitivity to the satisfaction of the majority of French voters has thus typically overwhelmed France's presidents and President Macron is no stranger to this rule; his own momentum for reform was punctured in his first term by the *gilets jaunes* movement (see Chapter 3) and then the COVID-19 crisis. He placed his bets from the outset of his first mandate on the power of the EU and France's place within it to find the road to economic salvation; a risky calculation at a time of declining support in France for European integration (see Chapter 3). This was not the first time that a French leader had looked to the EU to transform the French economy: French economic life has been sustained as well as constrained by France's membership of the European Union since its very beginnings in the 1950s, when French minds were behind the creation of the first community for the pooling of production and markets in coal and steel. The EU provides France with its key markets and is the source of the most stringent constraints on the freedom of the state to shape the French economic and business environments.

France in the European (EU) economy

The EU provides France with a market of approximately 450 million consumers. In 2020, this accounted for 54 per cent of all French export trade, and for the bulk of its agricultural exports (where it still enjoys a trading surplus). France is also the second-largest net contributor to the EU's budget, after Germany, contributing over €26 billion in 2021 (constituting one fifth of all EU member state contributions), despite also being the biggest beneficiary of the EU's agricultural subsidies (annually worth approximately €9 billion). France's immediate neighbour, Germany, remains France's number one trading partner and the two countries have established a highly institutionalized, bilateral relationship within the EU to foster cooperation and agreement across a wide range of policy areas. Nowhere is this more important to the smooth running of the EU and to the bilateral partnership itself than in economic matters; here, the two countries have long shared an interest in overcoming differences for the sake of peaceful and productive relations. The two countries were the key architects of the early European Communities of the 1950s and, in the 1990s, of the foundations of today's EU (see also Chapter 8). Following German reunification in 1990, France had to work harder to preserve its influence over Germany, and the two countries frequently clashed over macroeconomic policy at the EU level, including Common Agricultural Policy (CAP) reform, responses to the 2008–09 global financial crash and the COVID-19 crisis, and the EU's financial priorities in general.

In the 2020s, however, the balance of power between the two countries is undergoing a gradual shift as Germany has found itself weakened: destabilized in 2021 when Angela Merkel's long chancellorship came to an end; from 2022, economically disrupted by the impact of Russia's war on Ukraine; and challenged in its domestic politics by the disturbing rise of the far right. In this context, French president Macron had some success in persuading Germany to back EU-level spending, for example to mitigate the effects of the COVID-19 pandemic, as we see below. These developments were a key plank in Macron's ambitions to 'retool' the French economy and reduce its exposure to global economic and geopolitical shocks.

French farmers, the CAP and changing times

For nearly 30 years, European economic integration was largely limited to the highly expensive CAP, the common market in coal and steel, and the Common External Tariff, which established a 'Community preference' in virtually all trading with the rest of the world. In the late 1950s, when France agreed to extend the 1951 Coal and Steel Community to a broad spectrum of economic sectors, it negotiated important conditions and limitations. These constituted, principally, preferential agreements with its former colonial markets, and a good deal for its agriculture in the form of the CAP, which subsequently became part and parcel of the modernization and mechanization of rural France seen in Chapters 1 and 2.

De Gaulle himself played a large part in bringing to life the CAP, which, to this day, is the costliest of the EU's common policies and in which the supranational and independent Commission plays the pivotal role. The policy has, for five decades, cushioned France from the blows of an increasingly competitive global market for agriculture and its products and turned its biggest farmers into an important political lobby via their principal trade body, the FNSEA (National Federation of Unions of Agricultural Workers). But the policy and the times have changed, and French farmers find themselves suffering the financial hardships of inflation and tough retail pricing, as well as facing the challenges of adapting their practices to meet national and EU strategic targets for carbon neutrality and biodiversity protection. These prospects (such as French government plans to raise the duty paid on diesel fuel for agricultural use in 2024) have triggered agricultural protests in a number of EU countries, including France, where the agricultural heritage is so strong (see Chapter 2) and the sector so important to the economy. The CAP has indeed evolved in line with changing objectives. Where it used to take up over two thirds of the EU's budget, it now accounts for only 31 per cent of the total (EU 2021–27 budget). Direct payments to farmers still represent the bulk of the spending, but other expenditure is linked to environmental aims of sustainability and biodiversity, with large-scale ambitions for carbon neutrality by 2050 encapsulated in the EU's Green Deal. Supporters of the CAP in France point to its ongoing mechanisms for defending quality produce and its distinctive *terroirs* (such as protected origin labelling), from which French producers benefit, and to the size of France's subsidies, but critics see the need for a comprehensive overhaul of a system that is still structurally designed to benefit larger growers and producers, and where big business and its interests have an outsized voice, for example when it comes to (not) reducing the use of chemical pesticides. These difficult tradeoffs between farmers and consumers, between lobbies and the land and between domestic and EU politics are characteristic of France's economic integration in the EU.

From the single market to the single currency

Following the economic downturn of the 1970s and then the failure in France, in the early 1980s, of President Mitterrand's counter-cyclical, *dirigiste* relaunch of the French economy (see also Chapters 2 and 3), the European Community (EC) and subsequently the EU became an ever more important policy framework for French economic policy. In 1983, French president Mitterrand lent his support to EC-wide plans to 'complete' the European economic integration provided for in the original 1957 Treaty of Rome by removing existing barriers to trade between the EU member states. Mitterrand accepted this development as a way of boosting French trade and economic growth in general. He appointed the pro-European Jacques Delors as his minister for finance and the economy and subsequently nominated Delors for the role of Commission president, a post he held from 1985 to 1995. In that position, Delors drove the process of completion of the single market, persuading national leaders including German chancellor Helmut Kohl, UK prime minister Margaret Thatcher and French president François Mitterrand to come together and sign the 1985 Single European Act (Drake, 2000).

That treaty laid the foundations for a complex agenda characterized by the gradual and ongoing liberalization and deregulation of the EC/EU's internal market for goods, capital and services. The plan also included the opening of that market to the rest of the world, including in agriculture, as the EU sought to develop itself as a global trading player; as well as social measures designed to balance those market measures – principally of benefit to consumers and producers – with action designed to protect workers (such a maximum working week) and to boost social integration between people (such as educational exchanges in the case of what became the well-known ERASMUS programme; or the free movement of people within the EU, not only to study but to work, build families or retire).

Provisions for the extension of the Single Market into a currency union between the member states had existed since the early days of European integration but were still incomplete at the time of Germany's reunification in 1990s. That momentous development set in train many changes to the European integration project, at the heart of which were the plans to finally bring an economic and monetary union to fruition (and which again relied on Delors's role in ushering the national leaders into agreement, although he warned that the EMU as designed in the Maastricht Treaty was inadequately balanced between its fiscal and monetary measures on the one hand and the arrangements for political oversight on the other). During the 1980s, French governments had pursued a policy of pegging the French franc closely to the German Deutsche Mark, despite lagging behind German levels of competitiveness. This approach, accordingly, hurt French exports and contributed to the rising levels of unemployment in France. The EMU would reset this equation, diluting, in theory, German power over France's economy and extracting a sacrifice from Germany – the relinquishing of its strong currency – in exchange for French support both for German reunification and for Germany's ambitions for further political integration between the member states (including more power for the directly elected European Parliament, for example).

The result was the Maastricht Treaty, which in France in 1993 was only narrowly approved by referendum (barely 51 per cent supported it, as seen in Chapter 1) and which laid down a set of strict monetary and fiscal rules inspired by German monetary orthodoxy. These notably set limits for national government debt and deficit spending (the 'Maastricht Criteria') and ushered in two decades during which France and other member states – including Germany itself – struggled to meet its own targets, to the point where the rules were repeatedly broken. By 2024, the gap between rules and reality was critically stark: France's public debt had by then risen to 112 per cent of GDP, far above the rule of 60 per cent, and its deficit was around 6 per cent of GDP, double the 3 per cent rule. President Sarkozy, on coming to power in 2007, had authorized his government to announce that the date by which the French economy was expected to reduce its deficit in line with EU rules was to be postponed by two and then four years. These rules accordingly were renegotiated and supplemented on several occasions. The challenge was to provide more flexibility for EMU member states – diverging economies tied into an inflexible, single currency – while preserving the international stability of the single currency.

In 2015 this tension was at its most acute when Greece was maintained in the EMU at the cost of severe austerity measures imposed on its domestic economy by the EU, led by Germany, and in subsequent years Germany found itself challenged to relax its grip on the rules, as we see below in the case of the COVID-19 crisis response. During these years, the impact of EMU membership on France and its economy was mixed: economically it allowed successive governments to make the case for responsible government spending; politically, it created opposition to a process seen as lacking domestic democratic oversight; in 2010 and 2011 France was even deemed a 'flawed democracy' by the Economist Intelligence Unit for these reasons. These issues were compounded by responses in France to the enlargements of the EU in the 2000s to the ten former Soviet bloc countries of Central and East Europe: these developments became conflated with disquiet at the perceived costs of France's ever closer economic integration into the EU.

Winners, losers and crises

Opposition in France to European integration came to a head in 2005 when the country voted by referendum on the EU's Draft Constitutional Treaty. The treaty was rejected by 55 per cent to 45 per cent on a 70 per cent turnout of the electorate and the treaty in that form was never adopted. French government and mainstream opposition parties had campaigned in favour of the treaty but voters (and some party figures) rebelled and stopped the process in its tracks. The intended purpose of the agreement had primarily been to democratize and simplify the EU's institutional functioning as the EU enlarged, rather than further economic integration, and it had been prepared for the member state governments by a 'convention' – a forum including parliamentary and civic representation from across the member states – chaired by former French president Giscard d'Estaing. French negotiators had arguably secured a good deal for France but the text acted as a lightning rod in France for concerns and reservations about the ability of French governments to influence the direction of the EU in France's economic interests.

These focused on the gradual liberalization of the EU's services sector, where opponents to the treaty depicted a future France in which foreign service providers (the 'Polish plumber' was the figure invoked) would, in a mass migration of workers from the poorer and newer member states, undermine local work and wage conditions for the sake of 'competition' alone. France was not alone in expressing such concerns, and the EU's infamous 2006 'Services Directive' was subsequently watered down. In a similar vein, President Sarkozy personally saw to it that, in the renegotiation of the failed 'Constitutional Treaty' following the 2005 'no' vote, the expression 'fair and free (undistorted) competition' was excised from the preamble of the revised Lisbon Treaty, although it was confirmed in the form of a protocol to the treaty, to the effect that the internal market system ensures that 'competition is not distorted'. 'Competition', claimed Sarkozy, should not be treated as 'dogma' – even though it is a founding principle of European economic integration. President Sarkozy, notably, did not put the Lisbon Treaty back to a popular vote but ushered it through parliamentary approval (as did his successor, François Hollande, in the case of the 2012 TSCG, as seen earlier in this chapter), further entrenching the gap between French political and public opinion towards European integration, and providing opportunities for parties outside the mainstream to turn France's EU membership into a political opportunity (as seen in Chapter 3). France has in reality not been without influence over the course of European economic and monetary integration, as shown by its impact on the EU's response to specific crises. Indeed, French calls, at domestic and EU levels, for a more balanced political economy in which *dirigisme* has some part to play, found an opening in the world financial crisis that erupted in autumn 2008, at precisely the time when France was holding the chair of the Council of Ministers of the EU and could thus exert some control over the EU's agenda. This was an opportunity, at EU level, for France to rehabilitate the language of the strong state in the service of a *European* social model, even though the crisis had the effect of illuminating important differences between the EU's biggest economies – France, Germany and the UK – in precisely these matters. From the French chair, President Sarkozy called for an EU-wide plan for bailing out ailing banks, and for EU sovereign wealth funds to protect EU-based companies from hostile takeover bids. The mood was also favourable to the argument that salaries and bonuses in the financial services industries should be capped and taxed, and the sector itself far more heavily regulated. The crisis – from this perspective, popular in France – was in no small part a failure of the excesses of Anglo-American, *laissez-faire* economics and their admiration of untrammelled wealth.

The situation provided opportunities for debate on such matters, allowing the French argument to be heard. But, in real terms and by and large, the EU member states each took unilateral action to safeguard their domestic economic interests. Thus, British prime minister Gordon Brown implemented a VAT tax cut in the UK designed to boost consumption. This was criticized by President Sarkozy, who, in France, authorized a reflationary programme of infrastructure spending worth €26 billion, amounting to 1.3 per cent of GDP. This was shortly followed in Paris by a €6 billion package specifically for the car industry in the form of preferential loans, and a bank bailout scheme of €360 billion. These were all measures that increased France's public spending deficit and, in the case of the car industry bailout, President Sarkozy gave the impression at the time that this was conditional on companies such as Renault (in part state-owned) moving production units back to France from Eastern Europe.

Such strings are not allowed under EU law. Nevertheless, France and Germany managed to agree on how to curb bank bonuses (in the form of taxation); the 2008 French EU Council presidency succeeded in negotiating a Eurozone 'toolbox' of crisis measures, and President Sarkozy's tone throughout was combative, claiming a 'triumph' of French ideas over, in particular, the UK-style capitalism that was seen to have driven the EU's single market agenda for over two decades.

In the case of the 2020 COVID-19 crisis, and alongside a very costly domestic 'whatever it takes' policy of expenditure to support the economy, businesses and the working population, President Macron had an opportunity to put into practice a key plank of the platform that had seen him elected in 2017, namely a reworking of the EU's rules and ambitions such that it could operate as a 'sovereign' actor, as Macron saw it, on the world stage, including in the world economy. This was not sovereignty as the conventional, legally enshrined right of nation states such as France to protect their territorial integrity and decide for themselves (as stated in Title I of the French Constitution) but rather the capacity of the EU to act – through legislation, regulation and funding – independently (Macron sometimes used the term 'autonomously') of other world players in existential matters such as public health, food, energy and digital security, and environmental resilience. Clearly, this process of mitigating the risks of economic interdependence was an ambition for the long term and required significant political will on the part of the EU27. With regard to the procurement and distribution of the first COVID-19 vaccines, the EU showed weakness, but in response to the severe economic and social impact of successive lockdowns President Macron successfully won German support to lobby other EU member states to ultimately agree in 2018 on a €750 billion recovery package, unprecedented in particular in its provision for the EU to raise common debt. This package – named NextGenerationEU – of loans and investments is described by the EU as an opportunity to drive the transformation of its economy, notably to withstand the green transition, and a significant proportion of the package is targeted on delivering the EU's European Green Deal. France's 2022 presidency of the EU maintained this pressure on the EU to act on behalf of its member states in the face of numerous challenges, with some results such as the Digital Services Act (to regulate internet content and safety via cooperation between the EU and national authorities), although here too, as in the case of the EU's environmental targets, the French executive must balance specific domestic interests and concerns against the common EU good.

This balancing act has typified France's experience of European economic integration since the EU's beginnings. But, where France was originally one of only six founder member states and had an outsized say in the original shape of the institutions and processes of the early European Communities, and although it has successfully, over many decades, nominated French individuals to influential EU posts (not only Delors but commissioners and officials in key services including agriculture and the internal market) and is very experienced at EU politics and negotiations, it is today one of 27 member states with diverse economic and political interests. Its relationship with Germany, previously seen as the 'tandem' driving European integration, is far less predictable, with the Germany economy itself faltering where once it was the undisputed powerhouse of the block. Even the UK's exit from the EU (Brexit) in 2021, despite offering some opportunities for economic gain (in financial markets for example), and potentially removing a roadblock to some of the EU's more political ambitions, has negatively affected French exports and, as we see in Chapter 8, disrupted cross-Channel cooperation more broadly. France's impact on the rules of the EMU has fallen short of its long-time quest for a so-called 'economic government' in which the EU's national leaders would hold more sway over the European Central Bank and other central institutions than is currently the case, although it can be argued that the planning mechanisms underpinning EMU owe something to the French tradition of economic planning as discussed above. At home in France, finally, opposition parties are turning to the EU's own institutions, namely the European Parliament, as a platform for their campaigns to blame France's EU membership for domestic economic grievances and hardships, and to argue for a renationalization of France's economic fortunes.

Conclusions

Economic reform and planning are very much the hallmarks of President Macron's France, encapsulated in the country's €54 billion France 2030 investment programme to reverse France's industrial decline, 'massively' support innovative technologies and bring about the ecological transition away from fossil fuels. Alongside that programme are Macron's ongoing reforms to the labour market, designed to bring more cohorts, including regularized immigrants, into the workforce at a time of a declining French birthrate and ageing society, as seen in previous chapters. This scale of government and state intervention in the economy is superficially commensurate with France's traditional model of political economy, characterized as we have seen by a rhetoric of state capacity and social justice, and a toolbox of legislative and regulatory mechanisms to support these aims. In today's France, however, we have also seen that popular dissatisfaction with at least certain flagship reforms, notably to state pensions (but also latterly to the place of immigrants in the workforce and society more generally), has spilled out of the traditional framework of dialogue between capital, labour and the state to take the form of protest, often violent and/or prolonged. This was the case of the *gilets jaunes* movement, for example, and, although direct action of this kind is historically part of French political culture (as seen in Chapter 3), it now occurs in a context where the French parliament is unable to reach consensus (also see Chapter 3) and where French society is increasingly fragmented (as seen in Chapter 5)

The French state, for its part, is still expected to play its role in regulating, planning and balancing the economy and is still blamed when individuals – as workers, consumers, voters, pensioners, public servants, managers, directors, entrepreneurs, shareholders, investors – feel the pain of living in an open economy, and it is critiqued for its difficulties in carrying out structural reforms that many economists deem necessary for France to flourish in the 21st-century global economy. Yet the French state is manifestly only one of the many actors and forces shaping France's economic fortunes, a fact not lost on the French people who voted against the EU's Constitutional Treaty in May 2005; or the political parties, foremost of which the Rassemblement national, urging in 2017 for some sort of French disentanglement from the EU economy and blaming the EU for French economic difficulties; or on Macron himself, pleading in contrast for an understanding of French sovereignty that allows for greater EU-level common action in order to handle the immensity of the challenges posed by the climate emergency and the development of artificial intelligence alone.

Public unrest and painful socio-economic compromises are not exclusive to France, which, like many of its European counterparts and the EU itself, seeks to develop a discourse of political economy that incorporates factors other than GDP growth, such as social justice, sustainability and wellbeing. Furthermore, the importance for national economic survival of France's links to the global economy go well beyond the EU, to include its trading partners in the US, in Asia and in the fast-developing markets of countries such as Brazil, India and China, all with their own often nationalist agendas. In particular, the interests of big French business – in defence procurement, in nuclear energy and so on – are part of a bigger picture in which France seeks to project its influence across the wider world, using commercial, diplomatic, cultural and military means. In the economy, as in foreign policy, France likes to shape the debate, if not change the course of events.

8

France in the World

Introduction

France is a significant world player in cultural, commercial, political and military terms. As recently as the 1960s, Paris governed countries as large as Algeria and as distant as New Caledonia. Today, France possesses only fragments of its former empire but as a physical, political and administrative entity it still extends far beyond mainland France to the Atlantic, Pacific and Indian oceans, where 2 million French citizens live in France's remaining overseas departments and territories (as seen in Chapter 2). France's present-day identity as a world player is nourished by the country's 17th-century domination of Europe, often at the expense of the UK; by the revolutionary spirit of 1789, when France saw itself as a pioneer of democracy in modern Europe; by the 19th-century Napoleonic Wars that earned France the label of the *grande nation* (great nation) of Europe; and by the era when President de Gaulle (1959–68) developed a narrative of France's global *grandeur* (greatness) and *rang* (rank). Cogan (2003) argues that a sense of these historical achievements underpins contemporary quests for an influential French voice in international affairs, where History, with a capital 'H', is an ever-present force.

But contemporary France also remembers its 19th-and 20th-century mortal combats with Germany; its earlier, repeated losses of territory and pride to the British; its Cold War struggle with communism; and its many experiences as Europe's 'underdog' (Cogan, 2003). These events and relationships all revealed the limitations of French power, the virtues of collective security, and the possibilities of redemption. Beyond the continent of Europe, recent defections of French-speaking African states from the status quo, anti-French sentiments toward France's military presence on that continent and the very mitigated results of French-led military operations in sub-Saharan Africa, and violent unrest in several of France's overseas territories serve to underline the changing world dynamics that challenge the dominance of Western states, especially those with a colonial past as extensive as France. These shifts lead to the difficulty for these countries to fully, if ever, digest the consequences of that past. In the case of France, this extends to the troubled integration of successive generations of individuals and families from its former colonies, especially in North Africa (as seen in Chapters 2 and 5), as well as to a broader sense that France today must not only apologize for its actions of the past but rectify them. President Macron has put on the record that such sensitivities, however, cannot come at the expense of measures he sees necessary to put France – its military, its economy, its citizens – on a wartime footing in the coming years. According to Ramdani, moreover, Macron 'rules out apologies and never mentions reparations' (2023: 293), although perhaps his record will be more nuanced than that, as France slowly adjusts to new geopolitical realities.

Indeed, in the case of Africa, France sees its influence challenged by the growing influence of China, notably in the form of the latter's extensive investments in infrastructure and education, and by mercenary actors such as Russia's former Wagner group and its successors. In its own backyard, in Europe, France and its allies must contend with a belligerent Russia pushing at its eastern borders via its invasions and occupation of Ukraine, and its pressure by proxy on other parts of the region. France, finally, finds that it is appetizing to rich Gulf states seeking to establish themselves as today's newest global actors via ownership of assets that are economically and culturally significant, such as Qatar's acquisition of the iconic football club Paris Saint-Germain.

In this turbulent context, France typically seeks to amplify its voice and influence via its membership of significant international organizations, first and foremost of which the European Union (EU), to which President Macron has recommitted as an absolute priority, as Europe's crises and challenges pile up. There is also the North Atlantic Treaty Organization (NATO), which France fully rejoined at the turn of the 2010s after decades of semi-detachment;

the United Nations (UN), where it holds one of the five permanent seats on the Security Council and therefore a veto by virtue of its independent nuclear deterrent (known as the *force de frappe*); and la Francophonie, the French-speaking 'Commonwealth' of 88 members, associate members and observers, many but not all French former colonies, having 'in common' the use of the French language (as seen in Chapter 6). Membership of such organizations offers France opportunities to project its voice onto the global stage in matters of vital national interest such as security and defence. It also provides it with a voice in realms where it once exerted great influence, such as culture (as also seen in Chapter 6), and in fields such as technology and trade where it wants to shape the future, from philosophical norms to prosaic but vital regulatory frameworks.

At the same time, France's inclination and obligations to act multilaterally, in concert with other countries under the umbrella of such organizations, constrain the freedom of manoeuvre of French policy makers. It requires constant efforts to preserve France's place and voice in those bodies and, increasingly, to explain at home why it is cooperating with others when this can be seen as damaging to domestic interests, such as in the case of agricultural trade, increased military spending, or concessions of decision-making sovereignty to the EU level. This perilous balancing act between France's commitment to multilateralism on the one hand and its self-belief as a sovereign nation state on the other still jars with a sense of the recent past, where France, under the first president of the Fifth Republic, Charles de Gaulle, projected itself as an independent and sovereign actor in the world, free to chart its own course between the two superpowers – the US and the USSR – of the Cold War.

That Gaullist stance was always as much symbolic and rhetoric as real, but it constitutes what Sonntag (2008) calls one of the 'prison walls' of the French policy of seeking international prestige. The constitution does afford the president significant powers over foreign policy and during de Gaulle's presidency France left NATO's integrated military command, unceremoniously ejecting its Paris-based staff from the country; it maintained an unfashionable dialogue with the USSR; took a stance in the Arab–Israeli conflict – siding with the Arab cause – that set it apart from most of its Western allies at the time; and yet it knew that it was protected by the US nuclear umbrella. In today's France, traces of this belief in an independent, influential French voice, firmly inside the Western camp but with a unique room for manoeuvre and claim to leadership, are legion. Examples include President Macron's freewheeling diplomacy towards Russian President Vladimir Putin even as the latter invaded Ukraine in February 2022; his undiplomatic critiques of the West's security order (claiming in 2019 that NATO was 'brain dead'); his attempts, some successful, to reframe the debate on the future of the West, including his calls for European economic 'sovereignty'; his changing discourse on incorporating Russia's neighbours into the EU; his language for talking about France's global past; and France's newest definition of its international role as a *puissance d'équilibres*, literally translatable as a 'power of balances': an international actor with the power to bring others into balance (SGDSN, 2022; see also La Documentation française, 2023).

In this chapter, accordingly, we first review the many dimensions of the Gaullist legacy that still resonate in French foreign policy. These include presidential prerogatives; an uneasy balance between economic interests, notably served by arms exports, and a discourse of human rights; France's relations with Germany and the UK, its embeddedness in the EU; and its place in the wider world, including the African continent. But we also identify the limitations of that legacy, not only since the ending of the Cold War in the 1990s but also in de Gaulle's own day, when the US established its global domination and when France's empire unravelled, one bloody colonial conflict at a time. Second, we turn to current French strategy regarding its place in the new world disorder that has unfolded at speed in the first three decades of the 21st century. This includes the latest iteration of France's soft power diplomatic strategy, now stripped of its colonial connotations; France's renewed emphasis on EU-level action to address the threats from non-European actors that coexist with the existential crises of climate change, public health, runaway technological developments, and nuclear proliferation; and France's provisions for defending its territory, promoting its economic interests and readying its citizens to withstand the intensity of the conflicts it sees on the horizon. This strategy for national resilience leads us back, third, to the domestic dimensions of France's action abroad, past and present. How should today's French leaders engage with the legacies of their predecessors? Where are apologies due and what form should they take? How can the vicious blowback from its actions abroad – particularly in Muslim-majority countries – in the shape of domestic unrest, violence and terrorism be tackled? How can multiple voices and interests from across society be incorporated into the discussion of France's place in the world so as to generate a sense of national unity around France's international actions? We investigate these dynamics and the responses they have generated, including declarations of repentance and regret by the state for past actions.

The Gaullist legacy and its limits

Treacher (2003) notes how 'malleable' the 1958 Constitution is with regard to the president's power over foreign policy, to the point where de Gaulle, the first president of the Fifth French Republic, was seen as carving out a so-called 'reserved domain' for presidential foreign policy-making, typically insulated from democratic debate or dissent within France's core institutions, and of low electoral salience. Much has changed since de Gaulle's time, and the pace of change is ever accelerating as France tries to keep up with rapidly evolving world events. France's institutional framework for foreign policy-making, however, is remarkably similar to the earliest days of the Fifth Republic.

The power of the president

The French president remains the fulcrum of power for the conduct of France's international relations. This role is specified in the constitution and all presidents of the Fifth Republic have played their part to the full. According to Article 5 of the constitution, the president 'shall be the guarantor of national independence, territorial integrity and due respect for Treaties'. This is a supreme responsibility, on a par with that of the president of the United States. Accordingly, the French president, like his American counterpart, is also commander-in-chief of the armed forces (Article 15) and is given access to the country's nuclear missile launch codes on taking up office. Unlike the US, however, and as seen in Chapter 4, the French president is flanked by a prime minister who 'shall be responsible for national defence' (Article 21); she or he also heads a government that 'shall have at its disposal the civil service and the armed forces' (Article 20). In this tandem, nonetheless, it is the president who sets the strategic direction for France's foreign policy, including in periods when the president must cohabit with a prime minister from an opposing party.

This Gaullist legacy in French foreign affairs resides not only in the extent of presidential power but in the purposes to which de Gaulle put that power during his presidency (1958–69), namely the pursuit of French global greatness and rank (known respectively as *la grandeur* and *le rang*). De Gaulle sought to restore France – as he saw it – as a sovereign, high-ranking world player independent of both of the two Cold War superpowers, the US and the USSR, and to link France with its past glories after the catastrophe of its capitulation and collaboration with Nazi Germany during World War II (as seen in Chapter 1), in part by declaring such dark periods to be aberrations in an otherwise glorious past. Such goals were to be reached by developing an independent nuclear capacity, establishing friendships with countries of the 'Third World' and other non-aligned powers, courting Germany as a means to building an independent Europe, holding the UK at bay, and reinvigorating the long-held, colonial-era idea that France had a unique 'civilizing mission' in the world. At the same time, France's loyalty to the West during the Cold War was never seriously in doubt, neither was its dependence on the US and the transatlantic alliance for its security, nor its friendship, however troubled, with the UK. De Gaulle, in his day, therefore, became the voice and face of French foreign policy. The presidential powers and precedent that he created to this purpose are part of his legacy today, as are the guiding ideals of French foreign policy: independence and autonomy. Yet these were outdated even in de Gaulle's own days in power and, says Sonntag (2008), became a barrier – a 'prison wall' – between French diplomacy and the real world. In that real world, France needed European cooperation if it was to prosper and thrive, and de Gaulle set out to dominate the process of 'ever closer union between the peoples of Europe' that had begun in the immediate post-war years.

*French leadership of a 'political Europe': a reckoning with
Germany and the 'Anglo-Saxons'*

Indeed, France's unique role in the early 1950s in the founding
of what is now the EU formed a critical turning point in French
diplomatic history. This was a post-war solution to a century-old
problem, that of stabilizing relations with Germany for mutual
security, and it is impossible to underestimate its novelty or
significance. The new European institutions of the 1950s provided
the framework for a constructive partnership and, by the 1960s, the
Franco-German relationship was the backbone of the European
Economic Communities. With the backing of the US, without a
viable alternative from the UK, and thanks to the ingenuity of its
author, Jean Monnet, the declaration endorsed by French foreign
minister Robert Schuman on 9 May 1950 (see Box 8.1) took
France into an unprecedented experiment in the voluntary sharing
of decision-making power in the key economic sectors of coal
and steel, under the authority of new, European-level institutions,
notably the European Coal and Steel Community (ECSC) and the
European Economic Community (EEC). Over time, the Franco-
German partnership itself developed into a highly structured bilateral
relationship, framed by the Elysée Treaty of 1963, which signalled
a common intent to build a united Europe and established joint
working procedures. A joint Franco-German Council of Ministers,
for example, is held annually to facilitate political cooperation
in the specific fields of defence, security, the economy, finance
and the environment, as reaffirmed in the 2019 Aix-la-Chapelle/
Aachen Treaty, signed in January of that year between the two
partners. Genuine and sometimes unlikely personal friendships were
established between several pairs of French and German leaders, most
significantly Charles de Gaulle and Konrad Adenauer in the 1960s,
and François Mitterrand and Helmut Kohl in the 1980s and 1990s.

From a strategic perspective, France's friendship with Germany was
intended to allow France to exert influence in the form of leadership
on the European continent and, in turn, to enable Europe to operate
as an autonomous block with its own international strategy (referred
to by France as *l'Europe puissance* or 'Europe as a power') and its
own, European identity (defined in French as *l'Europe politique* or a
'political Europe'). De Gaulle himself spoke of the day when Europe

---

Box 8.1: The Schuman Declaration, 9 May 1950

French foreign minister Robert Schuman took virtually everyone by surprise when, on 9 May 1950, he made a short speech outlining a novel way of keeping the peace in Europe. The following extracts are the most famous parts of the Declaration:

"Europe will not be made all at once, or according to a single plan. It will be built through concrete achievements which first create a de facto solidarity. The coming together of the nations of Europe requires the elimination of the age-old opposition of France and Germany. Any action must in the first place concern these two countries. With this aim in view, the French Government proposes that action be taken immediately on one limited but decisive point. It proposes that Franco-German production of coal and steel as a whole be placed under a common High Authority, within the framework of an organisation open to the participation of the other countries of Europe. The pooling of coal and steel production should immediately provide for the setting up of common foundations for economic development as a first step in the federation of Europe ... The solidarity in production thus established will make it plain that any war between France and Germany becomes not merely unthinkable, but materially impossible [and] will lay a true foundation for their economic unification."

---

would reunite from the 'Atlantic to the Urals', making the East–West division of the Cold War a thing of the past, and bolstering Europe's strength. Germany was key to de Gaulle's notion of building Europe as a third source of regional power in the world at a time of extreme tension between the US and the USSR superpowers.

De Gaulle in his day argued for a strong Europe in the form of common European policies on matters of culture, education, the economy and defence. But he disparaged the European Communities' common institutions set up by fellow Frenchmen Robert Schuman and Jean Monnet, favouring instead cooperation between sovereign governments that would form a 'Union of States' (with a secretariat based in Paris, not Brussels). In the matter of European defence, for example, and when still out of power in 1954, de Gaulle had already incited his supporters in the French National Assembly to scupper a plan – devised in the mid-1950s by the French government itself – for a European Defence Community and a European Political Community. De Gaulle's argument was that these organizations would have left France exposed to binding decisions by a majority of which it was not part, in matters of national interest as vital as defence and national security. The Union of States idea was intended as a direct alternative to this, but it foundered in the face of opposition from all five of the other member states of the ECSC, including Germany. This defeat, at the height of de Gaulle's domestic powers, gave an early indication of the tensions at the heart of France's commitment to European integration via common institutions, and the limits to the willingness of other member states to concede to French interests.

In the 1960s, moreover, de Gaulle was similarly unable to persuade his German counterparts to diminish their commitment to the US as the sole provider of security for the West. He was just as unsuccessful in attempts to persuade the UK to see de Gaulle's France as an match equal to the US when it came to nuclear weapons and technology. By 1966, de Gaulle's isolation in these respects was such that he ordered the departure of NATO troops from French soil, inflicting damage on French prestige at large. At the same time, he withdrew French staff from the organization's joint command committees and pushed ahead with the development of an independent nuclear deterrent that was of questionable value in either the Cold War or post-Cold War contexts other than as an icon of French identity and a statement of power directed at the 'Anglo-Saxons', as de Gaulle and most of his successors liked to call the United Kingdom and the United States of America.

France's relationships with the UK and the US are marked by centuries of contradictory forces, including rivalry, jealousy, antagonism, incomprehension, friendship, fascination, mutual attraction and support. Language, food, agriculture, film, wine, music and foreign policy are all topics that episodically divide and enrage the governments of the US and France, but not necessarily their populations. Relations between France and the UK were stabilized 120 years ago in a written agreement, the Entente Cordiale, based then as now on both mutual self-interest (in 1904, regarding their respective colonial spheres of influence) and the attraction for both peoples of the other's country and culture. France and the 'Anglo-Saxons' operate far more frequently as global allies than as opponents, and certainly not enemies. Had Britain been willing to join de Gaulle in uniting Europe on French terms, then France would undoubtedly have looked across the Channel as well as the Rhine for a three-way 'triumvirate'. But de Gaulle drew lessons from the UK's exclusive commitment to its US partner in matters of nuclear and conventional defence and, on two occasions in the 1960s, rejected the UK's bid to join the EEC. In explaining those decisions, de Gaulle memorably caricatured the UK as the 'Trojan Horse' for American influence inside the Community. He also correctly predicted that, once inside the EEC, the UK would seek to change the rules providing for the protection of European goods and services in a globalizing market.

De Gaulle thereby legitimized a set of recurrent arguments relating to the identity of Europe (minus the UK) as culturally distinct from the English-speaking, specifically Anglo-Saxon world, and culture, here, extended to its broadest meaning of civilization. In France, under de Gaulle and for decades afterwards, globalization (the flows of people, capital, goods and ideas that threaten states' capacity to define an exclusive national identity) took on an 'American face' (Kuisel, 2001: 5): one that spoke in English, ate *la malbouffe* – junk food – and consumed Hollywood entertainment. In 1999, when French farmer José Bové dismantled the building site of a new McDonald's restaurant in Millau, central France (for which he was jailed), his argument was that globalization must be *altered* (hence the term 'alter-globalization' to describe the movement associated with him, as seen in Chapter 7) in order to balance out its overly American influences, including in agricultural production and trade. Sophie Meunier (2003) accordingly refers to the 'double talk' of French leaders on globalization: happy for French brands to benefit from global markets and happy to exaggerate their dangers. Ideas about French civilization therefore extend beyond the realms of economics and trade and are prevalent in any discussion of France's relations with the world beyond the north and west of the globe, many of which took shape during de Gaulle's years.

From la Françafrique *to la Francophonie*

France's traditional sphere of influence indeed extends far beyond the 'West' or the 'North' to reach into Africa (both North and sub-Saharan), Asia and the Pacific. France's bloodiest experiences of colonialism and then decolonization in the 1950s and 1960s were in these regions, particularly in what is now Vietnam, and Algeria. French colonization operated on the principle of cultural assimilation, and its decolonization occurred through strife, bloodshed and resistance, on both sides. France's relations with its former colonies in sub-Saharan Africa have been dubbed by critics as a family affair, known colloquially as *la françafrique*; the term has connotations of dubious diplomatic and commercial favours based on material interests and a determination to maintain French presence across the globe at all costs. During the superpower conflict of the Cold War, to this end, France positioned itself as 'champion' of the non-aligned countries, and the 'third world' (not to mention the Soviet satellite states), and President de Gaulle made a number of high-profile, often controversial, overseas visits in the 1960s to underscore this particular margin for manoeuvre from the Western 'camp'.

The years of de Gaulle's presidency were equally notorious for the tightness of Franco-African networks and the corruption and familiarity that these bred, and his successors in the 20th century did very little to reform matters. Thus, President Giscard d'Estaing (1974–81) became notorious for gifts of diamonds from a shady central African dictator, and François Mitterrand's family and close advisers were accused of having been implicated in arms and trade scandals. France's keen commercial interest in the manufacture and trade of arms, including to dictatorial regimes, is also well-known, as are the close personal relationships that have at times existed between presidents of the Fifth Republic and their opposite numbers in countries including Gabon, Libya and Syria.

Decolonization *à la française* has led to different sets of relationships between France and the regimes and peoples formerly under French rule, involving France in at least 30 military missions in as many years. Some of these, such as France's role in failing to prevent or to halt the Rwandan genocide of 1994, brought Paris international opprobrium and much ongoing domestic soul-searching. Other relationships – not exclusively with former colonies – have evolved into predominantly cultural links in the framework of the Francophonie organization based on the 'use of the French language in common' (see above). The organization operates a political agenda that goes beyond the promotion of 'cultural diversity' across the world (see Chapter 6); this aspect of the French-speaking world – la Francophonie with a capital F, denoting the organization that structures its activities – is both more and less than the British Commonwealth: less in that its common thread is the French language, and not allegiance to a head of state; more, given its claim to a voice in cultural and development politics. France's current role in the wider world, as well as its relationships closer to home, are subject to shocks and crises on a par with those experienced by de Gaulle in his day, but of a variety, intensity and speed that severely challenge de Gaulle's legacy of decisive action and illusory clarity.

France and the new world disorder

The Cold War provided a strangely stable climate for France and other countries to pursue their international ambitions. In contrast, the contemporary global era has, in so many respects, brought about an acute loss of 'Cold War comfort' for France, as Keiger put it (2005: 140) and a pessimistic sense in France of the decline of French influence (there was even a name for it: *le déclinisme*). The collapse of the USSR, German unification, the unilateralism of US foreign policy for nearly a decade after 9/11, the enlargement of the EU and the growing reach and pace of globalization, largely driven by China, all challenged France's global role. By the time of Emmanuel Macron's first presidential term in 2017, the world situation was more unpredictable still, symbolized by US president Trump's iconoclastic, high-risk approach to international affairs (2016–20), Russia's 2014 annexation of Crimea in Ukraine, China's squeeze on the freedoms of Hong Kong, Syria's civil war, the tentacular spread of Islamic State jihadi terrorism, and the growing awareness of the magnitude of the world's climate crisis. By the start of Macron's second mandate in 2022 the international context was highly perilous, further fragilized by nuclear proliferation, the impacts of the COVID-19 pandemic on societies and economies across the world, Russia's invasion of Ukraine in February 2022, and the simmering Israeli–Palestinian conflict, which in October 2023 erupted into extreme violence that reverberated through Western societies, including France. This third decade of the 21st century necessitated a rethink of the strategy that had only recently been updated to accommodate the novelties of the end of the Cold War. The so-called peace dividend that could have followed the collapse of the USSR in the 1990s soon gave way to the need for increased military spending (at a time of budgetary constraints following the costs of refloating economies after COVID-19) by France and its European allies; to a rolling update of national security strategies; to an expansion of EU and NATO membership to bolster the West on its eastern borders; and to a destabilization of democratic politics, in particular by populist forces capitalizing on international insecurity to clamour for more authoritarian and nationalistic policies, and to exacerbate divisions between domestic communities of different faiths and ethnicities.

Rethinking Europe part I: Maastricht, Germany and EU enlargement

France needed a rationale and doctrine to fit the post-Cold War era, and this revolved around the long-standing French notion of Europe taking responsibility for its own defence and security by becoming '*l'Europe puissance*', as seen above. Thus, former president Jacques Chirac marked his first term of office (1995–2002) by taking a number of key strategic decisions to slim down France's defences while starting the process of rejoining NATO (this was completed under his successor, President Sarkozy, in the face of considerable domestic opposition) and persuading the UK to think of ways to bolster NATO's European pillar. This latter commitment was enshrined in the 1998 St Malo declaration, signed by President Chirac and UK prime minister Blair, who jointly agreed that the EU must have 'the capacity for autonomous action'. In retrospect, this commitment on the part of the UK was not only a first but also a last: an anomaly for the UK that in so many respects – not only for its security but also for linguistic and cultural comfort – prefers to face the US and not Europe. Similarly, in the case of Germany, the momentous end to its division in 1990 spelt the beginning of a succession of firsts and lasts in the Franco-German relationship as it evolved to accommodate Germany's larger population size and growing influence within the EU and beyond, at considerable discomfort to France.

The 1992 Maastricht Treaty was both the first statement of the new Franco-German relationship and the last occasion on which France dictated substantial terms to its now larger neighbour; even then, the signs that the relationship would find a more balanced equilibrium over time were evident. At Maastricht and in exchange for his eventual support for German reunification on Germany's terms, French president François Mitterrand secured from his counterpart, German chancellor Helmut Kohl, a new Treaty on European Union (TEU) that represented a considerable step towards the Europe that French leaders had consistently called for, in the form of its establishment of the Common Foreign and Security Policy(the CFSP). The treaty also laid down the path to Europe's Economic and Monetary Union that, as seen in Chapter 7, was a German concession to France. However, the treaty also provided for European 'citizenship', including the right of EU nationals to stand and vote in local and European elections in another member state, and it was this provision that triggered a backlash against the TEU in France on the grounds of lost national sovereignty, arguments that almost defeated the treaty when it was put to a referendum by François Mitterrand, carried by only 51.04 per cent of the votes (see also Chapter 3).

That situation illustrated the contradictions inherent in French policy towards the EU and represented a parallel with French responses to the proposed European Defence Community in 1954 (see above). As in 1992, French leaders in 1954 had played a substantial role in proposing developments at the European level that would offer bold new solutions to new challenges: in 1954, a common European army in the face of the escalating Cold War; in 1992, institutions to generate a stable and strong Europe in a very unstable post-bipolar world order. In both 1954 and 1992, there was a backlash in France itself against the French-led proposals. Political opposition in both cases was central, not marginal, to the political system, and demonstrated in each case that the French pioneers of the European integration of the early 1950s had started a process that struck at the heart of traditional French identity, construed as an independent, sovereign nation in whose relationship with Germany France was the dominant partner.

When in 2001 Germany proposed that its voting weight in the EU's Council of Ministers should exceed that of France, now that Germany's population was one fifth larger than that of France, France successfully objected, agreeing instead to a compromise that entitled Germany to more (12) seats in the European Parliament (EP) against a loss of nine seats for France (the UK, Italy and Spain also lost seats in the change). Crucially, Germany's support for the EU's 2004 enlargement to the eight post-Soviet states to its east was not echoed in France: French public opinion remained consistently among the least favourable to enlargement in poll after poll at this time, and political opinion was also sceptical, especially among traditional pro-Europeans who feared that the French vision of a 'political Europe' was now definitively diluted. These fears and doubts surfaced in the 2005 French referendum on the EU's Draft Constitutional Treaty, decisively rejected (as seen in Chapter 7) in France by 55 per cent of the electorate. For now, France had faced the future by looking to its past, not only in European affairs but also further afield. The framework for change, for now, was the status quo of France's politics of prestige (Sonntag, 2008).

Beyond Europe: multilateralism and its limits

President Chirac's announcement in June 1995 that France would resume nuclear testing following his predecessor Mitterrand's moratorium on testing took France's partners by surprise, and created a furore of negative public opinion, particularly in those countries neighbouring the test site, including Australia and New Zealand, but also in France itself. However Gaullist in style this gesture, it nevertheless spelt the beginning of the definitive end of such testing, the subsequent signing by France of the Test Ban Treaty, and the downgrading over the following decade of the French nuclear deterrent. President Chirac also decreed the end of national service and conscription in a key move towards the professionalization of the French army, making it more compatible with other European armies.

The early 21st century also saw France scaling back military bases and operations in Africa and increasing its contributions to UN and EU-led peacekeeping operations instead, and to the collective attempts of the Western powers to combat international terrorism and nuclear proliferation. The UN is of particular significance to France's global role in that, for French policy makers, it offers an alternative source of legitimation for foreign operations other than US-led 'coalitions of the willing'. French foreign minister Dominique de Villepin's passionate speech made to the UN Security Council in February 2003 to deter a US/UK-led military intervention in Iraq without a UN resolution failed to prevent the operation but was an important marker, in this period, of France's commitment to initiating its own proposals for resolving international problems and hence taking a leadership role, intellectually at least. The 2008 White Paper on Defence and National Security commissioned by President Sarkozy was drafted in precisely this context and proposed a radical overview of both strategy and spending. By 2010, French troop numbers on operation throughout the world had already been cut by at least one quarter compared to 2006, especially in Africa, where President Sarkozy explicitly set about renegotiating all military agreements. In addition, France not infrequently found itself out of step with its partners in the EU and beyond – in its friendship with Putin's Russia, for example; in 2007, in new ties forged around defence contracts between France and Libya; or in seeking to lift embargos on arms sales, for example to China, a big and important commercial customer for France. At the same time, France sought to act in concert with its EU allies over attempts to prevent Iran from developing nuclear weapons capabilities. The opening in 2009 of a French military base in Abu Dhabi in the United Arab Emirates was also part of France's enhanced emphasis on shaping affairs in that part of the world.

Simultaneously, France's growing recognition of its limitations as solo peacekeeper, let alone peacemaker, in its former 'backyard' on the African continent (known as its *pré carré*) led it to support and foster local solutions in the form of regional peacekeeping forces such as Africa's RECAMP, launched in 1997. By 2006, France had approximately 14,000 women and men directly committed to military operations throughout the world, principally in Africa and central Europe; by 2009, the number of operational staff was closer to 10,000. Roughly half of these missions were multilateral (predominantly UN or EU) and included both military and civilian peacekeeping operations. Among these, by way of example, were UN missions in the Ivory Coast, the Democratic Republic of Congo, Darfur and Lebanon, and EU operations in Bosnia and Somalia. France, moreover, was a major contributor to the NATO-led operations in both Afghanistan (with around 3,700 troops stationed there by 2010, one third as many as the UK and one quarter fewer than Germany) and Kosovo.

However, the French-led Serval and Barkhane missions in the Sahel region of West Africa, initially launched in 2013 at the invitation of Mali's government to counter rising jihadi terrorism, ended in a withdrawal in 2023 that President Macron denied was a defeat. The evidence suggested otherwise: many French soldiers had lost their lives, the counterterrorism operations had had only limited results and, by the time the French forces retreated, sentiment and opinion in Mali and its neighbours had turned against the former colonizing power, rejecting its interference in both the French-speaking and neighbouring countries of the region. These developments fitted into a broader context in which the post-World War II 'Washington' consensus of international organizations, rules and norms, and the very notion of a Western-dominated international community, found themselves unravelling, prompting another reckoning for France and its European partners.

Rethinking Europe part II: shocks, crises and blips

Throughout the 2010s and into the 2020s, Europe was faced with external and internal challenges of differing severity and complexity. France initially approached these with familiar tools, such as close coordination with Germany to influence EU outcomes, but with each successive development France found itself having to revise and rethink the routes by which it navigated its external environment. President Macron's campaigns for election in both 2017 and 2022 insisted on the need for Europe to bolster what he variously called its sovereignty, or its autonomy, both a familiar message from the Gaullist past, and a realistic reappraisal of Europe's vulnerability to changes in its international environment, as would become most evident in the impact of Russia's war on Ukraine.

The aftermath of the global financial crisis of 2008–09 had created tensions between EU member states as they battled to preserve the Eurozone, with Germany establishing a path out that entailed harsh austerity measures for southern EU member states, notably Greece, and required all member states to commit to greater EU oversight of their fiscal policies (see also Chapter 7). That outcome was typical of this phase of the Franco-German relationship, characterized by the long, stable chancellorship of Germany's Angela Merkel, in power for 16 years between 2005 and 2021, in contrast to France, which in this period was governed by four different presidents (Chirac, Sarkozy, Hollande and Macron) from at least three different points on the political spectrum. But once Merkel's long term of office came to an end in 2021, Germany entered a period of political change and economic fragility. This was aggravated by the impact of Russia's war on Ukraine, which necessitated a jarring overhaul of Germany's defence and security strategies. In this context, the smooth running of the Franco-German engine at the core of European integration could no longer be taken for granted, and relations noticeably deteriorated.

Stability for France had also come from its relationship with the UK, which, since the UK's entry into the European Communities in 1973, had become institutionalized through regular bilateral summits and treaty agreements, and was greatly facilitated by their shared membership of the EU. In 2010, responding to the new environment taking shape at the end of the Cold War (see above), the two countries notably signed the Lancaster House Treaties. Those agreements provided for significant cooperation in operational matters of security and defence, including the creation of a Combined Joint Expeditionary Force and a commitment to collaborating on certain technologies, including those related to their nuclear capabilities. Cross-Channel relations had already been transformed by the opening of the fixed link – the Channel Tunnel – in 1996, which, in the context of the EU's provision for the freedom of movement of people and labour, had led to the settlement of hundreds of thousands of British and French citizens in each other's country.

Other agreements provided for 'juxtaposed borders' that allowed French and UK immigration officials to operate (side by side) on each other's sovereign territory, in part to assist with the regulation of irregular border crossings that by the mid-2010s had come to be seen as a crisis across the EU. The UK's surprise decision by referendum in 2016 to leave the EU was a shock, and many aspects of the Franco-British relationship were severely disrupted, from diplomatic communication to trade. Cooperation within the Lancaster House Treaties framework slowed, freedom of movement was curtailed, and the difficulties of handling the sad flows of asylum-seeking migrants crossing the Channel from France to the UK in unseaworthy vessels grew in complexity, with many lives tragically lost. In the face of the COVID-19 pandemic, moreover, the relationship soured as a post-Brexit UK championed its own vaccine strategy (from research and development to procurement to roll-out), freed, as the UK government saw it, from the solidarity binding France and its fellow EU member states to a common vaccine policy.

The Franco-British relationship was in any case perhaps already losing traction in the geopolitical context unfolding across the world, including on Europe's borders. Some of the Arab Spring uprisings of 2011 found themselves brutally repressed, as in Syria and Egypt, and in Libya they had taken France into a military operation alongside the UK and US that subsequently led to its leader, Muammar Gaddafi – who only in 2008 had been an honoured guest of President Nicolas Sarkozy in Paris – being killed by opponents, plunging the country into ongoing chaos. In 2014, Russia's President Putin illegally invaded and occupied Crimea, part of Ukraine. One of Putin's arguments was that this was a response to NATO's expansion to incorporate former Soviet states that, he claimed, posed a threat to Russia's security. In February 2022 he launched a full-scale reinvasion of Ukraine, generating a war still ongoing at the time of writing. In China in 2014, the regime hardened its approach to democratic freedoms in Hong Kong and by 2019 demonstrated just how severely it would limit those freedoms by law and by force. Islamist terrorism took root in north and sub-Saharan Africa and the Middle East in a battle to establish an Islamic State, and extended its violence into European countries including France, Spain and the UK. President Trump, in office in the White House in the US from 2016 to 2020, demonstrated little respect for the existing international order and clearly expected more from the US's European allies, a stance unlikely to soften in Trump's second term in office from January 2025.

In this context of growing insecurity, President Macron drew his own conclusions. In 2019 he had already and infamously pronounced NATO 'brain dead', meaning that its thinking was stuck in the past, unfit for purpose in the current climate. He proposed a new 'Paris consensus' to replace the post-World War II international order based on US dominance. He drew on the arrogance of the French president's powers (and, to his critics, of his personality) to improvise French diplomacy in the EU, rejecting its further eastwards expansion and undertaking prolonged dialogue with Russia's President Putin. He reiterated his belief that Europe must strengthen its capacity to exist as a 'sovereign' bloc in a hostile world of existential threats. It took Putin's full-scale reinvasion of Ukraine in February 2022 for Macron to revise some of his assumptions. In a sharp deviation from its earlier policy (see above), France now agreed to a renewed process of EU enlargement to allow Russia's smaller neighbour Moldova to join the queue of would-be EU members, alongside, potentially, Ukraine itself; and raised no objection to enlarging NATO to rapidly incorporate Sweden and Finland (Elysée, 2023). By 2024, in keeping with his habit of saying the unsayable, he raised the idea that European – including French – troops might be needed on the ground in Ukraine. When in 2021 Australia reneged on a contract with France for the supply of conventional submarines in favour of a tripartite Australia–UK–US (AUKUS) security agreement based on nuclear-powered submarines, France's options for independent influence in the Indo-Pacific region narrowed further still. But the diplomatic fallout with the US and Australia was a short-lived blip and in its National Security Strategy of 2022 France renewed its commitment to its Western allies and above all demonstrated its serious intent to put France on a wartime footing, ready for the intensity of conflicts and challenges of the times ahead. The Gaullist legacy no longer provided a reliable roadmap for navigating the international disorder – or the complexity of its domestic implications.

French diplomacy, domestic politics and the past

Sonntag's analogy of France's international politics of prestige seen as a set of prison walls (2008) identified the drag on change represented not only by the Gaullist legacy of greatness and rank but also by other features of French politics and society, including the elitism of its education system and a hierarchical culture of deference. Addressing these characteristics, alongside the challenge of coming to terms with France's recent past of colonialization, constitutes an ongoing issue for France as it seeks to navigate and shape the contemporary world.

Can diplomacy fix it? Influence, stakeholders and society

At the president's disposal is the machinery of French diplomacy, whose history far predates de Gaulle and is reflected physically in the home of the French Ministry for European and Foreign Affairs, situated on the banks of the Seine in Paris, and known as the Quai d'Orsay. In the splendour of its environment, and in its once-powerful status within the French core executive, the Quai symbolizes France's long past as a world-class diplomatic player when French was the language of global diplomacy and when the concept of *le rayonnement* underpinned its action abroad, including in its colonies; this was the hubristic mission of 'radiating' French values and norms throughout the world (much as the sun's rays illuminate the entire planet). This quest can still be seen in France' diplomatic network of embassies and consulates that the Quai d'Orsay describes as the second most extensive in the world (after the US). Beyond that reach, France counts on the presence of its representatives in key international organizations. Together with its permanent seat on the UN Security Council, France is estimated to hold around 9 per cent of the world's international civil servants. France also has a record of success in placing its men and, belatedly, women at the very top of other powerful international bodies. Christine Lagarde, for example, having served as France's first female Minister of the Economy from 2007 to 2011, went on to head the International Monetary Fund from 2011 to 2019 and then the European Central Bank (from 2019).

By its presence in such organizations, and also by a decades-old quest to maintain French as their working language, or one of them at least, France has sought to ensure its voice is heard abroad. While the fight to preserve the French language as a global *lingua franca* is now largely a rearguard action that brings little influence in its own right, it does ensure a French cultural presence across the world. This reach is enhanced by the global networks of French language schools and cultural centres and by France's 2006 decision to project itself in English, Spanish and Arabic as well as French on its France 24 television channel, the heavily state-subsidized alternative to CNN (as seen in Chapter 6). Beyond its public diplomacy, France turns to the tools of contemporary diplomacy by which states endeavour to promote their national image – or brand – and shape international rules and norms. In 2015, French diplomatic leadership played a key role in the groundbreaking Paris climate conference agreement to limit global warming to no more than 2 and ideally 1.5 degrees centigrade above pre-industrial levels (see Chapter 2), and in 2024, by hosting the Summer Olympic and Paralympic Games, France sought to showcase itself as a sporting nation that can host peaceful sports mega-events on an unprecedently green and inclusive basis. But such events – including France's bid to host the 2030 Winter Olympics at a time when the Alps are experiencing climate change at a more rapid rate than the rest of Europe (see also Chapter 2) – also point to a reluctance by France to rein in its diplomatic ambitions, thereby running the risk of exacerbating the chasm typically separating the world of French diplomats from society at large.

Indeed, underpinning the Quai's memories of France's glorious past is the specific organizational culture that typified the French foreign policy-making elite, and which has lent it an image of an arrogant country, prepared to act unilaterally to secure its national interests, at the risk of being caught off guard when reality bites. This is a world characterized by close-knit networks of diplomats and officials predominantly trained in the former National School of Administration (l'ENA). These individuals are imbued with a strong sense of hierarchy and encouraged to emphasize certain characteristics of French intellectual thinking such as the importance of powerful rhetoric and abstract, intellectual rationales for action. These are all qualities that have lent both strengths and weaknesses to contemporary French diplomacy, particularly with respect to how it is perceived by its partners abroad in a policy domain heavily marked by protocol and routine.

In France today, the president increasingly squares up to the Quai, appointing his own foreign policy advisers at the Elysée palace, outranking the foreign minister in important diplomatic decisions, and puncturing the myth of an all-powerful foreign policy elite immune from change. The diplomats' role today is to exert French influence rather than ooze prestige, and this has brought reforms. With regard to diplomatic training, for example, we saw in Chapter 4 that President Macron closed l'ENA itself (it had already been moved out of Paris to Strasbourg, on the border with Germany). He then initiated a reform to eliminate the very existence of a specific diplomatic corps (as seen in Chapter 5), opening the profession to generalists. To its critics, this development was seen as a dangerous attack on centuries of French diplomatic experience and know-how, risking France's international weight and security. The Quai, moreover, had already been subjected to cost-cutting, with savings to be made from rationalizing and reforming the functioning of the Quai itself, both in its premises in Paris and in its embassies and consulates across the world. Such changes and reforms fit into a context where the traditional pillars of French foreign policy-making, including the presidential voice itself, have had to make room for other voices, and where the blurring of domestic and European policy-making in particular has created opportunities for dissent.

Who speaks for France? National sovereignty in question

Democratic oversight of France's foreign policy is notoriously weak, exercised in the shadow of presidential power. Parliament's role in the foreign policy-making process is constitutionally limited to the ratification or approval of 'peace treaties, trade agreements, treaties or agreements relating to international organisation' (Article 53). However, it can and does raise its voice on foreign policy issues, such as its February 2024 sceptical response to President Macron's suggestion that Ukraine's allies could send ground forces to support the Ukrainian fight against Russia without escalating the conflict; the 2023 resolution against the EU's free trade treaty with the Mercosur countries of South America; its vote in 2014 supporting the recognition of a Palestinian state; and a vote in 2008 of no confidence in President Nicolas Sarkozy's decision to send more French troops to Afghanistan and to rejoin NATO's integrated military command. It is also part of the budget-setting process for all policy domains, including foreign policy. In the specific case of France's policy regarding the EU, moreover, the French parliament has gradually increased its powers, with constitutional amendments providing for oversight and scrutiny at numerous points along the policy-making process including standing committees and obligations on the executive to keep parliament informed. In foreign conflicts, moreover, such as the 2024 Israeli–Gaza catastrophe, votes from national parliaments as well as the EP are heard outside their home country and, as such, provide conduits for the expression of alternative views within the political system. France is not immune to these forces.

Furthermore, as we saw in previous chapters, the electorate itself has also had its direct say, specifically over France's EU membership. This has taken the form of three referenda (1973, 1992 and 2005) inviting public support on, respectively, the EU's enlargement to include the UK, Denmark and Ireland, the Maastricht Treaty and the EU's Draft Constitutional Treaty. We saw that, in the third of these cases, the French public voted 'no' (see Chapter 7). Subsequent EU treaty revisions were then not put to the popular vote in France but approved by parliament alone, to some disquiet. In the matter of its European policy, moreover, the French executive has had to accommodate landmark rulings by the French legal system, most notably and belatedly the recognition by the Council of State of the supremacy of EU over domestic law, and subsequent rulings interpreting and implementing that hard fact of France's EU membership.

Combined with the EU's powers to frame and sanction the fiscal policies of member states of the Eurozone (as seen in Chapter 7), these legal restrictions underline the fact that France's multilateral commitments, especially but not only to the EU, come at a cost, real or perceived, to its national sovereignty, to the point where the issue has become a fault line in French politics (as seen in Chapter 3). Indeed, it has long been a mantra of French leaders that it is possible to build Europe without demolishing or 'undoing' France (*faire l'Europe sans défaire la France*). For decades, French leaders have tied themselves into rhetorical knots to preserve that illusion when, as we have seen in previous chapters, France's EU membership has if not 'undone' France then certainly changed and complicated it to the extent that French presidents themselves deem the line between domestic and European politics to be blurred if not erased. Indeed, we have seen that France's EU membership has transformed the French economy, split its political parties, provided a scapegoat for populists and, in the case of fiscal policy, led the Economist Intelligent Unit to pronounce France a 'flawed' democracy, as seen in Chapter 7.

These are serious challenges at a time when President Macron correctly identifies the importance of national unity, not fragmentation, if the country is to be resilient in the face of so many external threats. President Macron has sought to sidestep the issue by insisting that the EU can be a source of European sovereignty – in energy supplies, in vaccine procurement, in collective security and so on – in an ever more turbulent international context. Framing the EU as an autonomous global player strongly echoes de Gaulle's attempts, largely unsuccessful, to persuade his European counterparts in the early 1960s to come together in a 'Union of States' with common policies in defence, culture and education (see above). Like de Gaulle, Macron's ideas for European-level sovereignty or autonomy – both terms have been used – have had the virtue of forcing debate between Europe's leaders on how to best tackle the challenges facing them now and in the future; like de Gaulle, this role also perpetuates perceptions of France as an unpredictable ally still confronting the demons of its history.

Acknowledging the past in France's future

In the specific case of its EU membership, we have seen (Chapter 3) how figures on the far right and left of French politics have normalized the idea that Europe is the reason for many domestic French problems. In the 2024 EP elections, the Rassemblement national won the most seats (see Chapter 3) with its campaign to regain control and influence over the direction of European integration, and opinion surveys revealed that, while a majority of the French public favoured European integration, they thought it should take a different direction. The contradictions inherent in France's 70-year historical experiment of defining itself by its leadership and tightly bound membership of a European entity were perhaps heading to a point of no return that could be reached were Marine Le Pen to go on to fight and win the 2027 presidential election.

Beyond its convulsions over Europe, France is facing the instability familiar to other former colonial powers. The Islamist terrorist attacks that shook France in the 2010s were not unconnected to France's colonization of north and sub-Saharan Africa and its more recent military interventions (as seen above) in the region, and in the Middle East. Author Emmanuel Carrère, in his account of the trials of those involved in the deadly terror attacks on Paris on 13 November 2015, reflects precisely on how certain of the accused invoked France's military attacks on Syria to justify their actions (Carrère, 2022). The ethnic, racial and religious diversity of France's population (as seen in Chapters 2 and 5), fed by the immigration that followed its conflicts of decolonization, has created an environment prone to division and conflict, particularly when encouraged by political opportunists seeking to wrest power from those representing a version of France's history they deem outdated; and especially in the midst of ethnically based conflicts elsewhere in the world, particularly the Middle East, that generate such strong emotions among diaspora and sympathizers in France and other European countries.

The manner in which certain former colonies – above all, Algeria – won their independence meant that France was subsequently home to both European settlers who fled the newly independent Algeria in 1962 and to indigenous Algerian individuals and families who had either fought with the French in the battle to keep Algeria French (some of whom are known as *les harkis*, as seen in Chapter 1) or subsequently come to France for work and a better life. The way in which France has chosen – and in many respects failed – to integrate such individuals and their families into the fabric of secular, republican French life is still a matter of much controversy (see Chapters 2 and 5).

Indeed, one specific aspect of the relations between today's France and its former colonies arises from discussions in France regarding how best to remember and commemorate these and other aspects of French history. An important part of President Jacques Chirac's legacy will undoubtedly be his part in a series of official apologies for France's past actions, especially in relation to French collaboration in the Holocaust (see Chapter 1). But this climate has bred a backlash, particularly regarding France's fight against Algerian independence; former French army generals have unapologetically 'confessed' to their use of torture in Algeria (already an established fact). Before becoming president, Nicolas Sarkozy had lent his support to a controversial clause in a 2005 bill regarding financial compensation for *les harkis*. The clause required French schools and universities to emphasize the 'positive role' played by France in its former colonies – meaning, principally, the benefits of *le rayonnement culturel*. Such was the opposition to the clause that Chirac subsequently withdrew it. It was then revived in other terms by Sarkozy, who, on the very night of his election victory, proclaimed that the time for 'repentance' for the past was over since, however misguided past actions might have been, it equated to self-hatred and was divisive and beneath the dignity of France. He would instead restore the 'honour' of the nation, and of French identity. Accordingly, President Sarkozy embarked upon a series of foreign visits intended to 'normalize' relations with, to begin with, Algeria and Rwanda. President Macron, for his part, embarked on his own presidential quest to reset relations with France's former colonies and spheres of influence, pronouncing on the campaign trail in 2017 that France's actions in Algeria constituted a crime against humanity but, once in office, significantly dialling back his expressions of repentance. Unlike his predecessors, he has seen France ejected, effectively, from its former backyard in Africa and, on an accelerated basis, subjected to the rapid spread of news and disinformation from across the world and to the global connections, positive and nefarious, produced by today's hyperconnectivity of technologies, ideas, grievances and suffering.

Conclusions

Many of the certainties stitched into the fabric of France's international presence would appear to be coming loose, if not unravelling. The EU remains the primary vehicle for the projection of French influence – and, by extension, identity – onto the world stage. President Macron bet his presidential career on his ability to lead the EU into the future in all its complexity. But the EU has been destabilized by the UK's exit, Germany's introspection and the pressures on the bloc to protect its eastern borders while satisfying the populations of its existing member states. In France, the 2027 presidential election will play out against a backdrop of division over European integration and its place in French politics, government and society. That election will also occur at a time when international affairs in general, and France's historical role in them in particular, will find their way into candidates' messages about the French nation and its identity. Once elected, the new president will find that presidential will alone is insufficient to unite the country around external challenges in the mode of former President de Gaulle, particularly if it fails to devise a process to accommodate the multiplicity of voices now clamouring for a say in how France positions and accounts for itself internationally. None of these challenges is entirely unique to France, but France is unique in the contradictory foundations of its EU membership, in the place it held in the Cold War era and in its mode of colonial power. It maintains many of its diplomatic assets and the brand *France* still has international cachet. Formerly an international player in a class of its own, conducting international relations in its own tongue, France now finds itself speaking the language of bilateralism, multilateralism and global partnerships in the face of the existential threats to its survival. Doing so in a way that maintains the unity of the nation is a challenge increasingly shared by many if not most of its allies in Europe and beyond.

Conclusions

It is, perhaps, impossible to take a neutral stance on France, such is the strength of the images it projects outwards to the world. It wants to be seen and heard, be identified and identifiable. Unsurprisingly, scholars have their own battles with the study of France, me included. First, France-gazing is arguably a saturated market. Two decades ago, Perry Anderson was already marvelling at the 'immense output on their society produced by the French themselves, on a scale undreamt of elsewhere' (2004). In the face of 'this mass of self-description, what', he asked, 'can the alien gaze hope to add?' (Anderson, 2004). The question was even more acute, in his view, when the 'alien' is not just a British writer but an *English* one, as in my case. This book is in part my attempt, in microcosm, to academically navigate that relationship between France and *les Anglais*, who for centuries have swayed between familiarity and estrangement, love and hate, attraction and repulsion. As in the previous book (Drake, 2011), there are undoubtedly biases and lacunae. One concerns crime and punishment as public policy; another is this book's focus on the *métropole* at a time, 2024, when France's overseas territory New Caledonia is burning; both beckon further research and comment.

A second challenge for the scholar, French and non-French alike, concerns the concept of the 'French exception'. Do we accept France's own telling of itself as special and, accordingly, place France on a singular, unique pedestal for the purposes of analysis? As early as 2009, Brouard, Appleton and Mazur saw 'French exceptionalism' as a perspective that can blind us to the fact that 'France ... lies no further outside the spectrum of advanced industrial economies than any other' (2009: xiv). Chafer and Godin are less categorical but still conclude that 'the French exception' was probably more parody than politics (2010: 239). Accordingly, this book has implicitly framed France in comparative perspective, asking not only how France measures up to its contemporary counterparts, especially in Europe, but also how it compares to its own past. We have seen that France is in step with much of the rest of Europe when it comes to the rise of populist politics, especially on the far right; the fragility of its representative democracy; and how it is at a loss in the face of immigration. From a historical angle, and from a distance, we see a France that is still very much France, at least in the sense that it is still highly attractive to the outside world, still speaking up for itself on the world stage, still resisting change for change's own sake, still exhibiting the impressive array of unique characteristics we would expect from such an long-established nation-state, and still nostalgic for the imagined past that exists in the eye of each beholder.

France is also still very much conditioned by developments occurring outside its own borders. We have discovered that probably the most incontrovertible dimension of contemporary France is the country's openness to forces and factors of all kinds, and the challenges and opportunities of living and legislating in such an open society. Mainland France is even the hexagonal shape it is because its geographical location in Europe has historically made it extremely vulnerable to its neighbours on all sides, including across the Channel but especially Germany, and it has had to fight over the centuries to secure and stabilize its external borders. Since World War II, military struggles have been supplanted by tussles over power-sharing arrangements with its neighbours, slugged out in the framework of the European Union.

Choosing this route to postwar reconstruction has taken France on an unpredictable journey to 'an unknown destination' (Schonfield, 1973) that has required some explaining by its political leaders. Emmanuel Macron and his predecessors have all argued that French membership of the European Union manages French exposure to all sorts of flows, including money, markets and migrants, and has amplified its voice internationally. President Macron opened a keynote speech in April 2024 with the very fact of France's international exposure, despite knowing that foreign affairs are rarely at the top of voters' concerns, repeating the familiar, presidential mantra that the future of France is 'indissociable' from the future of Europe (Elysée, 2024). France's integration into the EU has certainly added a layer to French national identity and framed a sense of belonging to a bigger entity with distinct values and visions of the world in the shape of a 'Franco-Saxon' European Union, in opposition to an 'Anglo-American counter-identity' (Hayward, 2007: 1–38, 335). At least, these have been the most compelling accounts of France's commitment to what it calls *la construction européenne* (European 'construction') over the last 60 years. In reality, the price of managing the outside world by means of common European rules has been high, as we have seen. It has necessitated constitutional amendments and created losers as well as winners. Economically, France has struggled to stay within EU fiscal guidelines that are themselves contested within the political class. When the EU is seen to fall short of French ambitions, or when French presidents fail to meet their citizens' high expectations, the potential for social conflict, political polarization and protest is high. This was the lesson of the 2005 referendum in France, which itself echoed the caution of former foreign and prime minister Georges Bidault, who back in 1953 had argued that 'Europe must not come at the price of unmaking France or its empire' (*'il faut faire l'Europe sans défaire l'Union française'*: Bossuat, 2006: 52, cited in Drake and Reynolds, 2017, 1). All French presidents, Emmanuel Macron most recently and fervently and with some success, as we have seen, have attempted to build EU capacity – to fight climate change, to manage immigration, to lead Europe's economies out of its polycrises – while giving the appearance of being in control of a process that Hayward has aptly described as 'leaderless' (Hayward, 2007: 342). In echoes of the UK's 2016 Brexit vote, political opportunists in France have seized on these difficulties, in the context of a rocky economy, to persuade many French voters that France may well be better off liberated from its international constraints, going it alone and 'taking back control'.

Such populist nationalism is only one aspect of the ongoing challenge for French leaders of securing the integrity of French territory and the indivisibility of the nation itself, as they are constitutionally bound to do. Boundaries within France, real and imagined, have proved to be as fragile as its external frontiers. France's overseas territories are restless and far from united regarding the relationships they wish to have with Paris and the *métropole*, mainland France. Even Corsica, counted as part of the mainland, periodically expresses a desire for greater autonomy, with some success. Further afield, the French-speaking world in the shape of la Francophonie cannot be relied upon to relay France's influence, let alone its language, throughout the world. Some members defect; all are courted by the world's rising powers. These developments remind French decision-makers of the diverse nature of both its population and territory, and the repercussions of its past. With an eye also on mounting costs, French governments have gradually decentralized important aspects of central administration. But, at the same time, open economies and advanced technologies pose serious, ongoing difficulties for the French state – as for any state – in its attempts to control flows of information, knowledge, trends, fashions, opportunities and funds within and outside its territory.

These developments are problematic for a country where the state has historically been so important for nation-building and where, as we have seen, expectations of it remain high. Yet the French state struggles to balance the three core principles of French republicanism – liberty, equality and fraternity – in the face of France's own diversity, let alone the impact of outside influences. There is no one single mix that can satisfy all demands. One result has been continuous and often controversial constitutional change to fine-tune the 200-plus-year-old revolutionary triptych. The state at least now acknowledges that it is pluralistic in its policy-making. It recognizes that gender discrimination is structural and deserves special treatment. It preaches tolerant attitudes towards difference. But this process is incomplete and inadequate. France experiences extraordinary and ongoing difficulties in catering for individuals and communities who emanate from France's colonial past. We have witnessed cultural battles over the notion of Frenchness, epitomized by the ban in 2010 that stigmatizes women in Islamic face coverings and evident in the festering discrimination against people of colour. We have seen an ever-tighter squeeze on personal freedoms in the name of national security, and witnessed how fears about immigration stoke a nervous national identity.

In these respects, France is not entirely unlike many other countries across Europe, which, as we have said, all face broadly similar challenges to established national identities and their power dynamics. But France must contend with a highly specific set of political parameters within which solutions must be found. French political culture still harbours practices that undermine its democracy, even allowing for the fact that all democracies are works-in-progress and incomplete. These include an unhealthy ideal of the individual-cum-saviour; a fixation with the personalization of politics and the cult of the celebrity, even in politics (to the point of coining a new term, 'pipolization'); and a lingering but persistent elitism. This mix translates into hopelessly high expectations of the office of the presidency, a role that, as Nabila Ramdani acidly but accurately notes, equates to 'the absurd reliance on a single alpha male with far too much influence over every field of national life' (2023: 308). Since the days of President Charles de Gaulle, France has expected something special, almost otherworldly, from its presidents. But presidents do not come much worldlier than Jacques Chirac or Nicolas Sarkozy, both of whom were convicted in criminal trials for corruption perpetrated while in public office. As for Emmanuel Macron, deemed by some to be the most haughty, arrogant and authoritarian – 'Jupiterian' – of the presidents of the Fifth Republic (quite some contest, given the nature of the role and the character of most of his predecessors), he has experienced virulent opposition from within the political class and from the electorate, amounting to what Sophie Pedder has called a 'stupefying degree of loathing' (2019, xviii).)

But, again, France is not really alone in these respects. The Barack Obama phenomenon in the US in 2008–09, subsequently outperformed by the Donald Trump spectacle; the UK's doomed love-in with 'Bojo', Prime Minister Boris Johnson (2019–22); India's enthusiasm for Narendra Modi; all these examples amply demonstrate a human weakness for charismatic figures who perhaps can change all lives for the better and who, when they inevitably do not, have far to fall. Furthermore, France's democratic institutions have evidently evolved since de Gaulle's day, and politics is conducted in a seriously altered environment. In France as elsewhere, politicians are exposed like never before to myriad voices raising a dizzying diversity of ideas, claims and causes, aided by technology that democratic states, unlike their totalitarian and illiberal counterparts, are no experts in harnessing for their own ends; these voices are spurred on by the high emotional content of contemporary human life.

Many French voters express distrust and disgust with politics, as seen in rising abstentionism and the collapse of support for previously mainstream, centrist political parties. In its polarization, its language and its very style, French politics enacts a symbolic form of violence that is echoed in the physical violence taking place outside, including between the state and its citizens. The notion that France is descending into savagery – *l'ensauvagement* – is no longer confined to the repertoire of racist politicians. The regime itself, the Fifth Republic, has been described by Ramdani (2023, 309) as a 'makeshift measure designed to get France through [the] exceptional circumstances' of the Algerian war of independence. Having survived for more than six decades since then, it has exceeded its shelf life, perhaps becoming as unloved (*mal aimée*) as its predecessor, the Fourth Republic (1944–58). Talk of a Sixth French Republic is not uncommon but, unsurprisingly, few contenders for presidential office have such an overhaul in their sights. President Macron's 'revolution' fell short of his own ambitions and his supporters' expectations and, at moments during the *gilets jaunes* movement, the president was targeted in his symbolic and physical existence, in echoes of revolutions past and, perhaps, as a warning of what is to come.

Faced with the prospect that 'yesterday's world is disappearing', President Macron after seven years in power called on France to 'retool' itself (Macron, 2023b) in every imaginable dimension. He also expressed his hope that 2024 would be 'vintage': the Notre Dame de Paris cathedral, burned almost to the ground in April 2019, would rise from the ashes. The summer Olympic Games would validate France's international standing. This would be his legacy. These entreaties to the French nation to move with the times and emerge from under their supposed comfort blankets (Drake, 2018); these hopes, looked set, yet again, to fall on deaf ears. France's battle for future survival will be fought both alongside its allies and with itself, and France will continue to hold others – English scholars included – in its thrall.

References

Ahearne, J. (2022) 'Emmanuel Macron and the reprojection of the French language', *Modern and Contemporary France*, 30 (3): 257–74.

Anderson, P. (2004) 'Dégringolade', *London Review of Books*, 26 (17) [online] 2 September, Available from: https://www.lrb.co.uk/the-paper/v26/n17/perry-anderson/degringolade [Accessed 20 October 2024].

Atout France (2024) 'En rétrospective: 2023, une année exceptionnelle pour le tourisme français!' [online], Available from https://www.atout-france.fr/fr/actualites/en-retrospective-2023-une-annee-exceptionne lle-pour-le-tourisme-francais [Accessed 25 November 2024].

Aubenas, F. (2010) *Le Quai de Ouistreham*, Paris: Éditions de l'Olivier.

Aubenas, F. (2023) *Ici et ailleurs*, Paris: Éditions de l'Olivier.

Baycroft, T. (2008) *Inventing the Nation. France*, London: Hodder.

Bayley, S. (2002) 'Am I getting a little Brazilian woman?' *The Observer*, Escape supplement, 17 February: 2.

Bossuat, G. (2006). *Faire l'Europe sans défaire la France. 60 ans de politique d'unité européenne des gouvernements et des présidents de la République française (1943–2003)*, Brussels: Peter Lang.

Brame, G. (2006) *Chez vous en France. Mille et une clés pour faciliter la vie*, Paris: Documentation française.

Brayfield, C. (2004) *Deep France*, London: Pan.

Brouard, S., Appleton, A. and Mazur, A. (eds) (2009) *The French Republic at Fifty. Beyond Stereotype*, Basingstoke: Palgrave Macmillan.

Carrère, E. (2022) *V13: Chronicle of a Trial*, J. Lambert (trans.), New York, NY: Vintage.

Chafer, T. and Godin, E. (eds) (2010) *The End of the French Exception? Decline and Renewal of the 'French Model'*, Basingstoke: Palgrave Macmillan.

Clift, B. (2009) 'Economic interventionism in the Fifth Republic', in S. Brouard, A. Appleton and A. Mazur, *The Fifth French Republic at Fifty*, Basingstoke: Palgrave Macmillan, pp 153–73.

CNC (2023) 'Bilan du CNC. Les chiffres clés de 2023' [online], Available from: https://www.cnc.fr/documents/36995/153434/3667_CNC_Bilan-chiffre+clés_V07.pdf/e0774239-3493-c9a9-14be-acb00cdf2 1cb?t=1715777181775 [Accessed 20 October 2024].

Cogan, C. (2003) *French Negotiating Behaviour: Dealing with la Grande Nation*, Washington, DC: United States Institute of Peace Press.

Cole, A. and Pasquier, R. (2021) 'Territorial governance in France: between recentralization and differentiation', in H. Drake, A. Cole, S. Meunier and V. Tiberj (eds) *Developments in French Politics Six*, London: Red Globe Press, pp 127–42.

Culpepper, P.D. (2006) 'Capitalism, coordination and economic change: The French political economy since 1985', in P.D. Culpepper, P.A. Hall and B. Palier (eds) *Changing France: The Politics that Markets Make*, Basingstoke: Palgrave Macmillan, pp 29–49.

Dabet, G., Epiphane, D. and Personnaz, E. (2024) 'Origine sociale, diplôme et insertion: la force des liens', Céreq Bref, no. 452, [online] May, Available from: https://www.cereq.fr/origine-sociale-diplome-et-insertion-la-force-des-liens [Accessed 20 October 2024].

Dickens, C. (2000 [1859]) *A Tale of Two Cities*, London: Penguin Classics.

Drake, H. (2000) *Jacques Delors. Perspectives on a European Leader*, London: Routledge.

Drake, H. (2011) *Contemporary France*, Basingstoke: Palgrave Macmillan.

Drake, H. (2018) 'Is France having a moment? Emmanuel Macron and the Politics of Disruption', *Political Quarterly* [Government and Parliament Blog, online] 14 September, Available from: https://politic alquarterly.org.uk/authors/helen-drake/ [Accessed 19 October 2024].

Drake, H. and Collard, S. (2008) 'A case-study of intra-EU migration. 20 years of "Brits" in the Pays d'Auge, Normandy, France', *French Politics*, 6: 214–33.

Drake, H. and Reynolds, C. (2017) 'Sixty years on: France and Europe from the Treaty of Rome to the 2017 elections', *Modern & Contemporary France*, 25 (2): 111–16.

Dubois, F. (2008) 'Cultural policy in France – genesis of a public policy category', *GPSE Working Papers (University of Strasbourg)*, 28 October.

Elysée (2023) 'Globsec summit in Bratislava' [online] 31 May, Available from: https://www.elysee.fr/en/emmanuel-macron/2023/06/01/glob sec-summit-in-bratislava [Accessed 20 October 2024].

Elysée (2024) 'Discours sur l'Europe' [online] 25 April, Available from: https://www.elysee.fr/emmanuel-macron/2024/04/24/disco urs-sur-leurope [Accessed 20 October 2024].

Fourquet, J. (2023) *La France d'Après. Tableau Politique*, Paris: Seuil.

Fourquet, J. and Cassely, J.-L. (2021) *La France sous nos yeux. Économie, paysages, nouveaux modes de vie*, Paris: Seuil.

Francophonie.org (2024) 'Organisation internationale de la francophonie' [online], Available from: https://www.francophonie.org [Accessed 20 October 2024].

Granville, B. (2021) *What Ails France?* Montreal: McGill-Queens University Press.

Hayward, J. (2007) *Fragmented France. Two Centuries of Disputed Identity*, New York: Oxford University Press.

Huc-Hepher, S. (2021) *French London. A Blended Ethnography of a Migrant City*, Manchester: Manchester University Press.

Hussey, A. (2015) *The French Intifada. The Long War Between France and Its Arabs*, London: Granta.

INSEE (2019) 'Tableaux de l'économie française. Édition 2019 [online] 26 March, Available from: https://www.insee.fr/fr/statistiques/3676870?sommaire=3696937 [Accessed 21 October 2024].

INSEE (2024) 'Naissances et taux de natalité. Données actuelles de 1982 à 2023' [online] 16 January, Available from: https://www.insee.fr/fr/statistiques/2381380#:~:text=à%20fin%202023.-,Lecture%20%3A%20en%202023%2C%20678%20000%20enfants%20sont%20nés%20vivants%2C,statistiques%20de%20l'état%20civil [Accessed 19 October 2024].

Jackson, J. (2023) *France on Trial. The Case of Marshal Pétain*, London: Allen Lane.

Keiger, J.F.V. (2005) 'Foreign and defence policy: constraints and continuity', in A. Cole et al. (eds) *Developments in French Politics 3*, Basingstoke: Palgrave Macmillan, pp 138–53.

Kuisel, R. (2001) 'The Gallic rooster crows again. The paradox of French anti-Americanism', *French Politics, Culture and Society*, 19 (3): 1–16.

Kuper, S. (2023) 'Paris, city of the future', *The Financial Times*, 7 December.

Kuper, S. (2024) *Impossible City. Paris in the Twenty-First Century*, London: Profile.

La Documentation française (2023) 'La France dans le Monde', *Questions Internationales*, 119–220, June-September.

Le Monde (2018) 'Catherine Deneuve: « Nous défendons une liberté d'importuner, indispensable à la liberté sexuelle »', 9 January.

Le Monde (2024) 'Que contient la loi relative à l'immigration? Comprendre en trois minutes', 10 November.

Léon, M. and Gallard, M. (2023) 'La société idéale de demain aux yeux des Français', *Fondation Jean Jaurès* [online] 16 November, Available from: https://www.jean-jaures.org/publication/la-societe-ideale-de-demain-aux-yeux-des-francais/?post_id=50803&export_pdf=1 [Accessed 18 October 2024].

Lequesne, C. (1993) *Paris-Bruxelles: comment se fait la politique européenne de la France*, Paris: Presses de la FNSP.

Lequesne, C. (2020) 'La Diaspora française de Londres à l'heure du Brexit' Les Etudes du CERI, 250 10.25647/etudesduceri.250 [online] July, Available from: https://sciencespo.hal.science/hal-03386603/file/2020-07-lequesne-diaspora-francaise-londres-etudes-ceri-250.pdf [Accessed 19 October].

Lombardo, P. and Wolff, L. (2020–22) 'Culture Études. Cinquante ans de pratiques culturelles en France', *Ministère de la Culture*.

Looseley, D. (1995) *The Politics of Fun. Cultural Policy and Debate in Contemporary France*, Oxford: Berg.

Maclean, M. (2008) 'French corporate governance in a globalised world: a changing business model?', in M. Maclean and J. Szarka (eds) *France on the World Stage. Nation State Strategies in the Global Era*, Basingstoke: Palgrave Macmillan, pp 144–61.

Macron, E. (2017) *Revolution*, London: Scribe.

Macron, E. (2023a) 'Message de M. Emmanuel Macron, président de la République, adressé aux Français, sur l'attaque terroriste perpétrée le 7 octobre par le Hamas en Israël, la réponse militaire israélienne à Gaza et l'antisémitisme, à Paris le 12 novembre 2023', *Vie publique* [online] 12 November, Available from: https://www.vie-publique.fr/discours/291761-emmanuel-macron-12112023-israel [Accessed 19 October 2024].

Macron, E. (2023b) 'Vœux du Président de la République aux Français', *Elysée* [online] 31 December, Available from: https://www.elysee.fr/emmanuel-macron/2023/12/31/voeux-aux-francais-pour-2024 [Accessed 20 October 2024].

Mayer, N. and Tiberj, V. (2021) 'Racial prejudice in multicultural France', in H. Drake, A. Cole, S. Meunier and V. Tiberj (eds) *Developments in French Politics Six*, London: Red Globe Press, pp 143–62.

Mendras, H. and Cole, A. (1991) *Social Change in Modern France. Towards a Cultural Anthropology of the Fifth Republic*, Cambridge: Cambridge University Press.

Meunier, S. (2003) 'France's double-talk on globalisation', *French Politics, Culture and Society*, 21 (1): 20–34.

Milner, S. (2021) 'Socio-economic policy and governance: the difficult and contested politics of reform', in H. Drake, A. Cole, S. Meunier and V. Tiberj (eds) *Developments in French Politics Six*, London: Red Globe Press, pp 163–77.

Milward, A. (2000) *The European Rescue of the Nation State* (2nd edn), Abingdon: Routledge.

Ministère de l'Agriculture et de la Souveraineté alimentaire (2024) 'Infographie – la viticulture française' [online] 13 September, Available from: https://agriculture.gouv.fr/infographie-la-viticulture-francaise [Accessed 19 October 2024].

Ministère de l'Intérieur et des Outre-Mer (2024) 'Les archives des rélections en France' [online], Available from: https://www.archi ves-resultats-elections.interieur.gouv.fr [Accessed 21 October 2024].

Morelle, A. (2021) *L'Opium des Élites. Comment on a défait la France sans faire l'Europe*, Paris: Grasset & Fasquelle.

OECD (2023) 'Country statistical profile: France 2023', [online], Available from: https://www.oecd-ilibrary.org/docserver/41ab3da5-en.pdf?expires=1729425220&id=id&accname=guest&checksum= 3436935CAD38E6E4E303C95696A927C8 [Accessed 20 October 2024].

Pedder, S. (2019) *Revolution française and the Quest to Reinvent a Nation* (paperback edn), London: Bloomsbury.

Ramdani, N. (2023) *Fixing France. How to Repair a Broken Republic*, London: Hurst.

Robb, G. (2007) *The Discovery of France*, London: Picador.

Roger, P. (2005) *The American Enemy. The History of French Anti-Americanism*, S. Bowman (trans.), Chicago and London: University of Chicago Press.

Sarkozy, N. (2009) 'Discours de M. Nicolas Sarkozy, Président de la République française, sur l'identité nationale, à la Chapelle-en-Vercors', *la Vie Publique* [online] 12 November, Available from: https://www.vie-publique.fr/discours/177210-declaration-de-m-nicolas-sarkozy-president-de-la-republique-sur-lide [Accessed 19 October 2024].

Schonfield, A. (1973) *Europe: Journey to an Unknown Destination*, London: Pelican.

Sciences Po (2024) *Cevipof* [online], Available from: https://www.sci encespo.fr/cevipof/en.html [Accessed 19 October 2024].

SGDSN (Sécretariat général de la défense et la sécurité nationale, 2022) 'Revue nationale stratégique 2022', [online] 29 November, Available from: https://www.sgdsn.gouv.fr/publications/revue-nationale-stra tegique-2022 [Accessed 20 October 2024].

Shields, J.G. (2007) *The Extreme Right in France. From Pétain to Le Pen*, London: Routledge.

Smith, A. (2021) *Made in France: Societal Structures and Political Work*, Manchester: Manchester University Press.

Smith, A.W.M. (2016) *Terror and Terroir. The Winegrowers of the Languedoc and Modern France*, Manchester: Manchester University Press.

Sonntag, A. (2008) 'The burdensome heritage of prestige politics', in M. Maclean and J. Szarka (eds) *France on the World Stage. Nation State Strategies in the Global Era*, Basingstoke: Palgrave Macmillan, pp 77–90.

Statista (2024) 'Countries with the highest number of international tourist arrivals worldwide from 2019 to 2023' [online] 4 October, Available from: https://www.statista.com/statistics/261726/countries-ranked-by-number-of-international-tourist-arrivals/ [Accessed 19 October 2024].

Steinberger, M. (2009) *Au Revoir to All That. The Rise and Fall of French Cuisine*, London: Bloomsbury.

Treacher, A. (2003) *French Interventionism. Europe's Last Global Player?* Aldershot: Ashgate.

Turner, L. (2024) *Lessons in Diplomacy. Politics, Power and Parties*, Bristol: Policy Press.

UNESCO (2024) 'France' [online], Available from: https://whc.unesco.org/fr/etatsparties/fr [Accessed 19 October 2024]

Vaïsse, M. (2009) *La puissance ou l'influence? La France dans le monde depuis 1958*, Paris: Fayard.

ViaMichelin (2024) 'Calais to Nice driving directions' [online], Available from: https://www.viamichelin.com/routes/results/calais-62100-pas_de_calais-hauts_de_france-france-to-nice-06000-alpes_maritimes-provence_alpes_cote_d_azur-france [Accessed 19 October 2024].

Vuillard, E. (2023) An Honourable Exit, Basingstoke: Pan Macmillan.

Weber, E. (1976) *Peasants into Frenchmen: The Modernization of Rural France, 1870–1914*, Stanford, CA: Stanford University Press.

World Bank Group (2024) 'France' [online], Available from: https://data.worldbank.org/country/FR [Accessed 20 October 2024].

Wylie, L. (1964) *A Village in the Vaucluse*, Cambridge, MA, and London: Harvard University Press.

Index

References to figures appear in *italic* type; those in **bold** type refer to tables.